Winston S. Churchill and the Shaping of the Middle East, 1919-1922

Israel: Society, Culture, and History

Series Editor:
Yaacov Yadgar, Political Studies, Bar-Ilan University

Editorial Board:

Alan Dowty, Political Science and Middle Eastern Studies,
    University of Notre Dame
Tamar Katriel, Communication Ethnography, University of Haifa
Avi Sagi, Hermeneutics, Cultural Studies, and Philosophy,
    Bar-Ilan University
Allan Silver, Sociology, Columbia University
Anthony D. Smith, Nationalism and Ethnicity,
    London School of Economics
Yael Zerubavel, Jewish Studies and History, Rutgers University

Winston S. Churchill and the Shaping of the Middle East, 1919-1922

Sara Reguer

BOSTON
2020

Library of Congress Control Number: 2020912385

Copyright © 2020 Academic Studies Press
All rights reserved.

ISBN 9781644693322 hardback
ISBN 9781644693339 paperback
ISBN 9781644693346 ebook PDF
ISBN 9781644693353 ePub

Book design by Kryon Publishing Services (P) Ltd.
Cover design by Ivan Grave

Published by Academic Studies Press
1577 Beacon Street
Brookline, MA 02446, USA
press@academicstudiespress.com
www.academicstudiespress.com

Winston S. Churchill and the Shaping of the Middle East, 1919-1922

Sara Reguer

BOSTON
2020

Library of Congress Control Number: 2020912385

Copyright © 2020 Academic Studies Press
All rights reserved.

ISBN 9781644693322 hardback
ISBN 9781644693339 paperback
ISBN 9781644693346 ebook PDF
ISBN 9781644693353 ePub

Book design by Kryon Publishing Services (P) Ltd.
Cover design by Ivan Grave

Published by Academic Studies Press
1577 Beacon Street
Brookline, MA 02446, USA
press@academicstudiespress.com
www.academicstudiespress.com

Dedicated to
My parents, Moshe Aron Reguer and Anne S. Reguer

In Memoriam of
Professor Jacob Coleman Hurewitz (1914–2008)
Sir Martin Gilbert (1936–2015)

Contents

Preface		x
Chapter 1:	Winston S. Churchill and the Middle East	1
Chapter 2:	Great Britain and the Middle East	6
Chapter 3:	The Secretary of State for War and Air	15
Chapter 4:	Middle East Dilemmas	34
Chapter 5:	The Secretary of State for the Colonies	57
Chapter 6:	The Cairo Conference of 1921	73
Chapter 7:	Approval of Parliament	91
Chapter 8:	Slow Progress	109
Chapter 9:	No Progress	126
Chapter 10:	Iraq: From Stalemate to Solution	144
Chapter 11:	Policy for Palestine	160
Chapter 12:	The Shaping of the Middle East	179
Endnotes		183
Bibliography		211
Index		221

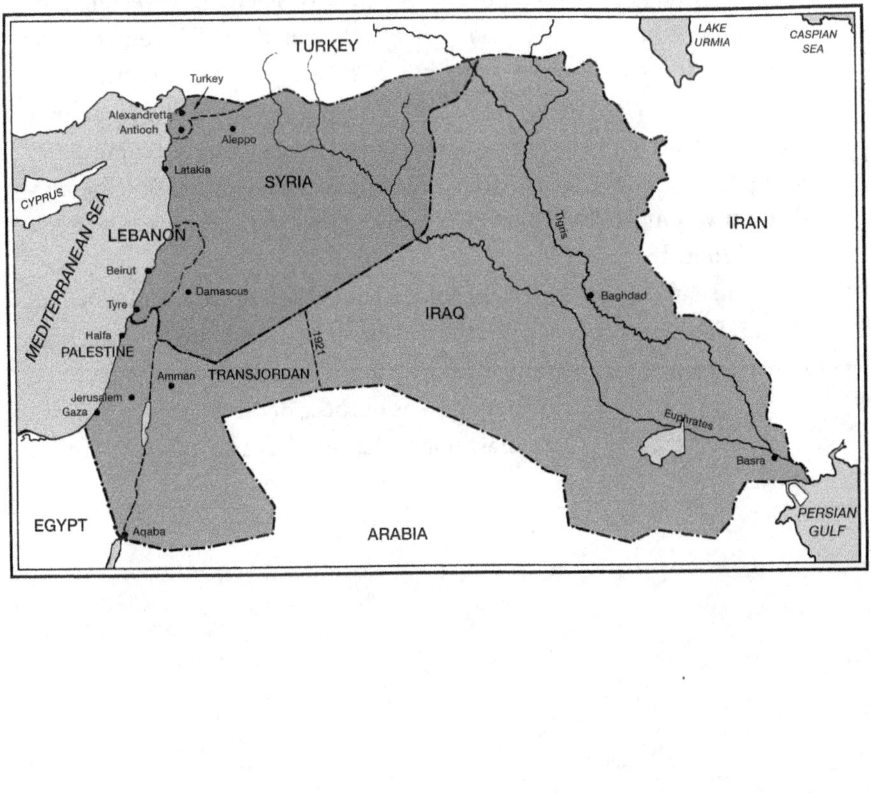

TURKEY
Turkey
LAKE URMIA
CASPIAN SEA
Alexandretta
Antioch
Aleppo
Latakia
CYPRUS
SYRIA
MEDITERRANEAN SEA
LEBANON
Tigris
IRAN
Beirut
Damascus
Tyre
Baghdad
IRAQ
Haifa
PALESTINE
1921
Amman
TRANSJORDAN
Jerusalem
Gaza
Euphrates
Basra
EGYPT
Aqaba
ARABIA
PERSIAN GULF

Preface

There are many people today who think that the political issues in the Middle East started with the creation of the State of Israel. However, the seeds for these issues were planted by the British and the French in the post world War I period. This book not only delineates the Western imperial policies that led to today's problems, but, by focusing on the activities of one of the most important political figures—Winston S. Churchill—it carefully traces their evolution. For Britain, it meant developing an overarching policy for Iraq and Palestine/Transjordan, because the main focus of British imperial power was India. The Middle East was viewed at that time as a strategic overland route to the Far East.

There have been many books written about the mandate period of both Iraq and Palestine, but most give the early mandate short shrift. There have also been many books written about Winston Churchill, but most focus on him through the lens of a biographer. The purpose of this book is to uncover the actual shaping of Middle East policy that still has an impact on today's realities.

CHAPTER 1

Winston S. Churchill and the Middle East

By October 1922, when the Lloyd George Government fell from power, the British Empire had reached its maximum territorial extent and seemed on the point of stabilizing all its imperial relationships. One of the newest areas to come under direct British control was a large section of the Middle East. The problem presenting itself to the British Government was how to deal with these new territories under the changed world conditions. There are innumerable elements to this problem and to treat the whole subject in equal depth for the whole period—from the acquisition of the Middle East until the end of Lloyd George's reign—would be a daunting task. The present attempt is more modest.

Winston S. Churchill's decision making shaped policies and events in the Middle East, and the unfolding developments there linked themselves to his career. He was introduced to the Middle East in 1898 when, as a war correspondent, he participated in Kitchener's campaign into the Sudan. The first opportunity he had to shape policy in the area came with his appointment as First Lord of the Admiralty in 1911. This study was originally planned to cover the decade 1912-1922, but after assembling all the material, it proved to be unmanageable. The present story begins in January 1919 with Churchill's appointment as Secretary of State for War and Air, and ends in October 1922 when, as Secretary of State for the Colonies, he loses his position of power and his seat in Parliament. The period is of major importance because it is one of flux: World War I loosened the hold of imperial tradition, and Churchill could experiment and innovate.

I am limiting the geographic scope of the study as well. Since the Fertile Crescent represented that part of the Middle East that was most substantially changed by World War I and its peace settlement, and since it was the area most directly under Churchill's control for the time period I am exploring, I am limiting myself to it. References to Churchill's activities relating to Egypt, the Arabian Peninsula, Persia and Turkey will be made only if they have direct bearing on the developments of the Fertile Crescent.

I have attempted to recreate the atmosphere of the time in this one area and to tell the story of Churchill's decision making in detail. It is not a biographical work; that was done by Martin Gilbert. I have examined the decision making process and the resultant policies, and have sought to assess Churchill's accomplishments. As import as the content of policy making is, once that policy is decided on, it would count for naught were it not implemented. No one in a high government position, or in any high administrative post, can hope to change things overnight or to carry out a new policy just by taking over a new position. The work involved in doing so is long and often arduous. Churchill was no exception to this rule. He was an exception in that despite the hurdles confronting him he did manage to implement a new policy for the Fertile Crescent. I have attempted to trace how he accomplished what he did and have uncovered an expert maneuverer with a broad array of methodological tools at his disposal. I have sought to assess both the multifarious and frustrating obstacles Churchill had to overcome as well as the arsenal of methodological weapons he used.

A question immediately arising is: can an individual make history? Or is the individual so governed by the situation which already exists when he moves onto the scene that his actions count for little? How large a part does chance play? Any attempt at writing a book about one person must deal with these three persistent elements and examine their interplay. Certainly the individual faces an existing situation, a product of earlier times, yet he may very truly affect events through his responses.

Winston Spencer Churchill has been, for over a century, an object of great interest. There are those who admire him as one of all-time blessings Britain ever received; and there are probably just as many who detest anything and everything about him. Anyone who evokes such polar responses must have been unusual and even his most ardent detractors have to admit, albeit unwillingly, that there was something indefinable that Churchill possessed separating him from the normal run of people.

In trying to find an answer to the question of whether Churchill influenced history, specifically, events related to the Fertile Crescent from 1919 through 1922, I found myself in a dilemma: How could I possibly get to understand Churchill's personality and his individuality. His own introspective observations, a primary source, very often have to be treated with great caution as many were written after the events occurred; yet, these observations do serve to show what the man was thinking at some point in time. As for the comments of contemporaries, another basic source for understanding the man, there were his admirers and his detractors, so again the material had to be treated with caution. The best sources, and the richest, for understanding Churchill and answering the basic question of whether or not he influenced the history of the Fertile Crescent are his deeds. But before letting the narrative take over, I believe it worthwhile, as part of the stage setting, to try to piece together some sketch of the man himself.

Churchill's admirers describe him as having a resourceful mind, full of such scope of vision and imagination as to place him in the category of genius. They point to his youthfulness with all its concomitant traits of enthusiasm, vivacity, vitality and lack of inhibition. "He must know all, taste all, devour all. He is drunk with the wonder and the fascination of living. A talk with him is as exhilarating as a gallop across country, so full is it of adventures, and of the high spirits and eagerness of youth."[1] His open ambition, self-confidence, as well as egocentricity seem to be the prerequisites for success for he firmly believed in his personal destiny and behaved like someone important thereby impressing others that this must be so. He was a man of great courage, an invaluable asset to all at the outset of the war. "When all looked black and spirits were inclined to droop, he could not only see but could compel others to see, the brighter side of the picture."[2]

Churchill's detractors mistrusted him for all the traits that his admirers valued. They feared the impetuous risk taker and despised his brusqueness, impatience and scorn and his disregard for personal sensitivities. They explained that "his mind was a powerful machine, but there lay hidden in its material and its makeup some obscure defect which prevented it from always running true."[3] They could not pinpoint exactly what it was, but when the mechanism malfunctioned, its very power caused disaster to himself, his causes, and his associates.

All agreed that Churchill's capacity for work and concentration was prodigious and that he was a master of detail, but it was his speaking ability, more than any other trait, that endowed him with such influence. "What people really want to hear is the truth—it is the exciting thing—speak the simple truth,"[4] taught Bourke Cockran, young Churchill's host during a visit to New York in 1895. Churchill greatly admired Cockran and modeled himself after him, mastering the New Yorker's lessons on the basic techniques of oratory and conversation.

Churchill learned how to express himself in lucid and compelling language. He developed a command of the beauty and imagery of the English language combined with magnificent epigrams and humor, and formidable invective and raillery into a powerful weapon to convince individuals, committees, the Cabinet, Parliament and mass meetings of his point of view. His oratory "is rich and varied in its essential qualities. The architecture is broad and massive. The coloring is vivid, but not gaudy. He strikes the note of gravity and authority with a confidence that one can hardly reconcile with the youthful face."[5] He was not an impromptu speaker and had a slight speech impediment, but he was adept at foreseeing the mood of Parliament, and possible questions and arguments that might be raised. His capacity for assimilating facts, reaching to the core of the matter, and framing plans or solutions, together with an initiative and determination added immeasurably to his ability to influence and persuade all who would listen.

The year 1919 introduced Churchill, the new War Secretary, gradually to the interconnected complexities of the Middle East problem: demobilization, economizing, the Bolshevik menace, opposition from other offices, opposition from his own office, France's ambitions, and the lack of a Turkish peace treaty. He developed his innovative policy to meet the challenge but was frustrated when he tried to implement it. No matter which way he turned in 1920 to settle the Middle East problem, which had now boiled down to a conflict between the aims of policy and economy, he was still frustrated. Solutions eluded him mainly because no one government office controlled the Middle East. His drive to empower the Colonial Office with control over the area in turn affected his career as he was appointed Colonial Secretary to solve the Middle East problem once and for all.

As Colonial Secretary, Churchill first set up his new Middle East Department and perfected the outlines of his policy for the region. Then he conferred with all the Middle East specialists at Cairo to work out details of his policy and took a side-trip to Palestine to negotiate with Amir 'Abdallah over custodianship of Transjordan. His next step was to obtain Cabinet and Parliamentary approval of this policy but before doing this he had to overcome many hurdles some of which proved to be unsurmountable. Once he gained Parliamentary sanction in mid-1921 Churchill felt that he could leave the daily running of Iraq and Palestine, his two major areas of concern in the Middle East, to his Department and to the two High Commissioners. His attention was drawn to other areas, especially to Ireland. Iraq progressed slowly along the lines drawn for it but Palestine hardly progressed at all and Churchill's disgust resulted in a policy of drift.

During 1922 Churchill wanted to give his attention to Ireland and party politics but a crisis in Iraq returned to his attention to this area. After a showdown between the Colonial Secretary and the king of Iraq, the issue was solved to Churchill's satisfaction. As for Palestine, the main role Churchill played was that of defender of the Balfour Declaration, which ensured that it would remain the basis of Palestine policy. His role in the formulation of the White Paper of 1922, known as the 'Churchill White Paper,' was a passive one.

An item basic to the success of Churchill's plans was peace with Turkey. The main reason why a definitive instrument had not yet been signed was the Turkish nationalist resurgence let by Mustafa Kemal. In the autumn of 1922, Kemal's westward move towards the Dardanelles and the warlike response of Lloyd George and Churchill caused a crisis which, in part, brought the downfall of the Coalition Government. Again, Churchill's career was affected by the role he played in shaping Middle East policy.

CHAPTER 2

Great Britain and the Middle East

When the First World War drew to a close and Great Britain began to shift gears slowly to a peacetime situation, she found herself in an uncomfortable position with regard to the Fertile Crescent. Britain had made numerous agreements during the war relating to the postwar division of the Ottoman Empire's Arab provinces and these agreements did not seem to dovetail one with the other. The variety of contenders for these provinces included the French, the Russians, the Italians, the Arabs, and the Zionists, and their aspirations often conflicted. Before the war there existed "no hard and fast agreements but there were notions, assumptions, and expectations, that if and when the Ottoman Empire came to be partitioned certain regions would go to certain Powers."[1] Which regions would go to which powers depended on different factors such as strategic or economic interests, or if a power had traditionally included a region within its sphere of influence. An examination of railroad agreements on the eve of the war, for example, shows that the Middle East was already in effect partitioned along lines of economic interests.[2]

Shortly after the outbreak of the war, Russia, alarmed that the British attack on the Straits could lead to British possession of Constantinople, initiated a series of diplomatic exchanges with the other Entente powers—Britain and France—aimed at securing her claim to those parts of the Ottoman Empire which were of vital interest to her, specifically the Straits. France had a long-standing claim to the Levant, recognized by most powers, but the area was not yet precisely defined. Britain had interests in the Persian

Gulf and its hinterland as well as in protecting Egypt and securing British communications with India.

The so-called Constantinople Agreement of the spring of 1915 which was a month-long series of diplomatic exchanges between Russia, France, and Britain, recognized Russia's claim to Constantinople and the Straits and the counterclaims of Britain to parts of Persia and the Arabian Peninsula as well as parts of the Ottoman Empire, and of France to parts of Syria and Anatolia.[3] But Britain felt that it was premature to discuss a partition in detail.

This was the first of the wartime secret agreements among the Entente powers aimed at partitioning the Ottoman Empire. Close on its heels was the London agreement, 26 April 1915, between the Entente and Italy. As part of the effort to bring Italy into the war on the Entente side, the Entente agreed to recognize certain Italian claims to parts of the Ottoman Empire as well as to other parts of the world.[4]

These agreements did not make partition of Turkey inevitable to the British.[5] The "Committee on Asiatic Turkey," headed by Sir Maurice de Bunsen, Assistant Under Secretary of State at the Foreign Office, was appointed right after the Constantinople Agreement was completed to clarify the British position on the Arab provinces. The report, presented in June 1915, favored a program aimed at maintaining the Ottoman Empire as an independent but decentralized federal state.[6] But, if Russia were to take a slice of the Ottoman Empire, then the other powers would follow suit and Britain would only be doing her duty by taking her chunk.

The third wartime agreement among the Entente powers, and central to the post-war disputes, was the Sykes-Picot Agreement. Britain informed France that negotiations were in process with Sharif Husayn, guardian of the holy places of Mecca and Medina—an important post both politically and religiously—which included an independent Arab state. Fearful that this might detrimentally affect her interests, France hastened into formal negotiations with Britain to delimit spheres of influence in the Arab provinces.[7] A provisional formula was drawn up, February 1916, by Sir Mark Sykes, adviser on Near Eastern Affairs to the Foreign Office, and Charles François Georges-Picot, French Counselor in London, and presented to Russia for agreement. Russia endorsed the Anglo-French plans in return for their approval of Russian claims to parts of northeast Anatolia.[8] According to the Sykes-Picot Agreement, the Arab provinces were to be divided into five areas: the "Blue" area, comprising coastal Syria and Lebanon, would be under direct or indirect French administration; the "Red" area, comprising the "vilayets" or provinces of Bagdad and Basrah, would be under direct or indirect British control; the "Brown" area, comprising much of Palestine, would be under international administration; and zones "A" and "B," comprising inland Syria, Transjordan and Mosul "vilayet," would be an independent Arab state with France having special economic and administrative rights in zone "A" and Britain in zone "B." This division was within the realm of the traditional European solution to the problem of disposing of wartime conquests acquired by an alliance of powers in that it provided for an authority to replace that which the allies were out to destroy. Arab independence without such a protective umbrella would invite anarchy or invasion. The agreement was kept secret partly because Turkey had not yet been defeated.[9]

The fourth wartime arrangement among the Entente powers again brought Italy into the picture to assure its desired share of Ottoman territory. The Saint-Jean de Maurienne Agreement of April 1917 incorporated Italian claims in a broadened Sykes-Picot plan, but Russia never endorsed the draft for the Bolshevik regime repudiated all tsarist international commitments.[10]

In addition to these four agreements among the Entente powers regarding the partition of the Ottoman Empire, Great Britain also entered into negotiations with two other parties, the Arabs and the Zionists. British negotiations via Sir Henry McMahon, High Commissioner of Egypt, with Husayn, the Sharif of Mecca, lasting from July 1915 through March 1916 (paralleling the Anglo-French discussions), were inspired in part by the desire of Secretary of State for War Kitchener to use an Arab revolt as a tool to hasten the collapse of the Ottoman Empire.[11] Husayn was prepared to agree to a military alliance on condition that Britain recognize the independence of the Arab countries the borders of which he proceeded to delimit. In order not to delay the arrangements for the Arab revolt, the political understanding between the two men, especially with regard to territorial reservations, was not clarified and its ambiguity caused much trouble in later years.[12]

The last of the wartime agreements affecting the Fertile Crescent was between Britain and the Zionists. The letter from Foreign Minister Arthur J. Balfour to Baron Lionel Rothschild, an acknowledged leader of British Jews, of November 1917, was inspired in part by strategic, in part by propagandistic, and in part by altruistic reasons.[13] The letter stated that His Majesty's Government favored the establishment in Palestine of a national home for the Jews on the understanding that nothing would be done to prejudice the rights of the Arabs.

Military partition followed the diplomatic partition. The Egyptian Expeditionary Force, under the command of General Sir Edmund Allenby, gradually overran Palestine, Lebanon and Syria, and Iraq was gradually conquered by the Mesopotamian Expeditionary Force led by General Sir Stanley Maude.[14] By the time the Ottoman Empire capitulated to the Allied powers and signed the armistice at Mudros, 30 October 1918,[15] Britain was in physical control of the Arab provinces. Allenby created three military administration zones corresponding roughly to the Sykes-Picot division but with marked changes in control. Except for Occupied Enemy Territory Administration West which conformed to the "Blue" zone and in which Britain allowed France to set up civil administration alongside British military administration, Britain remained in in firm control.[16] The three zones were governed by chief administrators directly responsible to Commander-in-Chief Allenby, who communicated with them through his chief political officer. The commander-in-chief was responsible to the War Office, but his political officer was responsible to the Foreign Office too, a situation which led to much confusion. Allenby tried to follow the Turkish administrative patterns as fully as possible as well as the international practices as prescribed in the Hague Convention.[17] In Iraq, Sir Arnold Wilson served as Acting High Commissioner responsible neither to the War nor Foreign Offices but to the India Office.

The India and Foreign Offices, which had been divided over aims and policies with regard to the Middle East during the war, were at loggerheads over which Office should control the area once the war ended.[18] The Foreign Office, conducting relations with independent foreign countries, sought to meet the susceptibilities of Britain's allies, to punish the Turks, and to devise a comprehensive foreign policy of which the Arab provinces were but one element. The India Office was concerned with the sensitivities of millions of Indian Muslims and with protection of Indian interests. The War Office was caught somewhere in the middle, anxious to attain its own goals. There was no clear cut decision on who was to decide Middle East policy let alone what that policy was. In the middle of the war there were eighteen separate individuals who advised on policy in an incredibly complicated line of authority.[19] While no central control was established in the Middle East, the Cabinet did at least create the Mesopotamian Administration Committee in March 1917 to coordinate policy there; this was soon enlarged into the Middle East (Administration) Committee in January 1918, which was in turn enlarged into the Eastern

Committee after two months and four meetings. There was a vast amount of work done between March 1918 and January 1919 and Lord Curzon, Under Secretary of State for Foreign Affairs, who served as chairman of the Eastern Committee, fought whatever he thought would undermine his role, thereby adding to the confusion over civil and military lines of authority on Middle Eastern affairs at the time of the armistice. Early in January 1919 the Eastern Committee was again reorganized, this time onto a less elaborate scale, into the Interdepartmental Committee on Middle Eastern Affairs, with Curzon still at the helm.[20]

Allenby provisionally recognized Faysal's Arab government in zones "A" and "B" of the Sykes-Picot Agreement, now labeled Occupied Enemy Territory East. This was done partly because Britain had made reassuring statements to the Arabs throughout 1918. These statements included a message by Lieutenant-Commander D. G. Hogarth of the Arab Bureau in [21] Cairo in the name of the British Government to Husayn—now King of the Hijaz—in January 1918, that the Balfour Declaration did not conflict with Britain's promises to the Arabs. A second statement was that of Sir Reginald Wingate, High Commissioner for Egypt, in the name of the British Government to seven Arab spokesmen from the Ottoman Arab provinces, June 1918, explaining British war aims in the Ottoman Arab provinces and the Arabian Peninsula. In this so-called "Declaration to the Seven," Britain recognized the independence of Arabian areas which were free before the war and those areas emancipated by the Arabs themselves during the war; in areas emancipated by Allied forces and those still under Turkish control, Britain would work towards setting up governments based on the consent of the governed. A third statement was made a week after the armistice in the form of a joint Anglo-French declaration promising self-determination to the Arab territories liberated from the Ottoman Turks.[22] These statements all served to undermine the Sykes-Picot arrangement and to compound the already complicated situation.[23]

When the victorious allies convened in Paris, January 1919, to draw up a lasting peace, Britain and France were already clashing over their Middle East objectives. These clashes were minor compared to the vaster problems of Germany, reparations, reconstruction and demobilization, and the enormous difficulties of the European settlement contributed to the failure to reach a settlement on the Middle East.

There were a number of proposals for the future of the Middle East prepared by Britain during the war and the Eastern Committee met in between the armistice and the peace conference to attempt to draw up Britain's approach to the issue. The Committee concluded that there should be no Turkish restoration and no Allied annexation, but there should be self-determination with some form of European advice. This would require cancellation of the Sykes-Picot Agreement. The Committee then disbanded for many of the leading ministers went off to Paris and Curzon had to fill in as acting Foreign Secretary. It was up to negotiations in Paris to settle matters.[24]

During the first three months of negotiating, Britain tried hard to push France into a change of policy on Syria, defining the Sykes-Picot Agreement as an elastic instrument. France, on the other hand, could not adopt anything but a rigid interpretation of the agreement as this was the major basis for any French claim in the Middle East. Early in December 1918 there was a secret oral understanding reached between David Lloyd George, the British Prime Minister, and Georges Clemenceau, the French Prime Minister, that seemed to include French acquiescence in the transfer of Palestine and the "vilayet" of Mosul to the British sphere in return for the assurance of assimilating zone "A" into the sphere of direct French administration and of the French procurement of the German share in the Turkish Petroleum Company.[25] This did not mean France was willing to renegotiate the entire Sykes-Picot Agreement, but rather that she was ready to make concessions on a "quid pro quo" basis and to keep the rest intact. Yet when France tried to convert this oral agreement into a written one, Britain was willing to conclude an oil agreement but resisted any French attempt to obtain a single mandate over Syria and Lebanon, and the consequent Anglo-French dispute came to a head at a secret meeting of the Big Four, 10 March 1919.[26]

To settle the dispute, President Woodrow Wilson recommended that an Inter-Allied Commission visit Syria and find out what the local opinion was on which power should become mandatory there. It was assumed by that time, that the area would be divided into mandates. But France refused to appoint delegates until French troops replaced British troops in Syria and until Britain fulfilled her part of the oral bargain of December 1918. France was also irritated by Britain's claim to a special role in everything to do with the Muslim world and saw all British actions as designs to encroach on the areas allotted to France.[27] Britain refused to send delegates unless France did the same. Although only the American members, Henry C. King and Charles R. Crane, went and although their inquiry proved to have no more than academic interest,[28] their arrival in Damascus, June 1919, encouraged Arab nationalists in the provisional Arab state under Faysal to convene a General Syrian Congress to frame a statement of their position. Their resolution rejected both a French mandate over Syria and a Jewish National Home in Palestine, and put forward the Greater Syria Scheme, namely one unified country that included Syria, Lebanon and Palestine.[29]

When the Versailles Treaty was signed, 28 June 1919, very little was clear about the Fertile Crescent aside from the principle of mandatory supervision. Faysal was still in Damascus, British troops were in Syria and Mosul, the administration of Syria and Palestine was still a military one. Iraq was developing along lines suggested by Arnold Wilson and the Foreign Office strongly objected to these Indian methods. The Foreign Office favored establishing a regime which would pass muster as an Arab government and would be workable, while at the same time would be under British control. Wilson's ideas were of the more traditional British protectorate type.

The Council of Four agreed to suspend consideration of Turkey until it could be ascertained whether the United States would be willing to assume a share of mandatory responsibility. The conference technically remained in session in the summer of 1919 but only subordinate delegates remained. Meanwhile Britain had to administer the area under her control as best possible.[30] That summer Mustafa Kemal, leader of the Turkish nationalists, invaded Armenia, the Wahhabis led by Ibn Sa'ud began expanding in Arabia and Bolshevism emerged as a real menace to the Middle East.

In September 1919 Lloyd George returned to France to discuss the military occupation in the Middle East. British ministers, military leaders and advisers met at his vacation home in Trouville, 11 September, and drew up a twelve-point memorandum stating that Britain was prepared to evacuate Syria and Cilicia starting 1 November handing over the garrisons according to the pledges made to the French and the Arabs, namely all to go to France except Damascus, Homs, Hama and Aleppo which had been promised to the Arabs. Palestine was to be defined by its ancient boundaries and if France opposed this, Britain was prepared to accept American arbitration. Britain was to have the right to construct and administer railroads and pipelines from Haifa to Mesopotamia.[31] This scheme was based mainly on the

Sykes-Picot Agreement thus breaking the deadlock with France that had existed since March.[32] The next day, Lloyd George discussed the memorandum over dinner with some of his chief advisers and the changes were put into a revised aide memoire the morning after, 13 September. Lloyd George presented it to Clemenceau later that day.[33]

At a meeting of the Supreme Council, 15 September, Clemenceau accepted the proposals for British evacuation of Syria and Cilicia but on the understanding that France was not committed to accept any other part of the arrangements; also, the agreement was temporary and would not prejudice the final peace settlement with Turkey.[34] This boded ill for Arab independence in Syria, but the way was clear for further negotiations on other suspended problems. By December an agreement giving France 25 percent of the Turkish Petroleum Company in return for railroad and pipeline facilities was reached. Lloyd George had in effect conceded to France and forsaken Faysal for he needed French cooperation for his Turkish and especially his European policies.[35] Yet despite all of these concessions France refused to accept the proposals other than British withdrawal from the "Blue" zone in November until it was agreed that France was to have the mandate for inland Syria as well, namely, zone "A."[36]

Nationalist pressures in Syria finally forced the two powers to come to terms. A second General Syrian Congress convened at Damascus, 8 March 1920, at which the independence of Syria was proclaimed, including Lebanon and Palestine, and Faysal was named king. This action was provoked by the preparations, in March, of the Allied Prime Ministers to assemble in order to work out a Turkish peace treaty and the Arabs feared that they would not be given an independent kingdom. A group of Iraqis passed a similar resolution on Iraq and chose the Amir 'Abdallah, Faysal's older brother, as monarch. These actions precipitated a crisis, forcing both Britain and France to end the drifting. The Cabinet met, 23 March,[37] to discuss what the Prime Minister might state in Parliament on the future of Iraq, anticipating an Allied conference on the Middle East early in April. The Cabinet approved announcing that Britain would accept a mandate for that country which had to include Mosul, the policy of Britain would be to develop an Arab Government based on representative Arab institutions and an Arab administration, Britain would not oppose Iraq's desire for an Arab ruler, and a large reduction of the garrison size was urgent.

The Supreme Council of the League of Nations met in San Remo, 19 April 1920, and Britain finally agreed to the French request for an enlarged Syrian mandate, and an oil agreement giving France a 25 percent interest in any concession that would exploit Mosul's oil resources quickly followed.[38] The mandates for Palestine and Iraq went to Britain. The mandates were assigned without first concluding a formal Turkish treaty and their terms had yet to be drawn up.

With the differences between Britain and France settled, the Supreme Council was able to agree on peace terms to be imposed on the Ottoman government. The Ottoman delegation reluctantly signed the instrument 10 August 1920,[39] in which all non-Turkish provinces and much of Anatolia were surrendered, a capitulatory regime was reestablished and an international commission was to control the Straits. But the treaty was never ratified for the nationalist regime under Mustafa Kemal at Ankara refused to have any part of it, and as time passed the imperial government at Istanbul gradually lost authority to the nationalists. Despite the absence of a peace treaty, Britain and France decided to proceed with their own plans for governing their mandates.

This is the Middle East setting in which Winston S. Churchill, first as Secretary of the State for War and Air, and then as Secretary of State for the Colonies, had to frame his policies. But there is also the setting on the home front that must be taken into consideration. One of the main administrative problems of the postwar government was the reduction of spending. Great Britain had loaned a fortune to her allies and had borrowed a fortune as well, especially from the United States. The internal debt was even more formidable and this dictated economy in every sphere of public expenditure. The short postwar boom broke abruptly in the winter of 1920–21, unemployment more than doubled, and industrial strife grew.[40]

The empire did not ease Britain's economic problems.[41] The Dominions, bound to Britain mainly by sentiment, all aspired to develop their own industries. Most of the African colonies were economic disappointments. Even India was becoming a liability for not only was she manufacturing her own cotton goods but was beginning to demand national independence. A graver nationalist challenge grew in Ireland where violence and bloodshed spread. The rise of a new British empire in the Middle East, with its oil and potential markets, seemed to offer the only optimistic note in a generally gloomy economic picture.

CHAPTER 3

The Secretary of State for War and Air

The year 1919 introduced Winston S. Churchill gradually to the interconnected complexities of the Middle East. His immediate task as Secretary of State for War and Air was the demobilization of the nearly three and a half million British soldiers scattered all over the world since the armistices in 1918 which ended the First World War. Such demobilization should be accompanied by enormous savings to the economy, Churchill's second task. Churchill was aware of the difficulties of the office but was "willing to undertake the v[er]y responsible duties," even thanking the Prime Minister for "the renewed proof of y[ou]r confidence wh[ich] such an invitation implies."[1]

David Lloyd George, Prime Minister of the Coalition Government since 1916, was Churchill's mentor who had fought to bring him back into ministerial ranks openly stating that it was unwise to allow such ability and talent to run to waste as it had since May 1915 when Churchill had lost his position as First Lord of the Admiralty.[2] In July 1917, despite strong hostility, Churchill was appointed Minister of Munitions, a position he held until Lloyd George asked him to take on the post of Secretary of State for War and Air, January 1919, again in the face of strong opposition.[3]

Energetically turning to his most immediate task, Churchill wrote a memorandum on demobilization within nine days of assuming office.[4] His task was a general one; it was up to him to develop the particulars and methods for realizing this task. What is unique here is that he planned for an army establishment—for six armies of occupation—before consenting to demobilization. Unless Britain wanted to lose the fruits of victory, there had to be armies of occupation strong enough to extract from Germany and Turkey the just terms which the Allies demanded. "The better trained and disciplined these armies are, the fewer men will be needed to do the job. We have, therefore, to create, in order to wind up the war satisfactorily, a strong, compact, contented, well-disciplined army which will maintain the high reputation of the British Service and make sure we are not tricked of what we have rightfully won."[5] This army would be one-third the war-size army and he listed how many should be retained in each of the six armies.

Before presenting these ideas to the Cabinet, Churchill urged Lloyd George to back his plan for his backing would influence the Cabinet to accept it. The discipline of the soldiers to be retained depended on their knowing that they had to stay in their new units for some time and that they were chosen on fair grounds. That way they would know that the pushing and shoving that had been going on would accomplish nothing and they would settle down to their job.[6] The Cabinet approved the Secretary for War's proposals in principle on 28 January.[7]

At this early post armistice stage, the Middle East concerned the Secretary of State mainly as one of the six are areas of the world necessitating an army of occupation. As a result of the war there were hundreds of thousands of British troops stationed in the Arab provinces of the Ottoman Empire as well as in Constantinople. Gradually Churchill realized that the Middle East was not only an area necessitating an army of occupation but an area needing a new policy.

Demobilization and economizing were Churchill's two basic tasks as Secretary of State for War and Air and therefore two basic ingredients in the recipe for Middle East policy. Again, he was given the order to economize but it was up to him to work out the details for realizing this. The struggle to reduce the expenses of his two departments colored most of his policy decisions during his two-year reign once the solution to the initial tremendous problem of demobilization was well under way. But Churchill was also administrator of the Crown's military forces and thus of the British Empire's security, and the overwhelming color looming up on this horizon was red—Bolshevism. This third ingredient of his Middle East policy was forced upon him from the outside and he had to work out how to cope with it.

It is doubtful if any minister of the British Government reacted as strongly as Churchill did against the Bolsheviks and his work at the War Office was dominated by the civil war in Russia until the Bolsheviks triumphed in 1920. Some, among them the Prime Minister, accused him of over-reacting, but Churchill contended that even if the Allies abandoned Russia to work out her own salvation, Russia would not abandon the Allies. "The bear is padding on bloody paws across the snows to the Peace Conference."[8] When Lloyd George told Churchill he wanted to invite the Bolsheviks to talks in Prinkipo, the reply was that "one might as well legalize sodomy as recognize the Bolsheviks."[9]

Churchill admonished the Cabinet, 17 March 1919,[10] for sitting still while the Bolsheviks were overrunning north Russia. The Bolsheviks were not sitting still and would roll over Siberia to Japan. Only when India herself would be threatened would the western powers stir and be prepared to put forward ten times the effort that at an earlier stage would have sufficed to save the situation. Churchill had written in this vein to the Prime Minister a few days earlier,[11] adding that it was the British Empire "with which we are particularly concerned" that would be threatened by a Bolshevik takeover of the Caucasus, Persia and Afghanistan."[12]

The red menace led to some of Churchill's most colorful speeches in this early period, as for example the one given in Parliament, 29 May 1919, during delivery of the Army Estimates. "... Bolshevism is not a policy; it is a disease. It is not a creed; it is a pestilence. It presents all the characteristics of a pestilence. It breaks out with great suddenness; it is violently contagious; it throws people into a frenzy of excitement; it spreads with extraordinary rapidity; the mortality is terrible; so that after a while, like other pestilences, the disease tends to wear itself out."[13]

It is not proposed to go into all aspects of Churchill's preoccupation with Bolshevism,[14] but it is important to try to find out if there was any basis to his fears with regard to its overrunning the Middle East. Within a month of the seizure of power in 1917, the Council of the People's Commissars of the Bolshevik regime issued an Appeal to the Muslims of Russia and the East which was signed by Lenin and Stalin. Analysis of this and other heavy propaganda artillery which was directed toward the Muslim East in 1917 and 1918 suggests that the Soviet Government believed that the success of the Bolshevik Revolution was contingent on its alliance with the Muslim East. The two were inseparable and interdependent. It was logical for the Bolsheviks to appeal to the largest Russian minority as Trotsky, plenipotentiary representative of Turkestan in Moscow, did by sending a telegram summarizing Lenin's principles to the committee of the soviets of Turkestan at Tashkent, 12 March 1919.[15] Great Britain, as the largest Muslim power in the world, thus became a main target of Soviet propaganda in its quest to aid the liberation of enslaved peoples from the domination of western countries.[16]

Intelligence reports flowed back to the British Government on Bolshevik activities, propaganda and feelers. Churchill kept himself informed of the major trends, especially the moves towards treaties with Turkey, Persia and Afghanistan. Later in his term of office as Secretary of State for War, more substantial moves were taken by the Soviets to woo the Muslim Orient and Churchill's fears seemed to be substantiated. Thus Winston S. Churchill's policies in the Middle East were formulated as much in response to the Soviet threat as to the instructions he received from the Prime Minister upon assuming office. He was a member of the school of thought advocating that Britain should remain a great world power and her imperial inheritance was an integral part of this position. That this inheritance in the Middle East was brand new made no difference to these imperialists, and it was to be protected against all enemies as strongly as longer held areas. When viewed through these dual lenses, now the one focusing clearer, now the other, Churchill's activities in the Middle East of 1919–1920 make sense and fall into a pattern.

Turning from why Churchill developed his policy to how he did so, the first thing to do is to determine the content of his policy. The first hint of this is in his correspondence in which he defended his dual position as Secretary of State for War and Air.[17] After stressing the point that combining the two offices in his hands was temporary and was geared towards efficient demobilization, Churchill made a second point soon to be further developed. He felt that the future garrisons of the Empire would "have to be reviewed in the light of the war and the increased responsibilities cast upon us by our victory." It was more efficient and harmonious to review the garrisons and air forces from a single standpoint "in order that the fullest use may be made of the new arm, especially in the East and in the Middle East, and that economy of expense and personnel may be effected to the utmost."[18] Churchill elaborated upon this a month later, previewing what soon became one of the pillars of his developing Middle East policy. The task ahead, he wrote to Lord Birkenhead,[19] was not only to demobilize but to reconstruct and redistribute Britain's fighting forces. "The Garrisons of Palestine, Mesopotamia and India have to be reconsidered from the point of view of the new technical inventions which the war has produced and of the general advance in the science of war." Only this way could there be economization. Airplanes especially would be very useful in maintaining order and suppressing revolts in "these large oriental regions." Southern Persia was the testing ground for Churchill's theories, for only with positive empirical proof could he hope to convince others to go along with his new ideas.

A key document summarizing War Office activities and problems of 1919 is a letter written by Churchill to Lloyd George at the beginning of September.[20] He dealt first with two main policy ingredients, demobilization and economizing. He was satisfied that his administrative branches were wholly concentrated on demobilizing the scattered army and reducing it to the "lowest level compatible with the safe and efficient discharge of the obligation laid upon us by the State policy." But, in answer to Lloyd George's complaint that it was not fast enough, this cutting down in numbers of men on pay and ration strength was delayed by about a dozen causes half of which related to the Middle East, introducing us to some new ingredients going into Churchill's evolving policy for that area. First, the delay in reaching a peace settlement with Germany required keeping ten divisions on the Rhine and three in France and Flanders until mid-July. Delay was caused, secondly, by the failure to reach a Turkish settlement and the continuous deterioration of Britain's position throughout the Turkish empire caused by Greek and Italian activities; thirdly by the unrest in Egypt due to internal causes; fourthly, by the unrest in Palestine and Syria due to France; fifthly, by the disorders in India and the threat from Afghanistan. These Middle East problems were mainly outside the realm of the War Office but by this time they had left the stage of relative minor concern to the War Secretary and were growing. No one could yet know what overgrown proportions they were soon to assume.

The next five causes for demobilization delay included Ireland, preparing for action in case of a strike, delay in repatriating prisoners of war, the shipping stringency, and the delay in disposing of stores scattered over all theaters of war. The eleventh cause listed was the need to proceed according to a plan which did not appear grossly unfair to the soldiers. Twelfthly, time was needed to create a new volunteer army and send the battalions out to India and the East to relieve the conscript troops. Last, Churchill listed that an overall complication was the difficulty of "arriving at fixed conclusions as to the size and cost of the post-war army, and by the uncertainty of the political as well as the military policy in Palestine, Mesopotamia and generally towards the Turkish Empire."

Such was the situation to date. But things were easing up a bit, and demobilization was up to 7,500 per day. War Office staff which had risen to 21,836 was reduced to 12,000 despite the rise in the volume of paper work. Garrisons of fortresses and coaling stations were reduced to skeletons, as were coast defenses. Repatriation of prisoners of war was proceeding.

Churchill then turned to the other very important task of his office, economizing funds. In an August cabinet meeting the Prime Minister had indicated that the total sum for the Army and Air Force under normal conditions was 75 million pounds. The Army Council and Air Council were both working on expenditure schemes and estimates would be completed as soon as possible. Then it would be up to the Cabinet to decide what action to take on the gap between money available and obligations with which the War Office was charged. This was a clever way, on the part of the Secretary of State, to point out that the funds allocated were much too few. A number of months earlier, Churchill had written to the Prime Minister that of the three forces it was the Navy that would have to reduce its expenditure most, because although the post-war force would be smaller, it would cost more because money was worth less, because pay was higher and because of its expensive scientific character.[21]

Since taking office, Churchill had concerned himself only generally with the Middle East, with the exception of his ideas on the use of airplanes. But by September, he was worried enough about one particular area to draw it to the attention of the Prime Minister because the problem had direct bearing on one of his two major tasks. He was greatly concerned over the cost of Mesopotamia.[22] With a population of about two million and a yearly revenue of two million, the country was costing Britain 25 million pounds in the current financial year. The General Staff had calculated the minimum force needed to hold the country and its cost would far exceed any return from the province. Therefore Churchill had directed that the whole question should be reexamined from a military standpoint. He suggested that a Cabinet Committee should also be appointed to examine the question in its economic, political and military bearing.

Churchill concluded that "after nearly 14 years' experience of administrative departments I have never seen anything to compare with the difficulties of the questions now pressing for decision, while the daily routine business in volume exceeds several times the greatest pressure known before the war."[23]

Churchill was even more defensive in his letter to Lloyd George of 6 September.[24] The Prime Minister had accused the Secretary of State of being preoccupied with Russia and Bolshevism. Churchill agreed that they caused him much distress, but that did not mean he had neglected his administrative duties. Quickly summarizing the problems detailed in his earlier letter, Churchill wrote that in these circumstances the progress in demobilization was remarkable and worthy of praise, not reproach. "The difficulties are immense. Abler men c[oul]d no doubt cope with them better; & if they present themselves they sh[oul]d certainly be used. But frankly I do not think I can do better work than I have done since I have been at the War Office. I am not capable of it. I have not the strength nor the ability."[25] Every point was fought over, and even imperative orders could only be executed at a certain speed and that only if there was constant effort from the top. This letter reveals further complexities that Churchill had to deal with in trying to formulate his policy, namely opposition from within and without. He had hinted at these difficulties in his earlier letter but after receiving Lloyd George's accusatory note, decided to spell them out. But although disgusted and momentarily disillusioned, it was not in his nature to remain so for long and Churchill plunged into his work and September proved to be an active month in the Middle East arena.

Since Mesopotamia was costing so much, Churchill focused his attention on it and the other aspect of how Churchill influenced policy, namely his methodology, comes to the fore. On 9 September[26] he telegraphed to the General Officer Commanding, Mesopotamia, General Sir G. MacMunn, that because of its enormous cost the present garrison of 278,000 had to be reduced at once by 98,000 which included 60,000 followers, as first step in reaching the permanent garrison size. The provisional after-war garrison should consist of two Indian Divisions, two Indian cavalry brigades and army and line of communication troops. The general had to make the best military plan in the circumstances. Churchill's figures were based on General Staff papers drawn up at his instructions of 6 August pointing the way to a policy of concentration on lines of communication and at decisive points.[27] The General Staff is the special military division of the War Office devoted to the study of the theory of operation, to collecting military information, and to the preparation and training of the army for war. Churchill was not giving general orders any more, but specific ones, probably hoping thereby to stimulate the response he wanted.

The general answered, 12 September, agreeing to reduce the garrison by 118,000 but only in the spring.[28] Churchill could not and would not accept this. He forced the issue in the return telegram by first detailing reductions in artillery, cavalry, infantry and machine gun corps,[29] figures which had been checked out by the Deputy Commander of the Imperial General Staff, Major-General Sir C. H. Harrington.[30] He then ordered the GOC to prepare a scheme for creating a special white police force and a small military instrument for maintaining internal order operating with light cars and motor launches carrying machine guns, in combination with airplanes and a native police force or gendarmerie. Otherwise Mesopotamia could not be controlled economically. Furthermore, the Prime Minister wanted, as an essential part of this arrangement, a system of payment of subsidies to local Arab chiefs contingent upon their good behavior and maintenance of order by means of local levies. This is how Churchill's policy for Mesopotamia had evolved by the autumn of 1919, and this is the military policy he adhered to as long as he dealt with the country.

General MacMunn replied, 6 October,[31] completely ignoring the War Secretary's untraditional plan that the provisional post-war garrison had to remain for the present owing to the disturbed state of Mesopotamia, but by the end of 1920 it should be possible to reduce the garrison to one division, one cavalry brigade at Baghdad, and one mixed brigade at Mosul. Somewhat satisfied that his ploy of giving such a radical order had forced the GOC to agree to reduce the troop level much more than the GOC had ever planned to, Churchill had all these telegrams printed and presented as a memorandum to the War Cabinet, 15 October, with a note that by the beginning of December the garrison strength would be down to 148,000, which included only 15,000 British troops.[32]

Closely tied to Mesopotamian troop reduction was the problem of that country's railroads which, along with planes and armored cars, formed a major part of Churchill's project for solving the question of how to control Mesopotamia without expensive soldiers. But Mesopotamian railroads fell within the domain of the interdepartmental Committee for Middle East Affairs and Curzon proved to be an unmoveable barrier to Churchill's plans. War Office interest lay in a "through Euphrates" project relinking Basrah and Baghdad via Hillah and Nasrieh, and an extension to the Persian frontier as far as Kermanshah. The committee had agreed, 11 January 1919,[33] to push ahead with these projects and details had been worked out by the War Office but everything became bogged down in the controversy over which department should pay the bill. If, as was anticipated, the railroads were to be transferred ultimately to civilian control, the War Office claimed it was not its affair. But since the actual transfer could not take place until a peace treaty was signed with Turkey, and the railroads were needed immediately for strategic reasons, the matter became more and more complicated as the months passed. The Treasury had decided, 19 March, that provision was to be made in Army Estimates for the expenses of the civil administrations of occupied territories until a peace treaty was signed.[34] This came as a blow to Churchill who was trying his hardest to reduce Army Estimates to the bare minimum, and it was not until 10 September that the Secretary of State for War personally gave orders again regarding this problem. The War Office at this time wanted to be in a position to undertake punitive expeditions against the unruly Kurds in Mosul Vilayet in northern Mesopotamia, and a railroad was essential to ensure a steady and economical supply of troops operating there through the winter. This would cost over a million pounds but, together with the Euphrates line, would allow for troop reduction down to five battalions from the present thirteen. This line would also be of the greatest value for civilian traffic.

These two problems had been communicated to Curzon who had procrastinated throughout July and August rather than settled policy.[35] When, at the end of August Churchill saw what Curzon had been doing, he insisted on being consulted before any further step be taken.

The Finance branch in answer to the War Secretary's prodding drew up a note on Mesopotamian railroads stating that the War Office was committed to the sum of three million pounds.[36] The Quartermaster General, Lt. General Sir Travers E. Clark, minuted that this was the time to press Curzon for an explicit view on the Mosul line and until then the General Officer Commanding, Mesopotamia, should be ordered to stop all work not explicitly sanctioned. He added that the Foreign Office should be told openly that if the railroads were not to be proceeded with the troops would have to be withdrawn further south.[37]

Churchill approved a multi-front attack to try to get the matter settled and sent a strong letter to Curzon pressing for an immediate decision on the northern railroad and requesting that he approach the Treasury to sanction its completion. He also ordered General MacMunn to cease all works not explicitly approved.[38] At the same time, Churchill circulated to the Cabinet a General Staff memorandum on Mesopotamia stressing the need for railroads and planes, a General Staff paper on garrisons there, and Sir John Hewitt's report of May on his impressions about Mesopotamia. In addition, a short statement on railroad policy was printed.[39] The War Secretary approved the four papers and in his preliminary note stressed the necessity for the Cabinet to lay down limits to the program of capital expenditure on railroad construction in Mesopotamia.[40] But even these strong measures failed to move Curzon to action in 1919.

Churchill faced even larger problems than these over his Air Force project. Railroads were a matter of dispute between a number of offices, whereas Air Force control over Mesopotamia gave rise to a dispute between Churchill and his own staff as well as with other ministries. This dispute exemplified his attempts to get his way through rational argumentation based on solid facts. To build up his argument, Churchill ordered the Acting Civil Commissioner at Baghdad, Lt. Col. A. T. Wilson, to write a paper on the possibilities of employing planes in substitution for troops in Mesopotamia and Persia, and had it in hand by 26 April.[41] Wilson highly recommended use of planes to control Mesopotamia, using South Persia as empirical proof of how well they worked and how much less costly they were than garrisons. Mesopotamia was a large rough country, sparsely populated, and full of turbulent tribes, and the ability to go on collecting revenue depended on maintenance of a force able to immediately repress trouble wherever it occurred, and this could be done effectively by planes. Wilson submitted, therefore, that the three squadrons allocated to Mesopotamia should be made up to strength quickly, with machines suitable for use in punitive operations at long distances. The Royal Air Force "should be in a position in future to do for us on land in the Middle East what the Navy have done for us in the Persian Gulf in the past."[42]

Wilson's paper confirmed Churchill's views, but Lt. Col. W. F. Nugent, a member of the Army Staff, disagreed with this paper,[43] writing that although the use of planes could modify the internal policing of Mesopotamia, it would be unsound to reduce the army of occupation on that account because that would be based on the wrong conception of the army's primary duty, namely protection against invasion. The Director of Military Operations, General

Radcliffe, concurred in this, as did the Deputy Commander of the Imperial General Staff.

Churchill responded to this contradiction to his views by minuting to the D.C.I.G.S. on 9 May[44] that the garrisoning of Mesopotamia had to be considered under two different aspects: disorder from within, and invasion from without. Regarding the former, "aircraft will certainly play an integral part in our arrangements and must, to the extent to which they are used, reduce our military force." As for the latter aspect, defense rested on the Empire's main power and not on a local self-contained field army. Then succinctly summarizing his overall policy in one sentence, the Secretary of State wrote that "the true principle requiring to be considered in Imperial Defence as a whole is to station in particular theatres only such troops as are necessary for immediate emergency, and to form at suitable points a central reserve which can proceed to any threatened portion of the British Dominions."[45]

In reply, Radcliffe drew up a report on 14 May, [46] agreeing that planes could eventually enable them to reduce troops but not greatly, as land communications were needed to maintain patrol dumps and repair facilities. Also, the effect of planes was transitory because strategic points could not be occupied, nor could offenders be arrested. Radcliffe agreed that Mesopotamia's defense depended on the action of main strategic forces, but a covering force was vital to protect the Baghdad railroad center because it would take time for troops to arrive.

Churchill quickly responded to these arguments, and 17 May wrote to both Harington and Radcliffe[47] that the latter's minute did not take into consideration the possibility, then within reach, of supplying plane stations direct from the air. A small number of planes could easily and rapidly establish landing grounds, repair shops, and petrol dumps at a distance of 100 miles from any road or railhead, and in a roadless country the cost of air transport would be less than that by road. "It is just because these possibilities are not studied in the light of the present and future developments that a limited view is taken." But, as with railroads, no progress was made here either.

Unfettered by the army's traditional way of thinking, the Secretary of State for War and Air was able to approach War Office problems with fresh, inventive, simple and far-seeing ideas. He then had to convince his General Staff, reluctant to move in new tracks, as seen above, and other ministries. The main issue between the ministries was money. For example, how much money could Churchill have to budget the Air Ministry, and how much money could he have for armored cars?[48] By September Churchill still had no clearance on a specific sum for the Air Force, and even by the end of November all he managed to get approval by the Cabinet was the survey of the air route from Cairo to Karachi, an item that had been proposed five months earlier.[49] Churchill's innovative plans for economizing in Mesopotamia were getting nowhere.

The lack of a peace treaty with Turkey further complicated the situation. Until August, Churchill was more concerned with specific details of War office problems, such as size of garrisons, supplies of animals, air routes, and land communications than with policy in Turkey and Syria. But the strain on military resources of maintaining these armies proved to be too much, and the War Secretary wrote so to Balfour, the Foreign Secretary,[50] urging a peace arrangement of a kind which would enable Britain to bring home her troops by late October. "I know how great your difficulties are, but I trust you will realize that the length of time which we can hold a sufficient force at your disposal to overawe Turkey is limited, and that I have not the legal power, nor the financial means, nor the political support necessary to extend those limits."[51] Delays in reaching peace had added over sixty millions to the Army Estimates, for which no Parliamentary sanction had been obtained and the people were becoming more and more disgusted.

Two days later he raised the issue in the Cabinet asking for a definite date for withdrawing from Turkey. Churchill would be relieved if the Cabinet decided to withdraw all British forces in the coming two months, but with usual prevarication all the Cabinet agreed on was that the War office was to submit a statement of what non-settlement of Turkey was costing, and what expenditure in Palestine and Mesopotamia amounted to.[52]

Balfour's answer from Paris was even more discouraging. The Turkish peace settlement was proving to be the most troublesome question with which the Peace Conference had to deal and could not really be dealt with until it was known what part America would play. Therefore he could not recommend a diminution of the forces especially as agitation was growing over the Greek invasion of Smyrna.[53] This Greek invasion of May 1918 was part of a wider Allied policy to break up the Turkish Empire according to secret wartime agreements. From Smyrna the Greeks seized control of a sizable hinterland. One result of the Greek occupation was the decision by Mustafa Kemal, one of the Turkish military heroes, to assume command of the nationalist movement and demand complete evacuation of Anatolia and Thrace by non-Turkish powers.

Deflated, Churchill wrote back to Balfour, 23 August, agreeing that if Britain stayed in Turkey it had to be in sufficient strength to be safe. He did not believe that America would undertake the mandate for Turkey "and I fear that we are waiting for something that will never come off."[54] This issue was then temporarily dropped as attention focused on settling the Syrian question with France, and Churchill was among the British ministers that gathered in Paris, September 1919. He played a secondary role to the Prime Minister and Foreign Secretary there and was concerned mainly with protecting War Office interests. These interests were geared at maintaining good relations with France but without detriment to the strategical position acquired in the war.

While in Paris, taking advantage of the presence of Allenby, Churchill asked him to write out proposals for interim and peace garrisons for Egypt and Palestine, as well as a scheme for a permanent apparatus for holding the two countries. Allenby's idea was a British civil police force in aid of the native police, with improved elevated roadways on which armed cars could travel and control the countryside by working in conjunction with armed motor launches and planes. Only a small garrison would thus be needed.[55] Churchill liked the idea very much for it dovetailed with his own ideas for economization. The Chief of the Imperial General Staff agreed, but only for Egypt and Palestine.[56]

In the midst of the negotiations in Paris we suddenly get a different picture of Churchill's activities. The Prime Minister wrote a long letter to his War Secretary, 22 September,[57] showing he was at his wits' end. Lloyd George was doing his best to comply with the legitimate demand coming from all over the country to cut down on expenditure. He had especially urged Churchill to apply his mind to the problem because the highest expenditure was military, because the War Office could make the largest immediate reduction without damaging public welfare, and because "I have found your mind so obsessed by Russia that I felt I had good grounds for the apprehension that your great abilities, energy, and courage were not devoted to the reduction of expenditure." Exasperated, Lloyd George felt that his appeals were in vain because the first communication Churchill sent after each interview related to Russia. Even after the Paris meetings to reduce British commitments in the Middle East, the War Secretary produced a lengthy memorandum on Russia. The last straw for the Prime Minister was a four page letter on Russia and a closely printed memorandum on Russia written by Churchill that weekend instead of the promised financial memorandum on the Middle East. Russia was thereby costing Britain not merely the sum spent directly on it, but indirectly in the failure to attend to the details of expenditure in other spheres. The Prime Minister made one last try to induce his Minister "to throw off this obsession which ... is upsetting your balance" and to concentrate on unjustifiable expenditures elsewhere. On a quieter note, he concluded: "I have worked with you now for longer than I have probably cooperated with any other man in public life: and I think I have given you tangible proof that I wish you well. It is for that reason that I write frankly to you."[58] This letter hurt Churchill deeply, and he responded that afternoon.[59] He had done his best and was ready to defend his actions in Parliament. Then he returned the attack on Lloyd George: If the latter had not been so pressed with other business he would have better understood and appreciated what the Army Administration difficulties had been what with having to restore an army from mutiny to contentment, to dissolve an immense army, to create a new volunteer one, and to meet the demands for troops at home and abroad. Reduction of garrisons would not be possible until policies were settled, as for example in Palestine, Egypt and Mesopotamia.

Turning finally to Russia, the War Secretary wrote that "I may get rid of my 'obsession' or you may get rid of me: but you will not get rid of Russia: nor of the consequences of a policy wh[ich] for nearly a year it has been impossible to define." He could not ignore the problem, concluding that "surely I am not wrong in writing earnestly & sincerely to my chief & oldest political friend to let him know that things are not all right & are not going to get all right along this road. Surely I was bound to do this."[60]

Yet Lloyd George's letter had the desired effect for Churchill threw himself into the task set before him. It is as though he needed sharp prodding every so often to keep him in line. The next day he ordered the CIGS and Adjutant General to draw up a memorandum showing proposals for retaining the military forces in Mesopotamia, Egypt and Palestine, listing the rate of dispersal of conscripts there and financial effects of the proposals.[61] He also sent off the telegram to the General Officer Commanding in Mesopotamia asking his views on intermediate and final garrison sizes.[62] Col. A. T. Wilson was asked for his opinion on the telegram to General MacMunn,[63] and the reply arrived, via the India Office, to Churchill, 29 September. Wilson agreed that the number of troops proposed by the General Staff was ample for maintaining internal order and suppressing frontier disturbances, assuming that peace with Turkey was permanent, the Kurdistan question was settled—namely, whether to stay there or not—the situation in Persia did not deteriorate, and that the French and Arabs did not clash in Syria.[64]

These incalculable assumptions, some of which were vital to Churchill's economizing plans, were reinforced by the telegram to Churchill from General MacMunn, received 7 October,[65] drawing attention to the fermentation going on in Mesopotamia because of Kemalist propaganda, pan-Islamism, pan-Arabism and Faysal's intrigues from Syria, other elements that could upset Churchill's plans. Until the future of the debatable provinces of the Turkish Empire was settled and the new mandatories grasped their provinces firmly the general considered that the provisional post-war garrison had to remain without substantial reduction as far as combatant units were concerned.[66]

Convinced by the opinions of the men on the spot that these seemingly minor ingredients had to blend into his recipe, Churchill noted to the Prime Minister, 7 October,[67] that he was about to issue the very far reaching orders for further rapid demobilization suggested to him by the Cabinet, but before doing so he wanted the Cabinet to formally accept responsibility for it. There would be no army reserve, he warned, no special reserve and no territorial force, that is there would be no reserve available for India, Palestine, Mesopotamia or Turkey in case of emergency. The Bolsheviks then surging forward to Turkestan trying to overrun the Middle East both by arms and by alliances with Afghanistan and the Kemalists in Turkey would cause that emergency. "The whole Turkish Empire outside Constantinople has passed beyond our control. Egypt, Palestine and Mesopotamia are intimately affected by the unrest in the Turkish Empire and Palestine in particular is likely to be disturbed by the French incursion."[68] Therefore, the War Secretary wanted it to be the Cabinet's responsibility for issuing the new demobilization orders so that should things go wrong he alone would not be blamed.

The report handed in the next day to the Secretary of State by the General Staff[69] on the retention of military forces in Mesopotamia, Egypt, and Palestine as ordered on the 23 September, reinforced Churchill's growing fears over those areas. The anti-British agitation could very possibly combine with Bolshevik activities and therefore it would be unwise to reduce the garrisons. In Mesopotamia the main factor affecting demobilization was completion of the railroad program, because poor communications necessitated large forces to police the country and patrol the undefined northern borders. The General Staff eagerly agreed to Allenby's plan for Egypt and Palestine, but again the actual rate of reduction could not be forecast because of so many unknown conditions.

Churchill made his red ink notes all over the report, demanding exact figures for Palestine and Egypt and ordering his staff to act on the figure of a 94,000-man reduction for Mesopotamia as agreed to by MacMunn. He also wanted all material on the three areas to be collated and a comprehensive survey made of the whole situation both for himself and the cabinet.[70] It is unsure how he expected to use this material because later that day Hankey, the Cabinet Secretary, sent a secret and urgent note to the War Secretary forcing his attention elsewhere.[71]

The Prime Minister thought that the time had come for the War Secretary to issue the necessary orders for the withdrawal of British troops into Palestine to Field Marshal Commander-in-Chief Allenby; communication would also have to be made to the French Government and to Amir Faysal through the Foreign Office. Churchill quickly gave the necessary instructions and alerted Allenby, 9 October, to prepare for the evacuation of British troops from Syria and Cilicia to begin 1 November 1919.[72]

A telegram was sent a few weeks later to Allenby[73] permitting him a few days delay in withdrawing from Syria provided that the British Government's main consideration was safeguarded, namely completing the withdrawal before climatic conditions rendered movement impossible. Allenby was requested to telegraph an appreciation of probable action by the Arabs should they decide to oppose France.[74]

Into this depressing scene of lack of movement in Mesopotamia economizing as well as premonitions of a French-Arab clash arrived a report, carefully drawn up by General Sir G. F. Milne, Commander-in-Chief of the Army of the Black Sea based at Constantinople, on the Turkish Nationalist movement. The military importance of the movement, wrote Milne, should not be underestimated because it had consolidated public opinion in Turkey, and its leaders were toying with the idea of armed resistance. Therefore it was advisable to contemplate a situation in which the use of military force might become necessary if the peace terms were drastic. To Mustafa Kemal there were three main 'non-Possumus' questions, namely evacuation of Smyrna by Greece and its return to Turkey, retention of Armenia and the return of parts of Thrace.[75]

Churchill was thoroughly downcast by the overwhelming interconnected complexities of the Middle East situation now that he was introduced to almost all of them, and their seeming insolubility. He wrote a long memorandum, 25 October, summarizing his reluctant conclusions.[76] Enumerating most of the problems, he wrote that Greece was on its way to ruin as a result of the immense military commitments in Smyrna Province; Italy was further disturbing Turkey; the French were about to overrun Syria and would soon be involved in a protracted and bloody struggle with the Arabs; the British were bound to sympathize with the Arabs incurring French wrath and accusations, injuring Anglo-French relations; the Jewish assumption that Britain would clear out the local Arabs from Palestine further upset the area. All of this, felt the minister responsible for the Empire's security, reacted on Britain's position as the greatest Muslim power and involved Britain in great expense and anxiety. Military establishments in Egypt, Mesopotamia and Palestine cost enormous amounts of money, gravely burdening Army Estimates. But if the forces were reduced, to economize, Britain ran the risk of a local disaster causing renewed war and expenditure. A strong force was also necessary around Constantinople and the Straits for an indefinite period.

He reluctantly concluded that the policy of the partition of the Turkish Empire among the European Powers was a mistake, for it would involve Britain, first, in abetting a crime against freedom, namely the conquest of the Arabs by the Turks, second, in deserting those Arabs who were their war allies, and last, in immense expense. Churchill proposed, as an alternative policy, that the European Powers should "jointly and simultaneously, renounce all separate interests in the Turkish Empire other than those which existed before the war," and should combine to preserve the integrity of the Turkish Empire but under the strict guardianship of the League of Nations, based in Constantinople.

> I know it will be found very hard to relinquish the satisfaction of those dreams of conquest and aggrandizement which are gratified by the retention of Palestine and Mesopotamia. ... The need of national economy is such that we ought to endeavor to concentrate our resources on developing our existing Empire instead of dissipating them in new enlargements. We can only compel the other Powers to give up their exploitation claims against Turkey by ourselves being willing to set an example.[77]

An analysis of this pessimistic memorandum shows that it was the economizing factor that outweighed all other reasons for proposing such a step for each problem eventually would cost a tremendous amount of money. On reconsidering the paper, Churchill probably realized that it was useless to suggest such a step and it was neither printed nor circulated. No matter what the cost, the British Government was not prepared to give up what it had won with so much blood and money. The document is important because it shows the state of mind of the War Secretary after less than a year in office.

In the last two months of 1919, Churchill focused once again on the Bolshevik menace to the Middle East. Intelligence reports informed him that Soviet agents had been trying to obtain connections with Mustafa Kemal and the two were in constant communication.[78] Lenin directed his speech of 22 November to the Muslim Communists calling for close contact between them and the Soviets. The Red Army's achievements would show the peoples of the East that against all odds "a revolutionary war waged by oppressed peoples may bring about so many marvels that it has become quite a practical policy to liberate the peoples of the East."[79] The struggle in the East would be one of oppressed colonies against international imperialism, and the task of the Muslims was to adapt communist theory and practice to Eastern conditions.

Furthermore, the Seventh All-Russian Congress of Soviets passed a resolution 5 December, greeting the representatives of Soviet Turkestan and Bashkiria [sic], regarding "their presence not only as proof that a feeling of solidarity with the toiling masses of the U.S.S.R. has penetrated the Muslim toiling masses, but that conviction has penetrated the Muslim East" that Soviet Russia "is their stronghold in their struggle for liberation from national oppression."[80]

How much this influenced Churchill's views can be seen from the ideas he expressed at a meeting of ministers called by Lloyd George on 10 December[81] to consult them on the line he should take at his meeting with Clemenceau the following day. Churchill said that any solution to the situation was better than none and now that the United States was out of the picture, an Anglo-French agreement on Turkish policy would be effective. A powerful British weapon over France was that it was by no means a foregone conclusion that Britain would guarantee French integrity. It should be used to force an agreement, now urgent, for there was a real danger of Bolshevist penetration, imperiling Britain's Middle East interests; also, the quality of British troops in Turkey was deteriorating. Churchill favored an

CHAPTER 3 • The Secretary of State for War and Air

Anglo-French administration over Turkey with certain concessions to other Powers. He also felt that the Sultan should be kept in Constantinople, and not allowed to be in Brusa with the secular government because he would then gather around him Mustafa Kemal, Enver and Trotsky who would help him build up huge hostile force and turn Asia Minor and Arabia into a seething cauldron of trouble.

An analysis of Winston Churchill's activities as Secretary of State for War and Air during 1919 in relation to the Middle East shows a growing awareness of the many faceted problem there and his gradual involvement in the efforts to solve it. Churchill advocated reliance on modern technology as a means of reducing dependence on expensive manpower. He visualized the combined use of airplanes, railroads, and armored cars and the concentration of small garrisons at central points, especially in the Fertile Crescent which gradually became an area of major concern to Churchill. He developed this policy in response to the tasks of his office—demobilization and economy—and to the task of an imperial minister to protect the empire from menace, in this case, Bolshevism. His methodology in promoting his policy for the Fertile Crescent was not fully developed in 1919 because the issues were still fairly fluid and because Churchill was still more involved in finding solutions to the more massive problems of Europe. A method already in use is the buildup of rational argumentation based on solid facts which Churchill wrote in order to convince his own department or his fellow ministers of his point of view. Another method used is that of direct orders to those below him demanding too much and therefore in the end attaining his real goal by a supposed compromise. A third Churchillian method is that of direct appeal to the Prime Minister. He was also concerned with protecting himself by forcing the Cabinet to share in the responsibility of what could be a dangerous step, in this case drastic troop reductions at a time of Bolshevik and Kemalist expansion.

The year 1919 is one of unproductive groping for a policy by Great Britain. Churchill is the exception, yet many of his carefully worked out proposals were opposed by other ministries which had a large voice in Middle East affairs, namely the Foreign and India Offices, and by ministers such as Andrew Bonar Law, Chancellor of the Exchequer, who felt the War Secretary's plans were too expensive. But by far the largest blockage to the implementation of his plans was the lack of a formal peace treaty with Turkey, a matter which lay beyond his control and seemingly beyond Britain's too, as the year 1919 drew to a close.

CHAPTER 4

Middle East Dilemmas

If 1919 introduced Churchill to the multiple problems of the Middle East, 1920 clarified the dimensions of these problems. The year 1920 was one of dilemmas and attempted solutions the warp and weft of which combined to form an interwoven pattern of many parts. At times the design is boring in its repetitiveness, resisting any change, but every so often this resistance is overcome and a new pattern begins to emerge in the complicated tapestry of the Middle East. Churchill's policy for the Fertile Crescent remained basically the same but the reasons behind his actions and his methodology widened. During 1920 his fear of the Bolshevik menace to the empire expanded to include a fear of the nationalist Turks who were gradually growing in power in Anatolia under Kemal's leadership. He advocated making peace with this force and then using Turkey to block the Bolsheviks thereby safeguarding the Fertile Crescent. Churchill's methodology in promoting the policy of replacing manpower by modern technology in the Fertile Crescent broadened and became more sophisticated. As his attempts to implement this policy were frustrated again and again by various Cabinet members who took turns setting up obstacles to Churchill's proposals, he would have a momentary spell of disillusionment and disgust, but then would be spurred into repeating his methods with variations once more. These methods are closely examined in order to try to recreate the atmosphere in which the War Secretary labored for only then can the reader clearly understand the steps proposed by Churchill at the end of 1920. By then, after two years of trying to work his way through a maze of stumbling blocks, he had reached the end of his tether. As a step preliminary to implementation of his policy, he

CHAPTER 4 • Middle East Dilemmas | 35

proposed creating a Middle East Department as part of the Colonial Office and thereby end the inter-office squabbling once and for all.

The year began with a flurry of activity on the Turkish peace treaty. A conference of ministers opened on 5 January to discuss the proposed treaty, but, as characteristic for the year, this dilemma led to another which in turn meshed with a third. Churchill drew the attention of the conference of ministers to the larger aspect of the case for and against keeping the Sultan in Constantinople, thereby forcing them to listen to his analysis of the Bolshevik danger to the entire Middle East, an issue that had preoccupied him in the closing months of 1919. The Bolsheviks had relatively strong forces in south Russia and would shortly be in touch with the Turkish nationalists. There were no military forces to oppose them, and Britain was almost friendless from Constantinople to China. "We could not, of course, stem all this by keeping the Sultan at Constantinople, but to turn him out would be to add one more spark to the spreading conflagration."[1]

He had elaborated upon the Bolshevik danger the day before in a speech at a Coalition demonstration held in Sunderland.[2] Reiterating his usual warning that they were out to destroy democracy, capital and religion, he also warned that the Bolsheviks aimed at agitating the millions of Indians against Britain. But there was an even greater immediate danger.

> A new force of a turbulent, warlike character has come into being in the highlands of Asia Minor, who reach out with one hand to the advancing Bolshevist armies from the north, and with the other to the offended Arabs in the south. A conjunction of forces between Russian Bolshevism and Turkish Mohammedanism would be an event full of danger to many States, but to no State in the world would it be more full of danger than to the British Empire, the greatest of all Mohammedan States.[3]

Churchill continued in this vein at the Cabinet meeting held the next day,[4] clearly setting forth the interconnected complexities of the proposed peace treaty and the reasoning behind his opinions. Constantinople and the Straits should be controlled by an international force, he stated, and the Government of Turkey should be controlled by an international commission. He felt that both the Sultan and the Government should remain in Constantinople, first, because the city was the best place from which to control Turkey, secondly, "because of the resentment that would be excited in India and throughout the Mohammedan world by the expulsion of the Turks from Constantinople. All our limited means of getting the Middle East to settle down quietly are comprised in the use of Indian troops. We must not do anything that will raise Indian sentiment against the use of these troops or affect their own loyalty."[5] The third reason was basic to his thinking: Churchill expected to see a hostile united militarist Russia in the near future, and if the Turk was in Constantinople, he could be used to prevent Russia's forcible acquisition of the city and the Straits. If the international force was the only defense, it would be valueless unless all the countries involved would be prepared to take up arms. Preventing the Russians from gaining access to the Mediterranean had been a pillar of British policy for centuries and Churchill moved in traditional lines when it came to imperial interests. The War Secretary's position was supported by the Chief of the Imperial General Staff.[6] Lloyd George agreed with the basic policy of denying Russia this access, but he proposed to do this with a Greek rather than Turkish barrier.

The Cabinet discussed the matter and compromised between the views of Lloyd George and Churchill: the Sultan should remain at Constantinople, but without any Turkish force, and the city and Straits should be garrisoned by an international force in which Britain would take part.[7]

While the elusive Turkish peace treaty and its attendant Turkish intrigues with the Bolsheviks form a separate dilemma seemingly begging solution, it is interwoven with a related dilemma facing Winston Churchill, namely that of conflicting aims of policy and economy. The Secretary of State for War began his campaign for policy decisions in the Middle East when he presented the Army estimates for 1920–21 on 7 February, explaining them in his accompanying memorandum.[8] The estimates divided into three headings: normal peacetime army, terminal expenses of the war, and expenditure of abnormal or quasi-war character arising out of temporary obligations, such as on the Rhine or in Constantinople, or out of new responsibilities, such as Palestine, Mesopotamia and Persia. The only possible field for immediate substantial reduction was the third category and the Cabinet had to decide on the policy to be followed. He enumerated the troop numbers and their costs for Constantinople, Egypt, Palestine, Persia and Mesopotamia to show just how expensive these troops were. Then he elaborated on the imperative need for a policy decision on Mesopotamia, the most expensive area of all, strengthening his argument by declaring that the General Staff did not feel it strategically important to retain Mesopotamia for Imperial security. He was, in effect, asking for evacuation, especially from Mosul, the northern "vilayet" or province.

Churchill ended his memorandum on an optimistic note now that his point was made. Although the cost of the Army was high and its fighting powers low, he wrote, "the remarkable fact is that an army capable of garrisoning the Empire should have been created on the voluntary system within the space of a single year." The raw recruits showed promise and within two years a good professional fighting force would emerge. "This is, in fact, the year when the expense of the peace time British Army will be at its highest and the results at their very lowest."[9]

The Finance Committee met, 9 February,[10] to discuss the Army estimates, but agreed that before any drastic decision could be discussed on evacuating Mosul, it had to receive the survey report regarding oil in Mesopotamia,[11] and the report from the new General Officer Commanding Mesopotamia reviewing the situation. The Committee also listed the conclusion of peace with Turkey as a prerequisite to any decision making. Pending these three things the Committee accepted Churchill's proposals on Mesopotamia. The Committee also agreed to withdraw the force from most of Persia, and to cut the cost of the Palestine and Egypt forces in half. Churchill's attempt to get the Cabinet to decide on policy succeeded partially, but failed again with regard to Mesopotamia.

Churchill's memorandum gave rise to a subordinate design, regularly reappearing within the larger pattern of conflicting aims of policy and economy: intraoffice disagreements. The Director of Military Operations, General Radcliffe, minuted to the Chief of the Imperial General Staff, 9 February,[12] that the immediate reduction recommended by Churchill for Mesopotamia would not be an economy in the end. As for Churchill's statement that the General Staff was not pressing for the retention of Mesopotamia on the strategic grounds of imperial security, that was no longer true. India was no longer surrounded by friendly and stable states, and if Britain were to pull out of Persia and Mesopotamia, there would be chaos and anarchy which would materially influence the defense of India.

Wilson passed this minute to the War Secretary who printed it for the Cabinet as a record of General Staff opinion.[13] The precondition of the

Genera Staff for any withdrawal continued to be peace with Turkey, still as elusive as ever despite the decision on 5 March of an Allied Conference at London to declare an official Allied occupation of Constantinople and the Straits.

Churchill was also concerned with a peace treaty, namely, "a peace which does not unite against us the feelings of the Mohammedan world."[14] But in March the dilemma of economizing his expenses weighed equally on his mind and divided his attention. He resumed the same tactics he had tried the year before perhaps hoping that by perseverance he would get his way. First, he set out to build up an impressive array of reliable data and memoranda which he could use to back up his arguments. So, he revived his favorite solution to the high cost of Mesopotamia by writing to the Chief of the Air Staff[15] to submit a scheme for maintaining internal security by planes, and then presenting his own well thought out ideas on the subject. He even went into details of architecture, strategic points for setting up guns and geographic prerequisites of base sites; special troop carrier planes were to be designed, and the results of chemical bombs were to be examined. Every effort should be made to enlist the cooperation of peaceful tribes, and Churchill suggested the total of 4,000 white and 10,000 native troops at between 5 and 7 million pounds a year aside from capital outlay.

Next, Churchill urgently requested members of his General Staff, on 5 March,[16] to plan emergency steps to reduce the Egyptian and Palestine garrisons to 43,000 from the then 90,000 men by 31 May. "Every day that these redundant men are left in Egypt and Palestine they are exhausting the limited funds available for the support of the permanent British Army." Estimates had to include shipping needs which Churchill would put a special demand for upon the Cabinet. The plan had to be ready in one week's time, slashing the garrisons to the core. It was, and by the end of the month all the details, including the shipping, were worked out.[17] The War Secretary made sure to note to his staff, however, that this was not a final reduction but merely an interim one."[18] In the midst of this promising situation for Egypt and Palestine, and the satisfactory notifications from Mesopotamia that troop reduction was 2,365 more than was asked for,[19] telegrams began to arrive from Allenby describing the convening of the Syrian Congress in Damascus which declared Syria independent and Faysal king.[20] The War Office and Foreign Office immediately telegraphed the General Officers Commanding Egypt, Mesopotamia and India that Britain did not recognize the right of the

Syrian Congress to settle the future of the Middle East; only the Allies could do so because they and not the Arabs had captured the area from Turkey.[21]

It took a crisis of these proportions to finally obtain an announcement of policy intentions. But activities in Syria, Lloyd George's later approval of holding Mosul, and the anti-Bolshevik collapse in Russia which was accompanied by the opening of the Caspian Sea to invasion all combined to frustrate Churchill's plans to drastically reduce the Middle East garrisons. Undeterred, he carried on his strategy of building up his store of data, and wrote a personal letter to General Haldane, the new General Officer Commanding, Mesopotamia, 1 April,[22] asking him to devise a cheap scheme for maintaining order and informing him that he very much favored the Air Force scheme for control of Mesopotamia and hoped that the General would also feel that way after examining the plan. The War Secretary was very anxious that the general should look at the question purely on its merits, without regard to its effect on his present command. He reassured the general that should control pass to the Air Force, he would "make every possible effort to find you another command equally suited to your rank and satisfactory to yourself." Churchill knew that without the approval of the general on the spot he could never convince his own staff, let along the Cabinet, to accept the air control scheme and reduce the expensive garrison.

As his next step in accumulating data, Churchill minuted to the Director of Military Operations[23] the following week that he wanted a map prepared showing the exact distribution of the forces in Mesopotamia, Britain and India, with a detailed explanation of the tactical and strategic object served by each detachment and an estimate of the numbers of the potential enemy in each district. Knowing Radcliffe's and the War Staff's opposition to drastic troop reductions in Mesopotamia because of the possibility of external invasion, Churchill carefully noted that "you need not take into consideration the external invasion of the country, but only the maintenance of its internal order, which is the phase I am now examining." He quickly added, however, to dispel any suspicion that he was ready to discount external invasion entirely, that he would be glad to receive a separate report on the possibilities of invasion by the Bolsheviks, the Turkish Nationalists, or the Arabs.

The report, concurred in by the Chief of the Imperial General Staff, was ready within five days,[24] and answered the War Secretary's direct questions while at the same time presenting the War Staff's view of the situation. Radcliffe's minute and report stressed that should it be agreed that the Royal Air Force take over, there should be no premature withdrawal or reduction of the garrison until the Air Force units were available in sufficient strength to relieve the military. Radcliff urged, in conclusion, "that no arbitrary reductions should be ordered contrary to the expressed opinion of the Commander responsible for the security of this territory," as if anticipating Churchill's next move.

There was one last memorandum he needed before approaching the Cabinet again, so Churchill ordered Haldane[25] at once to draw up proposals for measures necessary to effect the Cabinet's decision to reduce troops in Mesopotamia. Churchill realized that the units, brought up to full strength, would therefore have to be concentrated at a small number of important points on rivers and railroads, but there did not seem to be any alternative.

Churchill submitted the draft telegram to the Director of Military Operations and the Adjutant General for comments because it would help him very much to have General Staff concurrence. The Adjutant General, Lt. Gen. Macdonogh, in charge of personnel, merely amended the figures and pointed out that a great expense was the maintenance of 40,000 refugees.[26] Radcliffe, while agreeing generally with the Secretary of State, tried once again to point out that the policy of reduction of garrisons and consequent concentration would directly conflict with the political considerations constantly urged by Sir Percy Cox, Acting Minister at Tehran and Sir Arnold Wilson, Acting Commissioner at Baghdad, who felt that by withdrawing from occupied areas Britain might as well leave Mesopotamia and Persia altogether.

Churchill was interested in action and so ordered the dispatch of the telegram to Haldane copies of which should later be communicated to the Foreign Office, and to Bonar Law, Chancellor of the Exchequer. His excuse for not consulting them beforehand was that the matter had not yet reached the final stage of action.[27]

Final stage of action was reached in another arena. The San Remo Conference convened 19 April in reaction against the proclamations of Damascus, and by 25 April all major decisions with regard to the division of the Ottoman Empire were made; the Supreme Council also decided to allow the Greeks control of Smyrna and Thrace.[28]

Since so many long-standing questions were finally decided at San Remo, the War Secretary may have hoped that the British Cabinet would also be inspired to settle long-standing imperial questions. He submitted a memorandum on Mesopotamia, 1 May,[29] based on all the memoranda he had collected, proposing transferring all the military responsibilities from the Army to the Air Force as the best means of economizing on that overly expensive territory. He also proposed, for the first time, the immediate handing over of Mesopotamia to the Colonial Office, which would be responsible both for policy and expenditure. On 5 May, the General Staff added its pressure by drawing up a secret memorandum[30] asking for a decision between retaining the existing garrisons with no increase in responsibilities or contracting the areas for which Britain was responsible and thus allowing a reduction in forces. Otherwise, in the arena of conflicting claims of policy and economy, policy would outrun the military's resources.

At a Cabinet meeting that day, the whole field of British policy in the Middle East was discussed but to Churchill's dismay, again no conclusions were reached.[31] The following day, 6 May, both Henry Wilson and Winston Churchill tried once again and drew up new memoranda on the Middle East garrison which clearly illuminate the gulf growing between the two men's approaches to the dilemma of trying to reconcile the aims of policy and economy. Wilson,[32] basing his views on the delayed Turkish peace treaty, on inability to enforce its terms should it be made, on strained relations with Faysal, and on the unsettled interior condition of Palestine and Egypt, stated that it was most likely that Britain would not only reduce her garrisons but would have to reinforce every Middle East theatre, especially Mesopotamia. The C.I.G.S. conceded that if Britain had airplanes, personnel, armored cars, mobile machine gun units, wireless stations, railways and roads, they could commence a rapid progressive reduction of the garrisons; but Britain did not have them. Wilson's approach was the traditional military one.

Churchill,[33] on the other hand, while agreeing that much of the difficulties were attributable to the delay in making peace with Turkey and to the fact that the treaty offered a prospect only of disorder, and while agreeing that a reduction in garrisons also had to involve curtailment of responsibilities, rejected the basis on which Wilson's and the General Staff's calculations were made. They assumed that Britain was bound to occupy all or most of the mandated territories and aimed at reducing the country to order by means of a great number of scattered garrisons each of which had to be capable of resisting a maximum potential attack.

> I consider, on the other hand, that one single concentrated force at some convenient center point where there are good railway or river connections should be established, and from this base gradually in the process of years ... our influence should gradually be spread throughout the country. This process may be greatly assisted and accelerated by the use of air forces. It is, after all, the same processes which we have hitherto always followed in the development of our great Asiatic and African possessions. Never have we attempted to settle down all over the country at once with a large proportion of the army used for the purpose of conquest.[34]

The initial error of the General Staff fundamentally vitiated every subsequent calculation and its demand for forces would economically ruin the two new dependencies, continued Churchill. The only course which could save the provinces was "to break away altogether from the present arbitrary and conventional calculations, and to entrust the responsibility to a perfectly new department and new arm like the Air Force, which is prepared to adapt itself to new conditions and to the improvisations and partial measures which have always been characteristic of our colonial development." It was therefore up to the Cabinet either to accept the military calculations and ruin the provinces, in which case it was better to give them up, or to adopt a modest and patient method which would entail great contractions of responsibilities. His is a policy of withdrawal, disengagement and retrenchment under new and unconventional conditions.

The weaving of the Middle East tapestry began to assume violent and passionate colors throughout the summer of 1920 as each of the threads of Mesopotamia, Persia, Turkey, Palestine and Syria led into demonstrations, disorders and armed clashes. Instead of the warp of such events meshing with a harmonized weft of response from Great Britain, a fault began to develop within the pattern as the individual strands of the latter thread disputed over policy.

One of the threads, of minor annoyance at this stage, was Palestine.[35] The main concern of the War Office was the transfer of the administration from the military to the civil authorities as quickly and economically as possible, and to this end cooperated with the Foreign Office and the Treasury to set up a committee to deal with all such questions. The committee met 7 June,[36] with Generals Radcliffe and Thwaites, Director of Military Intelligence, as

War Office representatives, and details were worked out including separation of Palestine from the command of Egypt except on questions of coordination. The High Commissioner, Sir Herbert Samuel, would take over his duties 1 July and be directly responsible to the Colonial Office, and would carry the title of titular Commander-in-Chief with the proviso, insisted the War Office, that this did not give him any right of interference in details of operations or movement of troops.

Churchill contentedly left such details in the hands of his staff. He was concerned with larger issues of policy versus economy or with specific questions directed to him. He prodded Lloyd George to decide on policy in Palestine so that departmental action could proceed.[37] Palestine was costing six million pounds a year to hold and garrison reductions did not seem possible because of trouble from two sources: the French in Syria and Arab-Zionist friction. France was concentrating a considerable army in Syria aimed at imposing her will on Arabs. Once her position was secured she probably would turn to fomenting troubles between the Arabs and Great Britain; the Arabs would inevitably turn from the strong French battalions to attack the weak British ones, but Britain could not pull back for this would merely transfer the scene of future trouble from Palestine to Egypt, a more dangerous thing to deal with.[38]

As for Arab-Zionist friction, Churchill was well aware of the riots of 4–8 April in which there were 250 casualties, nine-tenths Jewish. Colonel Meinertzhagen, whom the Foreign Office had sent to Palestine, described to Curzon the policing role some British officers played in the riots, and explained that Allenby, though informed, had preferred to remain silent.[39] His honesty in criticizing the military administration evoked in response the strong antagonism of Allenby who tried to have him recalled, but the Foreign Office refused to cut short his tour of duty.[40] Vladimir Jabotinsky, an ardent right wing Zionist, who had taken measures to activate the Jewish defense organization against the Arabs, was sentenced to fifteen years in prison. The protest against the injustice of such a sentence for a man who had been a zealous British supporter during the war reached Cabinet level where it was decided that Churchill should ask Allenby to review the case.[41] When questioned on this issue in Parliament, 29 April, Churchill responded that he awaited Allenby's reply;[42] a week later he announced that Jabotinsky's sentence had been reduced to one year.[43] Allenby, however, absolutely refused to release him on parole despite Churchill's suggestion to that effect.[44]

This did not end the issue and Churchill set up a military court of inquiry, but by the time the report was ready, the civil administration was ruling and Samuel was loath to publish the report and thus revive the controversy.[45] Henry Wilson agreed and noted so to the War Secretary, who concurred in not publishing the report.[46] On the whole, however, Churchill's main concern in 1920 was with economizing on Palestine as in the rest of the Middle East, and so he must have been unhappy with the General Staff memorandum of 27 July[47] showing the liabilities of holding that territory especially financially. Henry Wilson, in an accompanying note, pressed for decisions of policy.[48] Nor was Churchill happy with Herbert Samuel's spate of telegrams throughout the month of August begging to be allowed to occupy Transjordan.[49]

Transjordan had been evacuated by the British in a vain attempt to induce the French to keep out of Damascus, Homs, Hama and Aleppo; therefore the Foreign Office, agreeing with Samuel, felt that Britain was at perfect liberty to reoccupy, especially as the Arab leaders invited them to do so.[50] Allenby also agreed it was a good idea for it would simplify the prevention of raids into Palestine.[51] But the C.I.G.S. opposed the move because it would be impossible to send reinforcements to back up the commitments that were certain to follow the occupation.[52] Lloyd George agreed with Wilson. The Foreign Office informed Samuel that he could only send political officers to as-Salt and Kerak to advise on local self-government, a step which Samuel immediately took and had to be satisfied with.

The War Office also refused to pay for the training of the Palestine Defence Force even though after training it would enable reductions in the regular garrison.[53] The proposal had been made by the Foreign Office based on recommendations of the Interdepartmental Committee on Palestine,[54] which met regularly during August and September to decide on details of the administration including the wording of the Palestine mandate and the frontiers.[55] If Palestine and Syria were relatively minor irritations, not so Mesopotamia, Persia and Turkey the first of which exploded into a full-scale uprising,[56] the second of which was invaded by Russia and the last of which seemed on the brink of a Bolshevik-nationalist coalition against the Allies. The flaw in the fabric developed over Mesopotamia and Persia as Churchill found himself faced with very strong opposition from Curzon, Milner and Montagu and the offices they headed, and over Turkey as Churchill and Lloyd George opposed each other.

Anticipating trouble in the Middle East, Churchill took steps to force some action by writing a long letter to the Prime Minister, 13 June,[57] advising him to devote at least two days entirely to this area and to the army strength related thereto. His tactic was to convince the Prime Minister of his views before trying to convince the entire Cabinet again. Action had to be taken soon partly because the Turkish nationalists had advanced towards Ismid, on the edge of the neutral zone of the Straits. A series of policy decisions had to be taken to enable the War Office to proceed. The first question was whether Britain would clear out of Persia or not, the next was whether to clear out of Mosul or not. "... [Y]ou must choose, & manfully face the consequences of either choice. We cannot go on sprawled out over these vast regions at ruinous expense & ever-increasing military risk. If it is decided to hold Mosul, the garrison of Mesopot [amia] must be fully maintained, the railway must be prolonged into Mosul, & Parliament must be told that the expectation of reduction in expense cannot be made good."[58] Third was the question of holding Constantinople and last was the problem of Palestine. Churchill wrote that it was up to the Prime Minister to say which costly commitment could be abandoned or maintained, but Lloyd George would then have to justify his choice in the House of Commons.

Churchill's tactic worked, and apparently agreeing that the time had come to make some policy decisions, the Prime Minister called a Conference of Ministers 17 June.[59] The nine ministers discussed the difficult situation in the Middle East and agreed to confer the next day with Henry Wilson and Trenchard who would be prepared to express their opinions on the military aspects of a policy which would first, authorize Greece to advance to east Thrace, give Greece control over Smyrna, and bring a Greek division to Constantinople; secondly, authorize the evacuation of Batum on the Black Sea and the transfer of troops to the menaced Ismid Peninsula which could then be held along with Constantinople; and thirdly, withdrawal from Persia and contraction to the railheads in Mesopotamia which would be controlled by the Air Force. Churchill's hopes ran high that at last major decisions would be made.

The nine ministers met the next morning[60] along with the C. I. G. S., the Chief of the Air Staff, the First Sea Lord and the Greek Prime Minister Venizelos. The appearance of Venizelos and his offer of troops convinced a majority of Ministers, especially Lloyd George that backing the Greeks was a sound policy. Reinforcements, both Greek and British, to Constantinople were agreed upon, but both Churchill and Wilson placed on record their view that military forces at the disposal of the British were insufficient to meet the requirements of the policies being pursued in the various theaters.

But this admonishment went unheeded as had all of Churchill's earlier ones about the unjustness of the Treaty of Sèvres. After France agreed a few days later to allow the Greeks to advance north and east from Smyrna, they proceeded to do so and by the end of June Greece occupied almost all of Eastern Thrace thereby halting the Kemalist forces outside the British occupied zones. They then advanced through western Anatolia and consolidated their position there well. Lloyd George's policy succeeded, and on 10 August the representatives of the Constantinople Government finally signed the Treaty of Sèvres. The Turkish nationalists disclaimed the action and Mustafa Kemal declared that the treaty was a direct act of aggression on Turkey by Britain, France, Italy and Greece. The Ankara Government was officially at war with the Allies. Churchill must have been very disappointed that so little resulted from all his tactics to get the issues before the Cabinet and that the one thing that was authorized was against his advice. But the ministers merely agreed that Cox should return to Britain immediately from Persia to advise on the situation in Mesopotamia; he was to satisfy himself before returning as to the measure of acceptance which the British proposal to create an effective Arab state was likely to obtain. Cox was also authorized to announce British acceptance of the Mesopotamian mandate and that he would return in the autumn as the Chief British representative to call into being an Arab Council under an Arab president and a General Assembly representative of the people. All military, financial and air questions were postponed, but Churchill managed at least to obtain Lloyd George's authority to forward a list of military decisions urgently required. He could still hope to accomplish something in the area of economizing to balance his failure to check Greek ambitions at the expense of Turkey.

That afternoon Churchill listed eleven directives to the Chief of the Imperial General Staff, the Adjutant General, and the Chief of the Air Staff to be put into proposal for action.[61] He refused to be defeated and was building up his arsenal for the next assault on the Cabinet.

Also, an appreciation arrived from Haldane 21 June[62] in answer to an eleven-question telegram sent him 6 June because of unease over the increase in unrest in Mesopotamia. Haldane replied that the disturbances were sporadic with no evidence of active cooperation between Bolsheviks,

Turkish Nationalists and Arabs. Haldane felt that the situation was in hand. The railroad between Basrah and Baghdad could be cut at any time but river passage would remain open, he felt sure. Security of Mesopotamia was not endangered by troop transfer from Persia and he intended to withdraw all forces by the autumn. Haldane emphasized that no troop reductions were possible, a matter with which the General Staff was in full agreement. He did not anticipate having to reinforce Persia but at the same time, did not feel that withdrawal from Mosul would strengthen the British position. The general felt that communications would play a main role in subduing an attack, again concurring in General Staff opinion.

Haldane had misread his intelligence reports completely. At the end of May the Arabs at Tel Afar, near Mosul, had reacted to the arrest of a local shaykh for debt by killing some British soldiers. The two armored cars sent to punish the Arabs were ambushed and their crews of over a dozen men were killed. This was the beginning of the Arab rebellion of 1920. The punitive force sent from Mosul drove the whole population of Tel Afar into the desert and the rebellion spread, with fierce fighting at Rumaitha and Samawa.

Despite the growing gravity of the situation in Mesopotamia little was done about it in London during July. The Cabinet decided not to withdraw yet from Persia and Haldane was informed,[63] as per Churchill's instructions of a month earlier, to suspend reductions in his force.

Henry Wilson kept receiving urgent reports from Mesopotamia and urged Churchill to dispatch a whole division from India to reinforce Haldane, not merely a brigade.[64] But Churchill was frantic over the expense this would entail and preferred to draw attention to telegrams showing successful action by the British against the Arabs.[65] Wilson finally convinced him by the end of the month and the Indian division was immediately ordered to Mesopotamia.[66]

By the end of July, too, the General Staff finally drew up the memorandum ordered by Churchill on 18 June, listing the decisions urgently required from the military point of view.[67] they concluded pessimistically that the garrisons throughout the Empire were beset by potential dangers which could far exceed their strength and that the sum of the liabilities was so vast, the War Office should be well advised to retain all the machinery of mobilization.

Henry Wilson added a note to this memorandum[68] summarizing the changes in the general situation during the summer in the Middle East pointing out to Churchill that the balance was disadvantageous to Britain.

Churchill vigorously protested to the Prime Minister at the delay in dealing with Mesopotamia and Persia and a Cabinet meeting was promised.

During the first week of August matters began to come to a head. The Finance Committee of the Cabinet met twice on 3 August[69] to discuss first Persia and then Mesopotamia where the position in Baghdad itself had become insecure. The Persian tribes, aided by the Bolsheviks, were attacking the British troops who were under orders not to take the offensive. The military advocated withdrawal but Cox strongly opposed it as it would endanger the Anglo-Persian Agreement which would hopefully be ratified by Persia within three months. The Committee ignored the military advice and decided to give Persia the time needed to ratify the Agreement. As for Mesopotamia, the Committee decided to concentrate strong British forces on the Lower Euphrates to sharply crush the rebellion.

News arrived that a small British column of some 400 men had been wiped out, so Wilson put much stronger pressure on Churchill for leaving Persia, concentrating forces and sending in reinforcements.[70] Pressured by his Chief of the Imperial General Staff, Churchill again tried the direct approach and wrote to the Prime Minister bluntly warning that a divided policy combining economy with the suppression of rebellion was dangerous.[71] All military advice to contract and limit British responsibilities in Mesopotamia and Persia had not been acted upon because of the decided opposition of the Secretary of State for Foreign Affairs and the Secretary of State for the Colonies. He felt, however, "that matters have now reached a point where my responsibility to prevent a great disaster has become a very real one."

Despite Churchill's pressure, cajolery and argument the Cabinet meeting of 6 August reached no decision except to send Cox back to report. Milner and Curzon made it clear that they would resign if Britain came out of Persia.[72] Further frustration followed at the Cabinet's Finance Committee meeting of 12 August[73] at which it was definitely decided not to withdraw British forces from Persia until the decision of the Persian Parliament on the ratification of the Agreement was known. Cox was to proceed immediately to Baghdad to be the High Commissioner.

Outvoted, Churchill had to do his best to make the policy succeed. He authorized the General Officer Commanding Mesopotamia to act up to the limits of his discretion on pursuing Britain's policy and repressing disorder; India was ordered to provide reinforcements.[74]

Yet the situation in Mesopotamia and Persia grew increasingly formidable toward the end of August. The railroad link with Persia was cut, new towns revolted and one of the Political Officers was murdered. Haldane now asked not only for the nineteen battalions already on the way but for two complete divisions and two cavalry brigades to work up from Basrah along the twin rivers. Churchill made plans to move thousands of troops from India, Palestine, Constantinople and the Rhine, but was wary of the dangerous situation this left Constantinople and India. He was also wary of an attempt to evacuate Mosul and feared that Britain was in for a long costly campaign in Mesopotamia that would strain military resources to the utmost.[75] Things were no better in Persia where the Bolsheviks had driven back the Persian Cossacks so that there was no barrier between the Bolsheviks and the tiny British force protecting Tehran. Any Russian reinforcement across the Caspian would compel British retreat; the rest of north Persia was in a great state of disorder. Therefore the British were in a position of jeopardy in both these countries.

Disappointed, Churchill summarized the situation in a long pessimistic letter to Lloyd George, where he complained that

> Week after week and month after month for a long time to come we shall have a continuance of this miserable, wasteful, sporadic warfare, marked from time and time certainly by minor disasters and cuttings off of troops and agents, and very possibly attended by some of very grave occurrence. Meanwhile the military expense of this year alone will probably amount to something like fifty millions, thus by this capital expenditure knocking all the bloom off any commercial possibilities which may have existed.[76]

He was even pessimistic about Percy Cox's ability to get things on to better lines, confessing that he felt no complete sense of confidence in him especially as all his recent prognostications about peace in Mesopotamia had been falsified.

Churchill wrote that he was doing his best to carry out the Cabinet's directions and every possible soldier was being sent to reinforce Mesopotamia to the utmost limits of available transport. There was nothing else to do, but the Cabinet should reconsider the whole situation when it reassembled.

In the end Churchill decided not to send such a pessimistic summary to his chief, perhaps because he was about to leave on a fortnight's holiday to the south of France and felt that things would look rosier after he had had a chance to relax a bit. But the document remains important in that it sheds light on the War Secretary's feelings of frustration with the Middle East situation at the end of the summer of 1920. Month after month, like a broken record, he had submitted memoranda describing the worsening situation and requesting policy decisions; almost each time committee or Cabinet discussions had ended in procrastinations. Frustrations piled up as Churchill was criticized by the press and in Parliament,[77] as well as by his leading opponents in the Cabinet, namely Milner, Curzon, and Montagu.[78]

Churchill was on holiday during much of September and Wilson was in charge of War Office business. While he was away the Mesopotamian rebellion gradually died and Haldane began the systematic punishment of the Arab tribes. In early October Sir Percy Cox reached Baghdad and became the Civil Commissioner, directly responsible to the India Office.

The last three months of 1920 saw a clear return to the dilemmas with which the year had started, namely the elusive Turkish peace treaty and its attendant intrigues with the Bolsheviks, and the intertwining dilemma of conflicting aims of policy and economy. The end of the year, however, saw a positive step to attempt to solve the problems of the Middle East, a step which Winston Churchill had been trying to get the Government to take for months and once taken overcame to a large extent the flaws which had developed in the weaving of the Middle East tapestry.

The Bolshevik spectre again lifted its head and the General Staff drew up two memoranda[79] on the Mesopotamian and Persian outbreaks which concluded that Bolshevik activities had taken advantage of Middle East discontent to further their own goals. At a Foreign Office meeting at Moscow, 9 May[80] attended by the leading Bolshevik Commissars and representatives of Turkey, Persia, Afghanistan, Azerbaijan, Armenia, Georgia and India, Lenin personally expounded his design for attacking British imperialism in the Middle East. "Our task is to root out the British Imperialistic spirit in Turkey, Persia and Asia generally. In India we must strike them hardest." A secret treaty was signed between Soviet Russia and these Islamic countries, and a separate one with Mustafa Kemal's government was signed 11 May.[81] The ties were further strengthened after the San Remo terms were known and thus by the end of May there were coordinated plans on foot for resistance in Syria, Mesopotamia, and Turkey plus a Bolshevik advance across the Caspian Sea. Therefore in General Staff opinion, as substantiated by dozens of intelligence reports,[82] the uprisings were not spontaneous.

The General Staff did not stop here but proceeded to bring proof of continuing Soviet activities in the Middle East. The Bolsheviks issued an invitation in late July to the Second Congress of the Third International or Comintern to be held in Baku in mid-August.[83] It was addressed exclusively to the workmen of Persia and the villagers of Iran, Anatolia, Syria and Arabia to come and deliberate how to free themselves from the English and French armies with the help of Russia. The Baku Congress met to create the machinery needed to implement the sovietization of the Muslim world. What the General Staff and Churchill could not know was that the Baku Congress marked a turning point by reviving the suspicions of the Muslims against the Soviet Union. The President of the executive Committee, Zinoviev, attacked Islam and Turkey thus destroying the illusion of a Soviet liberator, for the threat was then clear to the Muslims.[84]

The second memorandum drawn up in October by the General Staff[85] dealt more specifically with Bolshevik activity in Persia and used this as an illustration of Russia's foreign policy which was based fundamentally on the idea that Communism would die if confined to Russia and therefore had to be propagated throughout the world.

The two memoranda confirmed Churchill's worst fears, and he tried appealing to the public to act against Communism. In an interview by the Daily Telegraph, 5 November,[86] Churchill tied all the disruptive forces in the Empire together blaming them all on the worldwide Communist conspiracy. "Having beaten the most powerful military empire in the world, having emerged triumphantly from the fearful struggle of Armageddon, we should not allow ourselves to be pulled down and have our Empire disrupted by a malevolent and subversive force, the rascals and rapscallions of mankind who were now on the move against us."[87] Britain must be on her guard to recognize the danger and act with strong conviction against it.

As if to reinforce Churchill's fears still more intelligence reports arrived informing the War Office of further strong Soviet propaganda directed at the Middle East inciting revolt.[88] Churchill informed the Cabinet of all this and begged the Government not to give the Bolsheviks locomotives and uniforms in return for "stolen" gold at such a moment.[89] He appealed again to the Cabinet, 23 November,[90] figuring that the defeat of Venizelos at the polls 14 November and the subsequent return to power of King Constantine who had refused to help the Allies during the war would put Lloyd George and the Cabinet into a mood more receptive to his proposed solution. "We ought to come to terms with Mustapha Kemal and arrive at a good peace with Turkey which will secure our position and interests at Constantinople and ease the position in Egypt, Mesopotamia, Persia and India." Britain should abandon the policy of relying on the weak and fickle Greeks which only served to estrange "the more powerful, durable and necessary Turkish and Mohammedan forces." Thus Britain would recreate the Turkish barrier to Russian ambitions instead of encouraging the unnatural union of Russia and Turkey. Britain's state of financial stringency and military weakness dictated a policy of reconciliation and cooperation with the Muslim world. In this he was fully upheld by the Chief of the Imperial General Staff.

Churchill's pleas even though strongly backed by the Indian Secretary were of no avail. The Conference of Ministers which met 2 December[91] concluded that Britain should continue to press the Turks to ratify the Treaty of Sevres and should resist attempts to modify it; in the event of the subsequent non-fulfillment of certain terms of the Treaty, the opportunity should be taken to reconsider the situation in a light more favorable to Turkey. The War Secretary strongly dissented, saying that Britain should change her policy in the direction of procuring a real peace in the Muslim world, starting with the restoration of Smyrna to Turkish sovereignty, one of the five points Mustafa Kemal had written that he was willing to negotiate.[92]

Defeated again in his proposed solution to the Turkish peace problem, Churchill tried appealing directly and personally to Lloyd George, 4 December,[93] a ploy that sometimes worked. The tack he took was that the Prime Minister's line on Turkey would not commend itself to the House of Commons, particularly to the ever strengthening Conservative party which was much influenced by the Military circles and disagreed with Lloyd George's pro-Greek policy. "I do not often trouble with letters," Churchill wrote, "but I feel I owe it to you & to y[ou]r long friendship & many kindnesses to send a solemn warning of the harm wh[ich] y[ou]r policy—so largely a personal policy—is doing to the unity & cohesion of several important elements of opinion on wh[ich] you have hitherto been able to rely."

Concluding this long letter on a personal note, Churchill would never forget the service Lloyd George did him "in bringing me a fresh horse when I was dismounted in the war." Office did not attract him as much and so the counsels he offered were those of a sincere friend, "but of a friend who cannot part with his independence."

Churchill tried one last time to influence the Cabinet to change its Middle East policy. He drew their attention, in his memorandum of 16 December,[94] to the fact that Britain was simultaneously out of sympathy with all four powers exercising local influence there: the Bolsheviks, the Turks, the Arabs and the Greeks. This last was because of the return to power of King Constantine which severed the special relations Britain had with Greece under Venizelos. France and Italy were busy representing Britain as Turkey's sole enemy. All this came at a time when Britain's military forces were extremely weak. The solution proposed was one Britain had always utilized, that of dividing up the local powers so that if Britain had enemies, she also would have friends. It was obvious which of the two Britain should befriend: the Turks and the Arabs. As the greatest Muslim power in the world, it was Britain's duty to study policies which were in harmony with Muslim feeling. Lloyd George, however, clung to his pro-Greek policy, and backed by Curzon, carried the Cabinet with him. He asserted that it was impossible to change Britain's policy just because of a Greek election; the Treaty of Sevres would stand and Mustafa Kemal would not be negotiated with. Churchill had failed again.

Overlapping the Turkish dilemma was the Mesopotamian-Persian one. Churchill became increasingly disheartened as the time drew near for him to present the Supplementary Estimate for the Army because but for Mesopotamia he would have been able to show an actual saving on the Estimates of 1920–21 instead of an excess.[95] At the Conference of Ministers, 1 December,[96] Churchill complained that the War Office had to bear on its Votes the cost of policies over which it had no control, whereas it ought to be debited to the Vote of the department responsible for the policy. The discussion on the additional funds let to the conclusion that the House of Commons would grant the Supplementary Estimate only on receiving assurance that this was the end of the heavy military expenditure. Therefore the War Secretary would promise withdrawal of British troops from Persia as soon as the passes were open, and that the garrisons of Mesopotamia and Palestine would be cut to the core. The Cabinet meeting of 8 December[97] agreed with these conclusions. But before he had a chance to present the Supplementary Estimates, Churchill was given a telegram from Haldane[98] and a memorandum from Radcliffe[99] both strongly against these garrison reductions.

Churchill urgently presented this to the Cabinet, 13 December,[100] for it contradicted the statement he was to make in two days to Commons. The Cabinet rejected his proposal to withdraw to Basrah vilayet and the Persian oilfields but agreed to look into the situation further. Churchill should resist any demands for a declaration of policy in the debate set for 15 December; Churchill succeeded in this in his own inimitable fashion.

After a later Cabinet meeting, 17 December,[101] telegrams were sent to Cox and General Haldane informing them that there had as yet been no decision on the high cost of Mesopotamia, but that the Cabinet would like their opinions on withdrawal to the Basrah vilayet. With the strongly negative answer both from Cox and General Haldane to this proposed withdrawal, thereby reinforcing the earlier Cabinet opinion, the lines were clearly drawn between economy and policy. The Secretary of the State for War presented both sides of the case to the Cabinet meeting 31 December[102] and suggested that two alternatives presented themselves: either the Cabinet could decide to get back as quickly as possible to the Basrah line regardless of the political considerations and anarchy and chaos which would follow in northern Mesopotamia, or the Cabinet could create at once a Department the ministerial head of which should be responsible for the policy for the whole Middle East and obtaining the money to carry out that policy.

The second alternative was not a new idea. It had been raised at some of the meetings of the Interdepartmental Conferences on the Middle East as early as 1918, and even earlier, in 1917, by Montagu who was dismayed by the indecision over policy in Mesopotamia.[103] Churchill entered the fray, because of his disgust at the financial setup then in force in which the War Office had to pay out millions of pounds yet had no say in the policy for which the money was spent, by presenting a memorandum on "Mesopotamian Expenditure" to the Cabinet, 1 May 1920.[104] He argued for the transfer of the mandated territories to a central controlling body which "has a real knowledge and experience of the administration and development of these wild countries, which is accustomed to improvisations and makeshifts, which is accustomed to measure the territory it occupies by the amount of force at its disposal, and be measured by the exiguous funds entrusted to it." He favored placing the new department in the Colonial Office, rejecting Foreign Office control because mixing up the conduct of relations with foreign states with the administration of provinces would impair the discharge of both functions.

Churchill's memorandum touched off a round of memoranda dividing the Cabinet into advocates of Colonial Office control or Foreign Office control of the Middle East. Within the Foreign Office, Major Hubert Young wrote a note, 17 May,[105] advocating control by his Office and Lord Curzon incorporated Young's note into his own memorandum which he presented to the Cabinet 8 June[106] in reply to Churchill. Sarcastically, Curzon began by writing that if Mr. Churchill preferred the Colonial Office, he "must be very imperfectly acquainted with the views or interests of the States of the Middle East, if he thinks that such a transference would be contentedly acquiesced in by them, or would lead to an immediate solution of the difficulties by which we are confronted." The Colonial Office was equipped to deal with backward natives, not with states with pride in their ancient histories as Persia, or with communities as advanced and cosmopolitan as the Jews and Egyptians, or with countries that were focal points of international rivalry as Arabia and Syria. The mandated territories "would utter a cry of rage if their condition were, by even the implication of a misnomer, to be assimilated with that of British Colonies."

Within the Cabinet, Milner supported Curzon and Montagu supported Churchill. Outside the Cabinet, in Parliament, a number of prominent public and parliamentary figures also advocated immediate formation of a separate ministry to handle Middle Eastern affairs.[107]

Debate went on all summer and autumn over who should control the Middle East.[108] The problem became acute in December when Churchill forced the issue by pressuring the Cabinet over War Office expenses and the need to decide on policy. Finally, the full Cabinet met, 31 December,[109] in which the War Secretary presented the two opinions, as related above. The Cabinet discussed and rejected withdrawal to Basrah; as for a completely new Department, that was ruled out too. The arguments for and against Colonial Office and Foreign Office control were raised, and the Cabinet finally agreed that the responsibility for the whole of the administration of the mandates should be in one Department which would bear all expenses, both civil and military. By a majority vote, it was decided that the new Department should be a branch of the Colonial Office, and an Interdepartmental Committee should be set up immediately to work out details. Lord Milner refused to accept these new responsibilities and informed Lloyd George that he wished to leave his position as Colonial Secretary.

There is no evidence showing exactly when Winston Churchill agreed to head the Colonial Office.[110] He wanted to leave the War Office because of sheer frustration. He had tried for two years to fulfill his major tasks of demobilization and securing military economies, and had succeeded relatively well in both tasks except in the Middle East and Ireland. He had failed to convince his colleagues of the danger of Bolshevism to Britain's interests in the Middle East and of his concomitant plan to negotiate with Mustafa Kemal in order to set Turkey up as a barrier to Bolshevik ambitions. He had failed, too, to influence British policy in the Arab countries because of the rivalries and conflicting interests of the War Office, Foreign Office, India Office, and Colonial Office, each of which had a say in governing these newly acquired territories. He could not use his initiative nor take the bold steps which he wanted. It was at his insistence, when at his wit's end over how to accomplish anything, that the Cabinet finally agreed to place control of the Middle East in a new department of the Colonial Office. Perhaps because of this, and his constant inundation of the Prime Minister with memoranda on the Middle East, and Lloyd George's recognition that Churchill's varied constructive talents could be put to good use as Colonial Secretary that Churchill was offered the position. It is known that Lloyd George found it difficult to work with both Curzon and Montagu, but easy to work with Churchill, who had proven himself a man for difficult tasks. It was logical therefore for the Prime Minister to ask him to take the responsibility for the most difficult and problematic areas at that time. The earliest piece of evidence of Churchill's new role is a letter by Sir Arnold Wilson, written 17 December after lunching with Churchill: "I think we are very lucky to have him in charge of the Middle East. A great improvement over any other Minister I have seen and determined to make as good a show as he possibly can."[111]

A new chapter was about to begin in the history of the Middle East one which at the outset gave cause for optimism that at long last the dilemmas were about to be solved.

CHAPTER 5

The Secretary of State for the Colonies

Winston Churchill plunged into his new job at the start of the new year though he did not exchange the seals of office until mid-February 1921. The challenge of the new position with its wide range of responsibilities excited his imagination; Churchill devoted much thought to strategies for meeting the Middle East challenge since this was a main reason for his change of office. His goal as minister of Lloyd George, to realize economies and to reduce commitments was balanced by his goal, as a minister of the British Empire, to uphold the honor and imperial interests of Great Britain.

Setting up his figurative easel, Churchill busily began mixing his colors to start his creative painting. But before applying the paints he had to sketch the colorless yet vital outlines of the picture of his imagination on the blank canvas. These outlines were the new Middle East Department of the Colonial Office and the clarification of his own ideas on the many issues of the Middle East, especially of the Fertile Crescent. Churchill had the unique opportunity of creating a new department and he tried to make it as efficient and all-encompassing as possible. He did this by recruiting the most able men he could to represent every possible point of view, and by putting to use all the years of experience he had as a public servant. He wanted the department to have the initiative and effective control over all Middle East policy.

As for clarifying his ideas on Fertile Crescent issues, he built upon his War Office policy of the use of modern technology to replace manpower, expanding this policy to include a special police force and cheap Indian troops. This he had to interweave with the burden of Britain's wartime and postwar commitments that he inherited, and Churchill gradually concluded that the best way to construct viable Arab governments was through a Sharifian policy, namely using the members of the family of Husayn, guardian, or Sharif, of the holy cities of Mecca and Medina, whose sons—Faysal and 'Abdallah—had helped the Allies during World War I.

To achieve his goals both in the creation of the new department and in the creation of the expanded policy, his methods were generally direct ones. He appealed straight to Lloyd George, Curzon, and Faysal, and via telegrams to Cox and Haldane thereby overcoming the few obstacles that cropped up. Then he collaborated with his new department of experts to clearly outline all aspects of this policy.

Churchill insisted from the first, upon accepting the task of clearing up the situation in the Middle East, that he must have the power and the means of doing so. In a note to the Prime Minister, 4 January 1921,[1] he presented ten carefully thought out points, hoping that Lloyd George would be able to give him the aid and authority required. The first point, as could be expected, dealt with the Mesopotamian entanglement. Churchill insisted on having "authority at once to give *general directions*, within the scope of Cabinet decisions, upon the Mesopotamian position, whether in civil or military matters," including evacuation of north Persia. This last was a source of contention with Curzon who constantly wrangled with Churchill over withdrawal, and had just done so in a Cabinet meeting held before Churchill wrote this memorandum.[2]

The remaining nine points sketched details of his transfer to the Colonial Office and of setting up the new Department: the India Office should continue ordinary administration and the War Office should continue to bear the military costs for the while; a committee should be set up under Churchill's supervision to implement the Cabinet decision to form a Middle Eastern department, and Churchill outlined the committee's terms of reference as well as suggested that Sir James Masterton-Smith should preside over the officials representing the Departments concerned; the exchange of seals of office should take place in early February but should be announced earlier; until the Imperial Conference scheduled for that summer, Egypt should remain under the Foreign Office. Churchill wanted a representative in the House of Lords to aid in Colonial Office business dealings, and suggested the name of Sir James Stevenson. His last point was that he should visit Mesopotamia "at a very early date in order to take decisions on the spot aimed at securing our position as Mandatory without undue expense."[3]

CHAPTER 5 • The Secretary of State for the Colonies

Lloyd George promised his as yet unofficial Colonial Secretary most of the points listed above, and four days later Churchill wrote privately to his Prime Minister that he had put all matters in train.[4] The Interdepartmental Committee on the Middle East, presided over by Sir James Masterton-Smith, soon to be appointed Permanent Under Secretary of State of the Colonial Office, was set up and given its terms of reference.[5] Churchill sent to the High Commissioner of Mesopotamia, Sir Percy Cox, and the General-Officer-Commander in Chief, General Aylmer Haldane, a private and secret telegram informing them of his new position and defining his task for their guidance.[6] This telegram clearly sets forth Churchill's thinking on the Mesopotamian issue in early January and begins to give body to his sketching. His primary concern was reducing the high cost of holding the country and so he warned that unless an economical method could be devised by 1922, Britain would retire and contract to the coastal zone. Since large military forces had to remain until that time to safeguard the retirement from northwest Persia into Mosul, Churchill hoped that their presence would help the setting up of an Arab Government, "through whose agency a peaceful development of the country may be assured without undue demands upon Great Britain. It is to this policy that we must devote our efforts." He contemplated the formation of an Imperial Mesopotamian Police Force of exceptional individual quality and the formation of Indian military units to work in conjunction with a system of air control. "I trust that by these methods, in regard to which action will be immediately begun, it may be found possible for us to do justice to the mandate which we have accepted."[7]

The telegram shows that Churchill was just beginning to view Mesopotamia in a context wider than a military one. He had asked for advice on his new responsibilities as well as for detailed information on the Middle East as soon as he had accepted the new position. He studied the facts and figures as well as the policy instruments. His future actions as Colonial Secretary were bound by the terms of the many commitments made by Britain during and after the war, the San Remo decisions and the rules of the League of Nations.[8] A conquering nation could no longer march in and colonize. The key phrase was now "self-determination" and the Allies firmly believed that their protection of the liberated peoples of the Middle East was what the people themselves wished.[9]

France and Britain had promised to help establish national governments in Syria and Mesopotamia according to the Anglo-French Declaration of

1918[10] and Churchill's reference to the development of an Arab Government shows that he was absorbing the background material of his new office.

He began action, as he had telegraphed, by ordering Adjutant General Macdonough to examine the possibility of using African troops in Mesopotamia, instead of or as well as Indian troops.[11] He also set up a committee headed by Macdonough, to frame a scheme for immediately raising an Imperial Mesopotamian Police Force of 2,000 men to start with; the committee was also to frame a scheme for raising, from Indian volunteers, a number of cavalry regiments and infantry battalions for special permanent service in Mesopotamia.[12]

In noting to the Prime Minister that he had all matters in train Churchill added that he needed "a little more time & consideration. ... before definitely launching Feisal. I must feel my way & feel sure of my way."[13] Churchill was referring to the Cabinet decision of 31 December to open secret negotiations with the Amir Faysal over his possible candidature as king of Mesopotamia. Faysal had been ousted from Syria the previous summer by the French and was in London pleading his cause. The strongest advocate of making Faysal king was T. E. Lawrence,[14] who backed the claims to an Arab kingdom of Husayn, Sharif of Mecca, and his sons 'Ali, 'Abdallah, Faysal and Zayd. Another important Sharifian was Hubert Young, a member of the Eastern Department of the Foreign Office and secretary of Curzon's Interdepartmental Committee on the Middle East. The two men and their sympathizers organized their propaganda well and created for Faysal a reputation for statesmanship and moderation as well as a belief that he had claims on the gratitude of Britain for helping fight the Turks.[15] Curzon became a partisan of Faysal and wrote favorably of him to Churchill while keeping the Colonial Secretary informed of the negotiations with the Amir.[16] The Director of Military Information and the Chief of the Imperial General Staff also favored Faysal.[17]

Before committing himself to Faysal, Churchill had to make sure that the French would not object to the idea of placing the deposed "King of Syria" on the throne of Mesopotamia. He, therefore, touched on the issue during general discussions on Germany, Eastern Europe and the Middle East with Alexandre Millerand, the new French President. The talks took place during a stopover in Paris while Churchill was on his way to the south of France for a fortnight's rest. Churchill wrote a detailed letter describing the conversation.[18] His impression was that France was sick of pouring out money and men into Cilicia and Syria, and was ready to be conciliatory to Britain. Churchill showed that they had a common interest in appeasing the area and should plan for the future. Millerand agreed and said that the first step should be an arrangement with Mustafa Kemal. Churchill carefully worded his reply, that Britain was not opposed to such negotiations, "if an accommodation could be come to which resulted in the Turks calming down and not disturbing or threatening us any further ... ."

Churchill then told Millerand that Arab sentiments also had to be appeased, hinting at the Faysal issue. If France and Britain did not work together then they would both lose everything. But when Churchill said a major cause of Arab unrest was French occupation of Damascus, Homs, Hama, and Aleppo, Millerand countered that it was Zionism in Palestine that was disturbing the Arab world. Yet all in all Churchill felt that the time was right for France to be accommodating and he hoped that the opportunity would not be missed.

In a private letter to Lloyd George reporting on the above conversation,[19] Churchill added that the more he studied the Middle East problem the more he was convinced that the new Department should be vested with the conduct of British affairs in the entire Arab peninsula within the Jerusalem-Aden-Basrah triangle because it was one interwoven problem and "no conceivable policy can have any chance which does not pull all the strings affecting them." He was confident the Cabinet would agree and did not doubt that the Masterton Smith report would demonstrate the impossibility of any divided authority.

Churchill now needed two more pieces of information before deciding definitely on Faysal. First, he telegraphed to Sir Percy Cox:[20] "Do you think that Feisal is the right man and the best man?" Cox should not worry about French objections because Churchill was optimistic that the French could be placated "provided matters are handled with them candidly and courteously."

Then he awaited Lawrence's report about the negotiations being carried on between Faysal and the Foreign Office.[21] Churchill had to know whether the Amir would act in Britain's interests as king of Mesopotamia. Lawrence had agreed to become the Colonial Secretary's adviser on Arabian affairs and was present at the negotiations in this capacity. Lawrence stated in his report, on 17 January, that Faysal had, in effect, agreed to set aside all questions of pledges, thus opening the way to new and constructive discussions.[22]

While awaiting replies to his many queries Churchill tried to recruit the cooperation of the head of the other Office controlling parts of the

Middle East, Lord Curzon. Tactfully, Churchill addressed the older man: "I am sure I can count upon y[ou]r help in the difficult & embarrassing task I have undertaken. It has been imposed upon me by circumstances & the Prime Minister after I had more than once declined it. I look forward only to toil & abuse. But I hope at least to have some measure of control. I shall greatly value any advice that you may be willing to give me, & also the aid—indispensable at so many points—of the Foreign Office."[23]

Foreign Office cooperation was needed because it was in charge of relations with Turkey and France, countries central to Churchill's economizing plans, and because the work of the two offices overlapped. He aired his innermost thoughts to his wife that "Curzon will give me lots of trouble & have to be half flattered & half overborne. We overlap horribly. I do not think he is much good. Anyhow I have the burden on my back. We are quite on good terms personally. I shall take lots of trouble to bring him along."[24]

Encouraged by Curzon's reply that he did "not know whether to congratulate you or commiserate with you on taking over these ventures," but wished him "a better return" than he had received,[25] Churchill wrote again a few days later. He would be very grateful if Curzon would give him, especially in the early months ahead, the benefit of his counsel "based as it is on so much knowledge, and thus put me in a position to discharge the obscure and tangled task which I have the temerity to accept."[26] Curzon readily agreed to render his help and cooperation.[27]

The first thing to get tangled was the telegraphic correspondence between the Secretary of State and the High Commissioner at Baghdad. Upon receipt of Churchill's 8 January[28] wire, Cox answered that he could not agree with the Government's plans of withdrawal, mistakenly believing that the Sharifian plan that he wanted was rejected; therefore he would have to resign.[29] Haldane replied critically as well, that he could reduce the troops no further until the Arab forces had proved themselves.[30] These telegrams crossed two private and secret ones from Churchill on 10 January and 15 January.[31] In the earlier one he pressed for the departure of every unit that could be spared, while beginning to apply some of the principles of the air scheme; he also informed Cox and Haldane that committees were framing a 2,000-man Imperial Mesopotamian Police scheme and an 8,000-man Indian army scheme,[32] and asked for their opinions. In the telegram of 15 January, he asked for Cox's opinion of Faysal's candidature and on the proposed National Assembly.

Cox's reply to the proposed drastic troop reductions dampened the Secretary of State's enthusiasm somewhat. Cox stressed that premature evacuation would cause the collapse of the provisional Government and the whole machinery of civil administration, because the future of the Government depended on its ability to collect revenue and the tribes would not pay unless the central Government was in a position to enforce payment in the last resort.[33] The most he was prepared to risk was reduction to one division and one brigade in Basrah provided a division was maintained in Baghdad and Mosul.

On 23 January[34] Churchill sent a long personal telegram to Cox regretting receipt of his resignation telegram and hoping this was due to a misunderstanding. Churchill in fact intended to try his utmost to preserve British control of Mesopotamia and only if every scheme for reducing the enormous military expenditure was rejected by those on the spot would Britain retire to the coast. Cox had been wrong to suppose that his scheme of setting up one of the Sharif's sons as a local ruler had been rejected as a whole and had he waited to receive Churchill's further telegram this would not have happened.

Churchill understood Cox's difficulties, but Cox should in turn try to realize the difficulties existing in Britain. He did not think there was the slightest chance of the Cabinet agreeing to pay the 12-14 million pounds per year which Cox's military scheme would cost for a country which Britain was pledged to return to the Arabs at the earliest possible moment.

> I have undertaken very reluctantly to face this storm and difficulty in the hope that all British work and sacrifice in Mesopotamia may not be cast away, and I have a right to loyal aid and support from the men on the spot. I am not committed to any particular alternative method of providing the force necessary to sustain the Arab Government, but I am determined that every avenue shall be promptly and thoroughly explored. For this reason I have set up without a day's delay the Committees which are necessary.[35]

Churchill clearly nailed his point home by asking why Cox should assume that the only form in which the requisite element of force could be supplied was the ordinary one of regular troops organized in divisions and brigades and with their lavish and ponderous staffs? Surely it was worth considering whether the special police force, Indian troops, and Air Force scheme would be just as effective. He ended this long telegram by saying that Cox would take a great responsibility if he deprived Britain of his local knowledge and influence by resigning., thus gravely diminishing the chances of a satisfactory solution.

Cox replied briefly, 26 January, that he was ready to cooperate in exploring every avenue provided that during the period of investigation no premature action in the direction of withdrawal or reduction below the safe minimum was taken.[36] Two days earlier Cox had definitely chosen to back Faysal's candidature.[37] By that time Churchill too, had decided to back Amir.

Satisfied that the issue with Cox was settled, Churchill turned his attention to Haldane asking him to comment on what the maximum rate of withdrawal to Basrah town would be from September to December. The Secretary of State could not understand why it should be difficult to move 90,000 men along a railroad and two rivers in three months' time, assuming Basrah port would be kept fully supplied with the necessary shipping.[38] He added, two days later,[39] that one of the reasons for the huge expense was the list supplied by the Quartermaster General showing that as of December 1920 Britain was feeding a total of 225,785[40] people and 53,198 animals. Churchill wanted a program of total evacuation as soon as possible, but Haldane continued to resist this.

Disgusted with trying to settle questions by an interchange of telegrams which in effect necessitated constant erasures, thereby messing up his canvas, Churchill finally decided once and for all on a conference to be held in Egypt, not Mesopotamia, at the beginning of March. He wired to Cox of his decision[41] asking him to come and bring along Generals Haldane and Ironside as well as his chief financial adviser.

Lord Milner, the former Colonial Secretary, was very much in favor of Churchill's proposed trip to the Middle East to see the situation for himself, and wrote to Sir Herbert Samuel, High Commissioner for Palestine, that "he is very keen, able & broadminded & I am sure, if he only gives himself time to thoroughly understand the situation, he will take sound views & you will find him a powerful backer."[42] Samuel too was optimistic,[43] as was Sir A. T. Wilson, former Acting High Commissioner for Mesopotamia, who reassured Cox that the general belief was that "Winston ... having made 2 mistakes cannot afford to make any more, is out to make a good show, not only of the dominions ... but also of the Mandated Territories, if by any means he can."[44]

The Masterton Smith report was presented to Churchill on 31 January, who distributed it to the Cabinet, 7 February, urging earlier consideration.[45] The Committee recommended that the new Department should be responsible for directing policy for the whole Arabian peninsula. The scope of the new Department should be administration and policy in Iraq, Palestine and Aden, policy in all other Arab areas within the British sphere of influence, delimitation of boundaries, and all expenditure, both civil and military. Further, the War Office and Air Ministry should continue to advise on military requirements and to conduct operations during the transitional period, but would be repaid by the Colonial Office except for withdrawal from Persia. Detailed recommendations were made with regard to the civilian services including loans from parent services.

The Foreign Office was disturbed over the territorial sphere recommended by the Report for the new Department which left the Foreign Office as the channel of communication merely for the Hijaz government; it insisted on having a hand in questions of international politics. The War Office was even more upset over the recommended military arrangements which were intended to put an end to the unsatisfactory system under which the War Office had to bear the cost of Middle Eastern operations while the policy necessitating such operations was conducted by other Departments of State. The War Office viewed the new principle introduced by the Committee quite as objectionable as the evil it desired to remedy, namely the ultimate removal of the Middle East defense forces and military policy from War Office control after the transitional period. The Director of Military Operations was appalled at this prospect, fearing that the contemplated gendarmerie could neither control internal matters nor defend the mandated territories from the external aggression so sure to come. These fears totally counteracted "the laudable object of saving expenses on the assumption that the Colonial Office will be able to produce a cheap substitute for regular troops—a sort of military margarine in fact—and so reduce the cost of living in their Middle Eastern household."[46]

Defending his actions as War Office representative on the Committee which had made such recommendations, Sir Herbert Creedy, Secretary of the War Council, noted that he had been placed in a delicate situation since although Churchill had been War Secretary at that time, his thoughts and interests had been directed to his new Department.[47] "Mr. Churchill's original idea was to have a sort of War Office of his own with military and military-finance departments. With characteristic thoroughness he wished to be completely master in his own household. He took a great personal interest in the deliberations of the Committee and did not conceal from them the lines on which he expected their recommendations would be framed."[48]

The framework was good, but before dealing with it in the Cabinet, Churchill drew up a short report on Middle Eastern affairs including in it eighteen private telegrams on Mesopotamia and presenting four points which the Cabinet should approve in principle.[49] Taking no chances, he wanted the Cabinet to approve the Masterton-Smith Report, clearly affirming that the initiative and effective control of all policy within the Middle East would be vested in the Secretary of State for the Colonies; he wanted the Cabinet to approve the Egyptian conference, and that the Colonial Secretary should have the power to replace the Commander-in-Chief in Mesopotamia by a junior officer. Finally, the Cabinet should state what a suitable grant-in-aid for Mesopotamia would be after the evacuation of the main body of troops. The four points were vital ones of power and control so very essential to the success of the new Colonial Secretary, and would enable him to finalize the charcoal sketch of his planned picture of the Middle East and begin painting.

Churchill presented both papers to the Cabinet, at noon 14 February,[50] orally summarizing certain points and asking for approval. The Report was approved on the understanding that the proposals affecting the Government of India be approved by them as well and that the Foreign Secretary and Colonial Secretary were to consult on reaching a working agreement on the initiation and development of Arabian policy. The Egyptian Conference was authorized, and the Mesopotamian grant-in-aid was to be further considered as was a new name for the Colonial Office.

The Colonial Secretary immediately commenced the official formation of the new Department trying to have every point of view represented. He wanted Sir Arthur Hirtzel to be his senior adviser but Hirtzel declined to leave the India Office. Instead, on Hirtzel's advice, John Shuckburgh, of the India Office, became the Assistant Under-Secretary, the man in direct control of the three subdivisions. Major Hubert Young, of the Foreign Office, became the head of the first division, in charge of political and administrative work of each individual area, and was directly in charge of the men controlling the policy of Palestine, Mesopotamia, and Aden and the Arabs. T. E. Lawrence became the Arab Advisor. Eric Forbes Adam and Reader Bullard were principal officers. Churchill ran into a few snags when he tried to recruit men to head the military and financial subdivisions of the new Department because the Board of Education refused to release Roland Vernon to head the financial division and because some of the men approached found it difficult to decide as quickly as Churchill wanted them to. A rushed announcement of the "provisional" appointments had to be made despite the lack of formal concurrence in order to quash the press accusations that Churchill was setting up a grandiose office. *The Times*, for example, had published an editorial praising his new appointment but clearly warning him that there were "suspicions that he is ambitious to rule on an Oriental scale and that he may prove to be extravagant, and may seek constantly to magnify British commitments in Palestine, in Mesopotamia, and in Persia."[51] The communiqué thus released, 25 February,[52] stated that total personnel of the entire Department was to number about fourteen.

As usual, Churchill also immersed himself in all the details of his new office. He not only ordered a uniform system of spelling Arab names, a large map coloring differently the various areas, a genealogical tree of the Sharifians, and a rundown on religious differences between the Shi'is and Sunnis,[53] but he also gave minute instructions as to office papers and the form the minutes should have.[54]

To counteract one of the major shortcomings he had experienced as War Secretary and to complete the Department's framework Churchill formed a purely official Group Council, comprising Shuckburgh, Young, Vernon and Lawrence, to consult once a week with representatives of the Foreign, India and War Offices in order to be in continuous touch at early stages of policy formation.[55] Earlier he had received permission to see intercepted naval telegrams and secret service reports.

In informing Curzon of all these administrative matters, Churchill also pointed out the necessity of coming to a clear understanding with France before going to Cairo. French representatives were coming to the London Conference scheduled for 21 February to discuss possible modifications of the Treaty of Sèvres, and Curzon should take advantage of their presence to present Churchill's plans. Churchill knew that Curzon was willing to do so because before handing over the Foreign Office files on Husayn and Faysal, the Foreign Secretary had written a long minute clearly setting forth his opinions on the Middle East.[56] It should be noted that many of Curzon's views, which had been reflected in Foreign Office action until then, were adopted by Churchill in modified forms. Curzon felt that excluding the governing factors of the British mandate for Palestine (including the bargain with the Zionists) and the French mandate for Syria, Britain would like to redeem her pledges not only as a matter of honor but also because it was in her interest to have an independent and friendly Arabia. Such a state could be composed of five elements, two of which—Transjordan and Mesopotamia—were under British control, one under French control, one already independent i.e. the Hijaz, and lastly the remainder of the Arabian Peninsula which was in the hands of independent chiefs. Britain was willing to see an Arab state in Transjordan provided that the Arab ruler did not involve Britain in trouble with the French and that he did not squabble with Palestine. In Mesopotamia the framework of the new Arab state was being rapidly created and Britain would welcome a Sharifian ruler, again provided he abstained from embroiling Britain with the French. As for French opposition, Curzon proposed to tell them quite frankly that Britain meant to carry out her pledges as far as possible and the above plan seemed the only feasible way; it even safeguarded the French position.

Churchill noted to Shuckburgh, his Assistant Under-Secretary, 17 February,[57] that he wanted a proposal for action on Curzon's minute, and received a reply the same day.[58] Shuckburgh, Young—the new Political Secretary—and Lawrence—the Arab Adviser—had discussed the question of the attitude to be taken up towards the French Government in regard to the Sharifian policy in Mesopotamia and had decided, as Curzon had minuted, that Britain should present it to France with the utmost possible frankness. No other policy offered any prospect of reducing the Mesopotamian situation within reasonable time to a state in which Britain was able and willing to deal with it. The Arab ruler was sure to be either Faysal or 'Abdallah, and France had less to fear from a brother enthroned and occupied "than from a disappointed and unemployed free lance with every temptation to make mischief."

Churchill dismissed the tentative suggestion that France set 'Abdallah up in Damascus. 'Abdallah had arrived in Transjordan soon after the French defeat of Faysal, threatening to take military action against the French in Syria. Britain was interested in dissuading him from such an action fearing it might provide an excuse for France to move into British-claimed Transjordan. Lieutenant-General Congreve, Commander of the Egyptian Expeditionary Force, had written to Churchill that holding Transjordan could prove very expensive and had recommended giving up the Palestine Mandate east of the river Jordan.[59] By the time Churchill took over control of Transjordan, British policy favored an Arab state in the area. Therefore, after examining the alternatives, Churchill agreed to allow 'Abdallah to consolidate his position in Transjordan provided he was ready to act in general accord with the advice of British political officers.[59a] Such a policy in Mesopotamia and Transjordan was the only one possible, in Churchill's opinion, showing that he was a convinced Sharifian.

Two days later Shuckburgh wrote another memorandum to the Colonial Secretary stating that the Allied Conference about to assemble in London offered an opportunity of settling all questions still hanging in the air such as the future of the Arabian Peninsula excluding the Hijaz.[60] Faysal was in London trying to get permission to plead the case of the Arabs at the Conference, so it would be advisable to take him into the Colonial Office's confidence on planned Arab policy. Churchill agreed to bringing up the subject at the next Group Council to get Curzon's concurrence, but doubted whether it was wise to confront the French with Faysal. He was right for France refused to meet Faysal who was therefore barred from attending the Conference.[61]

Blocked on this road Churchill invited Faysal to lunch with himself and Lawrence, 22 February to present, in a veiled manner, proposed Colonial Office policy.[62] He had entrusted preliminary talks to Lawrence who had the full backing of the Middle East staff on this policy,[63] but the idea of Faysal serving as king of Mesopotamia was now so central to his picture of a settled Middle East that Churchill felt that he himself had to handle the crucial discussion. The skillful series of delicate thrusts and parries began with Churchill "regretting that the Emir had lost his beautiful Arab clothes. The Emir replied that he had also just lost his beautiful Arab country." Steering the conversation toward the agitation in Transjordan, Faysal said there was every prospect of peace with France; he had been warned by Lawrence a week earlier[64] that all prospects of British support for the Sharifian family could be destroyed if 'Abdallah persisted in aggressive action against the French. His comment obliquely showed that 'Abdallah agreed to Britain's demand. Churchill then touched on relations with Ibn Sa'ud, and Faysal stressed the need for money and mobile defense to keep the peace in Arabia. Churchill finally moved the discussion on to the issue central to both men: Mesopotamia. The Amir thought that it was practicable to create a local government there.

> Mr. Churchill said he respected Arab prowess in war, poetry, science, imagination: but he was not convinced that they possessed the more ordinary virtues of organization: the power to run trains to time, for example. The Emir said he had his own doubts about Arab exactness and system. ... Mr. Churchill suggested that perhaps a division of responsibility and spheres was indicated. The British might organize, the Arabs imagine and execute. The British might work the technical services and administrative services, while the Arabs took charge of religion, war, etc.[65]

Neither man fooled the other by this polite circumlocution of the facts. Faysal was being told that Britain would run things in the proposed Arab state, but the Amir had little choice for he needed British backing to gain the throne.

Assured of Faysal's and 'Abdallah's cooperation and satisfied that the construction of the new Department was proceeding well, Churchill went ahead with his plans for the Cairo Conference. The Conference was the logical sequence to the formation of the new Department. The artist in Churchill insisted that he personally survey the scene he was painting in order to really experience it and not merely try to apply the colors according to someone else's impressions. The primary Conference goal was radical economizing both in the military and financial spheres which necessitated a comprehensive examination of Britain's position in the Middle East to clear up confusion, reduce commitments, and set up a firm foundation for administration by clearly defining policy. The new lines of procedure would have to be balanced against Churchill's need to maintain and consolidate the territorial gains and strategic vantage points won in the Middle East as a result of a vast outlay of British gold and treasure. Strategic interests included secure communications and trade, for example oil, air routes, and a base near the Suez Canal, which was part of the water route to India. An additional factor to be taken into consideration was British honor: how to fulfill British obligations and pledges as much as possible within the more important objectives of good government and strong empire. Churchill touched upon these goals in a letter to Sir George Ritchie, president of the Dundee Liberal Association, written 25 February[66] and published in *The Times*, 4 March, concluding that he hoped that by means of an Arab Government supported by a moderate military force Britain could discharge her duties without unjustifiable expense. But nothing more could yet be elaborated on in public.

Churchill began working on the Conference by writing out a rough agenda for Shuckburgh to fill in.[67] Starting with Mesopotamia he listed seven major points to be discussed, five of which he had already telegraphed to Cox at the start of the month.[68] The Department view on questions to be discussed differed from Churchill's mainly in emphasis: the Colonial Secretary stressed the questions of the new ruler, the makeup of the future garrison, the scale of the civil administration, and especially the timetable of immediate military economies. But where he listed the questions of the total amount of the grant-in-aid and the extent of territory to be held and administered as a result of the above decisions, the Middle East Department listed the foreign relations of Mesopotamia under the mandate, and included the questions of Kurdistan, amnesty for political offenders, refugees, and Indian labor under a coverall heading of "special subjects."[69]

Churchill ordered Shuckburgh to draw up a similar agenda for Palestine, as well as a short discussion on the places to be transferred from the India Office, the position of Somaliland, and the general relation of the Middle Eastern Department with the officers serving abroad.[70] The provisional agenda drawn up as a result of this order provided Churchill with a rationale for dividing Palestine. In 1915 Britain promised to support Arab independence in the vilayet of Damascus, whose western boundary was the river Jordan; in 1917 Britain promised the Jews a national home in Palestine without mentioning specific boundaries. Both these pledges would be fulfilled if the territory west of the river became the Jewish national home and the territory east of the river became an Arab state. There was legal justification in the Mandate itself for such a policy: the preamble stated that nothing shall be done which may prejudice the civil and religious rights of non-Jewish communities, and article 3 obliged Britain to encourage self-government for localities consistent with the prevailing conditions. The two clauses justified setting up two different political systems because in Transjordan the system had to be Arab in character. Churchill's advisers recommended that an Arab ruler should rule Transjordan, and at the same time recommended developing Palestine's industrial potential.[71]

This provisional agenda which had been discussed point by point by the Middle East personnel of the Colonial Office was handed to the Colonial Secretary as he was setting out on his journey to Egypt. He was handed, too, an appeal from Dr. Weizman,[72] asking Churchill to include western parts of

Transjordan as well as the area between Beersheba and the Gulf of Aqaba in the boundaries of Palestine. Before leaving, Churchill also tried to arm himself with clear proposals for establishing an independent financial authority under the High Commissioner of Mesopotamia with wide powers over both civil and military expenditure, and with proof of the value of trying to establish Air Force control over the mandates. To obtain the former he asked for the opinions of Sir Arthur Hirtzel and Sir Charles Harris only to receive opposing views. Hirtzel noted that an expert financial adviser should control British military expenditure in Mesopotamia as well as keep watch over the Arab government's expenses to ensure self-support.[73] Harris accused Hirtzel of contemplating that the High Commissioner would be a little Viceroy, with his own military department, administering the army whether it was British or not; he felt that it was for the War Office to continue to control the armed forces and its finances.[74] Churchill clearly noted that it certainly was his intention "that once we set up our own Vote for Mesopotamia, the High Commissioner will be in every respect in the position of the Indian Viceroy," and asked Shuckburgh's advice on equipping Cox with a high financial officer who would have the power to investigate in detail every branch of the military expenditure especially the waste on followers and staffs, and on whose report Cox would have the power to send out of the country those who were not wanted.[75] But Shuckburgh could not render such advice at that time because the Masterton-Smith report did not deal with control over Mesopotamian expenditure during the transition phase, and it was necessary to clearly define the powers of a financial adviser before making an appointment. Churchill thus had to proceed to Cairo without the power to effect this aspect of control and reduction of expense, but he did take with him optimistic reports of the value of the Royal Air Force in reconnaissance, tactical cooperation, pursuit, distant attack, demonstration, and especially communications.[76] He took with him Air Marshal Sir H. Trenchard, Chief of Air Staff, to forcefully present the case for air control of Mesopotamia, a major part of Churchill's plan to reduce expenses in that territory. To Trenchard, Mesopotamia was the arena where the R.A.F. could consolidate its claim to equal treatment with the army and the navy, therefore he was "very keen to insist on the withdrawal of a lot of the little detachments, to accept a certain amount of chaos in part, but to hold the central line, and by gradual peaceful penetration spread over three or four years to regain what we give up."[77] No wonder Churchill insisted he accompany him to Cairo.

CHAPTER 6

The Cairo Conference of 1921

The Cairo Conference opened on Saturday, 12 March 1921. The detailed agenda had been worked out by Churchill and his staff on the long journey to Egypt,[1] and after a short assembly presided over by the Secretary of State, the conference divided into two committees sitting simultaneously: the political committee and the military and finance committee.[2] Stress will be put on the role of the Colonial Secretary as director of the conference in painting his scenario to suit himself. By guiding the conference Churchill ensured that the policy outlines he had worked out would be filled in to his liking and he found no real obstacles in his path. He also guided the direction his policy took outside the conference by traveling to Palestine to meet with 'Abdallah and with representatives of the Zionists and Palestine Arabs.

Churchill served as the bridge between the conference and London, for without the sanction of the Prime Minister and the Cabinet no decision reached at Cairo could be implemented. It was a difficult task, as it had to be done via impersonal telegraphs to a Prime Minister who was loath to commit himself. In contrast, Churchill's face to face attempt to convince Amir 'Abdallah to stay on in Transjordan on Churchill's terms was much easier for the Colonial Secretary, and tied up one more loose end of his policy. Although the conference did not deal with basic Palestine policy, merely confirming earlier British decisions, Churchill either felt that the time had come to clarify his position on Palestine or this was something he simply could not avoid. Therefore, while visiting Jerusalem he made his first public statements as Colonial Secretary on Britain's policy there, balancing the two parts of the Balfour Declaration and hinting at what later became known as the economic absorptive capacity principle.

The first five days of the Cairo Conference were devoted to Iraq[3] and related areas. The small Political Committee, composed of Churchill, Cox and his Political Secretary Miss Gertrude Bell, Young and Lawrence quickly attended to the first item: the immediate reduction of British military commitments. Cox and Haldane had already agreed on preliminary troop withdrawals and therefore it was unnecessary to discuss alternatives, so the committee moved on to the second item, namely formation of a local government of real prestige and authority for this was central to further substantial military reduction. Cox described his activities in Iraq and presented the list of candidates for ruler although all of the committee members had already agreed on a Sharifian ruler, the Amir Faysal. Churchill's argument in favor of the Sharifian policy openly reveals part of his calculations in acting so: it enabled Britain to bring pressure to bear on one Arab sphere in order to attain other ends in another sphere. If Faysal knew that not only his father's subsidy and protection of the Holy Places from Ibn Sa'ud's attack, but also the position of his brother in Transjordan was dependent on his own good behavior, he, as well as 'Abdallah and Husayn, would be easier to deal with.[4] Churchill insisted that at some stage and somehow the British had to approve the ruler and not merely acquiesce to an election by the Legislative Assembly. This process of selection and a timetable of the procedure to be adopted in the event of Faysal's appointment were discussed the next day after which Churchill sent a personal and secret cable to Lloyd George[5] asking for his assent so that a definite plan of action could be drawn up. The committee suggested the following formula: "In response to enquiries from adherents of Emir Feisal the British Government have stated that they will place no obstacle in the way of his candidature as ruler of Iraq and that if he is chosen he will have their support."[6]

Concurrently the much larger military committee met, under the chairmanship of General Congreve, to discuss the program for the immediate withdrawal of a substantial part of the military force, as well as to consider Trenchard's proposals for controlling Iraq until the Air Force takeover was complete.[6a] The eight squadron plan was approved as well as Haldane's detailed plan for reduced military commitment by concentrating defenses on the Mosul-Baghdad-Basrah line.

It was at the first meeting of the combined Political and Military Committees, 13 March, that Churchill really began to hammer home in bright colors his major goal of realizing economies. He stated that troop reductions proposed by Haldane must be accelerated by all means and he would spare no effort to supply the shipping so necessary to this acceleration. He was as good as his word and while the military committee sat to examine a place by place distribution of forces, Churchill wired to Lloyd George of the need for confirmation that the Shipping Controller would meet Churchill's requirements.[7] He also asked if he could assume that Turkey would stay away from Mosul, for this would greatly simplify troop reduction in that sector. Churchill still feared that if Turkey were alienated by Britain, she would spoil his peaceful settlement in the Middle East. He had aired his fears of Lloyd George's pro-Greek attitude before leaving for Cairo, but the Prime Minister continued to encourage the Greeks to remain in Thrace and Smyrna. By asking Lloyd George if he could assume that Turkey would stay away from Mosul, Churchill tried to force him to go on record to this effect, making it clear that an Iraqi garrison to ward off outside aggression was not Churchill's responsibility.

Returning to the meetings, Churchill adamantly refused to aid the refugees financially, and decisions had to be arrived at as to their future. He was not content with the proposed reductions and felt that every item must be enquired into to discover why expenditure had not been adequately reduced, even suggesting many ways to reduce costs, such as selling stores and using lower paid junior officers. He stated that the entire policy of reduction would be reviewed in October when further savings would be made to bring the garrison down to 15,000 men.

While waiting for Lloyd George's answer to his telegram, Churchill met with his Political Committee, 15 March, this time including Major E. W. C. Noel, the Kurdistan consultant, to discuss the issue of Kurdistan. Cox and Bell wanted Kurdistan to form a part of Iraq but Noel favored setting it up as a buffer state. Both Lawrence and Young felt the area should not be placed under an Arab government. The Chairman agreed on the value to Britain of Kurdistan as a temporary buffer zone between Iraq and Turkey, and anticipated the formation of Kurdish regiments to protect the area, but was ready to defer to the views of Cox and Bell.

The military Committee met to work out the details of the second troop reduction to take place in October, as noted to them by Churchill, while a subcommittee on finance met to discuss what to do with Iraqi railroads. All conclusions were discussed at the meeting of the combined political and military committees held that afternoon. Reiterating that their object should be to secure a further saving of three million pounds during 1921–22, Churchill stressed that development of local forces capable of relieving the garrisons and acting in conjunction with the Air Force should have priority over other considerations. Everything else should be drastically reduced and railroads should be repaired to increase troop movement to the ports where ample shipping would be available.

Churchill anticipated correctly that Lloyd George had informed the War Office of his shipping needs[8] but Lloyd George wriggled out of committing himself to keeping Turkey out of Mosul. More important, Churchill was wrong in anticipating the Prime Minister's approval of the plan to endorse Faysal: Lloyd George insisted that the initiative must come from Iraq.[9]

Unaware of this and impatient at Lloyd George's tardiness in replying to his 14 March telegram, Churchill decided to send another wire informing the Prime Minister of progress to date. His telegram of 16 March,[10] which crossed the Prime Minister's, presented definite proposals for action for the first state of the troop reductions, for the second stage—if Iraq was quiet internally, if the Arab government was successful and if there was progress in the levies and the Arab army—and for Faysal's timetable.

In the midst of meetings geared towards settling the Kurdish question, the cross-desert aerial-railroad-pipeline route, and subsidies to Ibn Sa'ud, King Husayn, the Imam of Yemen and the Idrisi, the Prime Minister's telegram insisting that the initiative for choosing Faysal must come from Iraq must have hit Churchill hard. He telegraphed back, 18 March, that the formula suggested about Faysal was not intended for publication "but as a definite indication of the limits within which our policy could be framed."[11] His telegram of 16 March contained the procedure for Faysal's adoption, a procedure devised by Cox, Bell and Lawrence which had the unanimous approval of the authorities gathered in Cairo. There was no doubt of the value of the Sharifian system and Faysal was the best candidate, and would be accepted by the people if he appeared there partly because of the mere fact that he was allowed to return. All of Churchill's proposals hung together and by rejecting the part about Faysal, all was in effect rejected. "I do hope you will give to me personally the support to which I am entitled in a task which I certainly have not sought."

So important was the Faysal question that Churchill reiterated the thrust of this telegram in yet another one the next day in reply to Lloyd

George's short telegram approving troop reduction but needing time to further consider the issue of Faysal.[12] Their policy had to be viewed as an interdependent whole, and in accepting one part and postponing another, Lloyd George was "simply asking me in Egyptian phraseology to make bricks without straw."[13]

Churchill could not afford to wait for Lloyd George's reply, vital though the issue was, and the Conference continued as scheduled. The Palestine mission arrived, led by Sir Herbert Samuel, and the first meeting of the Palestine political and military committee took place 17 March. Churchill, as chairman, opened the meeting by announcing that the committee had to discuss British policy in Palestine under two aspects: the general and external aspect as affected by the policy in Iraq and Arabia, and the aspect of local development with particular reference to the Zionist question. The Departmental view was aired, namely that a distinction should be drawn between Palestine and Transjordan under the mandate, and the meeting was thereafter devoted to a discussion of Transjordan.

The Chairman hoped that the decisions of previous meetings with regard to Iraq might prove the solution of Transjordan too; the Sharifian cause was the best course available, despite the French view that "by supporting the Sherif we were building up, like Frankenstein, a monster which would eventually devour us."[14] It was inevitable that Britain should adopt a policy elsewhere which would harmonize with her Iraq policy. "If we were to curb the activities of Abdullah," reasoned the Colonial Secretary, "while allowing him to remain in Trans-Jordania, we must obtain the goodwill of the Sherifian family and place them as a whole under an obligation to His Majesty's Government in one sphere or another."[15] To guarantee that there would be no anti-Zionist disturbances and no anti-French ones, the Arab leader in Transjordan had to be given support, either in money or troops. The military committee would have to devise a scheme for a force across the Jordan that Britain could financially afford yet not be too small as to be unsafe.

Discussion followed, and Samuel declared himself against an independent Transjordan; but Churchill out-argued him. The statement by Major Somerset, British Representative in Transjordan, that it would be impossible to get rid of 'Abdallah from 'Amman was a decisive point bringing Samuel over to Churchill's point of view. All major questions were to be dealt with by subcommittees and their conclusions reported on. So the committees met all afternoon and Palestine members also participated in the discussion of the Royal Air Force scheme for the defense of Iraq.

At the Palestine political and military committee meeting sitting the next day, 18 March, Churchill hammered home, as he had done earlier at the Iraq meetings, the necessity of economizing through drastic troop reduction. The need to aid Transjordan would necessitate temporarily increasing the garrison but only until the local defense force to be created by the Palestine administration was ready to take over, say in six months. Against this temporary increase Churchill trusted that it would be possible by a careful scrutiny of arrears and terminal charges to meet the additional expense involved. In the long run the local defense force would prove to be an economy because it would be fit to replace the permanent garrison.

When the Palestine committee moved on to the relatively minor problems of tracing the frontiers of the mandated territories, and deciding on the clauses to be added to the mandates on administering Kurdistan and Transjordan, Churchill left it to attend the meeting of the Iraq political committee which was to decide on subsidies to Arabian leaders. These subsidies formed an important part in Churchill's policy for controlling the Middle East at a relatively cheap price. Ibn Sa'ud, ruler of the Nejd in Arabia, had great capacity for doing harm for he could invade Iraq, Kuwayt, the Hijaz or other parts of Arabia; British interest lay in refraining such action. Cox, Lawrence, Scott and Cornwallis, who made up a special sub-committee to examine subsidies, therefore recommended increasing his subsidy. Sharif Husayn, as guardian of the Holy Places, had much influence on the Arab world and unless he accepted the Allies' decisions on Arab areas he could cause great unrest; his subsidy would be paid if he ratified the Allies' treaties, did not commit acts of aggression in Arabia, and improved the pilgrimage conditions. It was also in British interests to pay small subsidies to minor Arab leaders to keep them quiet. This issue was carried over to the next day's meeting when Lawrence presented a memorandum on the question of the relations between Britain and the Imam of Yemen. It was in Britain's interest to make peace with the Imam because it would remove a threat to Aden, on the southern tip of the Arabian Peninsula, thus enabling a reduction in the garrison there. A peace treaty would keep the Imam away from al-Idrisi, ruler of 'Asir, with whom Britain had treaties. It would also reduce the chance of French and Italian intrigue there. Britain could achieve this by paying a small subsidy and

CHAPTER 6 • The Cairo Conference of 1921

guaranteeing present boundaries. Churchill wired the proposed subsidies to Lloyd George for approval.[16]

As each committee reached its conclusion, Churchill had to telegraph back to London for approval. He informed Lloyd George, 18 March,[17] that there would be no further troop reduction in Palestine, and asked for his approval in occupying Transjordan and in making arrangements with 'Abdallah for the control of that territory. The Colonial Secretary tried to offset this cost increase with the assurance that Palestine only cost four million pounds, not seven as reported in Commons, and by 1922–23 the cost would not exceed two million. Churchill needed the Prime Minister's authorization on the above before being able to approach 'Abdallah at the end of the month. He had planned to visit Palestine anyway, and now intended to take advantage of the visit to meet 'Abdallah too.

Churchill also telegraphed to the Colonial Office, 19 March,[18] that it was time to approach France about setting up a commission to delimit the boundaries of the mandates. The Colonial, Foreign and War Offices immediately started putting the proper channels in motion, and despite the fact that there still was no reply from the Prime Minister about the key issue, Faysal, the meetings moved ahead. The combined political and military committee met twice, 19 March, to agree on the cross-desert route, the formation of Arab defense forces in Iraq, and the most suitable station for the British garrison if the Air Force scheme was accepted. The same day saw the first meeting of the committee on Mesopotamian finance which dealt with details of all military and civil charges.

No meetings were held on Sunday, 20 March to give the participants a brief rest in which to catch their breaths and go about their own interests. Lawrence wrote to his brother: "Here we live in a marble & bronze hotel, very expensive & luxurious (Semiramis Hotel); horrible place: makes me Bolshevik. ... We have done a lot of work, which is almost finished. ... We're a very happy family: agreed upon everything important: and the trifles are laughed at."[19] But it was not a trifle that by the next day Lloyd George had still not confirmed the choice of Faysal as Churchill had requested. Churchill meanwhile chaired two meetings, one on the sale of Iraq railroads in which he decided that no decision could yet be given, and one on the question of civil service for countries under the Middle East Department.

Alerted to a Cabinet meeting to be held the next day, Churchill telegraphed the Prime Minister pressing for reconsideration of the handling of Faysal's candidature in Iraq. He stressed again that there was no doubt of Faysal's acceptability, but the situation was delicate for Britain had to give Faysal some assurance that she wished him well.[20] The Middle East Department added its own argument to all of Churchill's which Marsh sent to Lloyd George, averring that "any attempt to ascertain 'the wishes of the people' in Mesopotamia would not only be dangerous locally, but would be futile vis-à-vis the French."[21] The French would claim that Britain had engineered the whole business. Britain should candidly inform France that the Faysal solution was the only one possible; otherwise Britain would have to clear out.

The Cabinet met on Tuesday morning, 22 March to consider the Colonial Secretary's various proposals.[22] The main question at issue was whether Churchill's plan did not cast the initiative for choosing Faysal too definitely upon the British Government; this would incur strong French hostility. But the collective force of Churchill's recommendations and the total picture it set forth impressed the Cabinet enough to accept them. To facilitate Britain's arrangements with France, the order of events were to be: Cox was to return to Iraq and set going the machinery which could result in the acceptance of Faysal's candidature; Faysal was to return to Mecca after an informal intimation to him that the post of ruler over Iraq was vacant and if he were offered the position by the people, Britain would welcome their choice, subject to the double condition that he be prepared to accept the terms of the mandate and that he would not use his position to attack or intrigue against the French; Faysal then was to appeal to the Iraqi people announcing his candidature, and Britain could tell the French that there was no ground for protest.

The Prime Minister telegraphed these conclusions to Churchill that afternoon[23] along with the conclusions on the Transjordanian and other proposals. No immediate decision could yet be taken in appointing 'Abdallah nor in occupying the territory, because the Cabinet had misgivings on political and military grounds: politically France would see the simultaneous installation of two brothers as a menace; and militarily, such an occupation would involve a new commitment, the extension and duration of which it was impossible to forecast. Also, it was unsure if 'Abdallah would accept the setup. The Cabinet approved the south Kurdistan proposals as well as those on military reductions and shipping. Only the issue of subsidies was reserved for discussion with Churchill in person.

The next day, 23 March, before leaving Cairo for Jerusalem to put the finishing touches on his painting, and at the time when the committees were discussing the transfer to the Colonial Office of Aden and Somaliland and the refugee problem, Churchill telegraphed Lloyd George[24] thanking him and the Cabinet for approving the general policy in the Middle East. He did not expect 'Abdallah to be governor of Transjordan but he should concur in the governorship of whoever was nominated. Churchill was firm in insisting on a small British force there or Transjordan would not be stable, an indispensable condition preliminary to further troop reductions. He added that General Gouraud, the French commander-in-chief of Syria wanted to meet him in Jerusalem, and concluded with a message to be delivered to Faysal in London if Lloyd George agreed: "Following from Lawrence for Feisal. Things have gone exactly as hoped. Please start for Mecca at once by quickest possible route. ... I will meet you on the way and explain details. Say only that you are going to see your father and on no account put anything in press."[25] Meanwhile Lawrence accompanied Churchill, Samuel, Sir Wyndham Deedes—his Chief Secretary—and Young to Jerusalem, 23 March, where he left them to meet Amir 'Abdallah at as-Salt, east of the Jordan River, to escort him to Jerusalem. "It was an amusing performance, for the people of Salt & Jerusalem were very enthusiastic & excited, & nearly mobbed the car in their anxiety to welcome Abdulla."[26]

The first of his official conversations between 'Abdallah and Churchill was held at Government House in Jerusalem, Monday 28 March,[27] and Churchill opened with an explanatory statement of his Sharifian policy, carefully coming to the point that Faysal's rule would be agreeable to Great Britain. It was hoped that the people of Iraq would acclaim him, said the Colonial Secretary arriving at his first main point, and it would help if 'Abdallah also supported Faysal thus officially giving up his own claims to the throne of Iraq as had been originally planned by Britain.

'Abdallah appreciated all this but his first point was the problem of the Arabian Peninsula. As a son of Husayn he wanted to know what Ibn Sa'ud's position was in the eyes of the British. This issue was so important to 'Abdallah that it is the only time in his memoirs of the conversation that he describes Churchill's actions: "He rose from his chair and walked over to the window, and with his left hand on his side, turned to Lawrence and said, 'Tell the Amir that I cannot reply to his question before asking the Cabinet.'"28 The Secretary's report, however, merely shows that Churchill tersely replied that Britain could not force Ibn Sa'ud into anything but could only hope to influence him by making him financially dependent on Britain.

Satisfied, the Amir then responded to Churchill's first point and declared that he was delighted with the policy for Iraq and would cooperate. Churchill could now move on to his second main point: Transjordan should be constituted as an Arab province of Palestine under an Arab Governor responsible to the High Commissioner. Now the fencing started. First 'Abdallah suggested that there should be an Arab Amir over Palestine and Transjordan in the same relation to the High Commissioner as Faysal to Cox. Churchill pointed out that Palestine had been entrusted to the administration of the mandatory whereas Iraq had been provisionally recognized as an independent state so the positions were different. The Amir countered by asking if Britain wanted to establish a Jewish kingdom and turn out the non-Jewish population? Churchill calmly assured him that Jewish immigration would be a very slow process and the rights of the existing non-Jewish population would be strictly preserved. 'Abdallah tried one more time and suggested that if Palestine-Transjordan could not be like Iraq, Transjordan should be cut off from Palestine and combined with Iraq, adding that he could not advise on an Arab Government if the territory remained under Palestine. Churchill now put all his cards on the table clearly explaining the position and responsibilities of the Arab Governor who would recognize British control as Mandatory: he would abstain from and repress anti-French activities; he would accept British policy west of the Jordan; he would be appointed by Samuel after 'Abdallah agreed to the nominee; chief officials and assistants would be chosen with the High Commissioner's approval and all important measures would be subject to his ultimate sanction. Transjordan would not be part of the Palestine system and therefore Zionist clauses would not apply. To help the Arab Governor keep peace, Britain would be prepared to put a British force at his disposal at 'Amman, the force being there to secure Palestine interests and to calm French fears as well as to ensure good administration, but only if the Governor would make himself responsible for the safety of the line of communications with Palestine. Local forces would also be needed and Britain would help the Governor organize, equip and maintain them.

Finished with his description, Churchill turned to 'Abdallah with a veiled threat:

> He was taking a great responsibility as the new Minister in charge of the Middle East in advising his colleagues to join hands with the Sherifian family. He had been advised by certain other people that this was a very dangerous policy. He had been told that His Majesty's Government would be better advised to split up the Arabs into distinct and separate local Governments. This had been the policy of Rome and of Turkey in the past and appeared to be to some extent the policy of other Powers at the present time. He wished to impress upon the Emir that a very grave choice had to be made within the next few days by His Majesty's Government, namely, whether they should divide or unite the Arab peoples with whom they had to deal.[29]

Faced with such an overwhelming array of arguments, proposals and threats, 'Abdallah had no choice but to give in as gracefully as he could and accept Churchill's policy, claiming that first he had to consult his father and brother. Churchill accepted this, adding one more point before the close of the conversation, that by setting an example in the British sphere it was possible that France might also adopt a Sharifian policy.

At the second conversation held later that day 'Abdallah raised the point that anti-French action would continue as long as France continued her present policy, implying that he could not prevent such activity. Churchill replied that Britain was only concerned to see that France was not annoyed from Transjordan; he wanted to be able to say that it was precisely because Britain had adopted a Sharifian policy that the Sharif was no longer hostile to France. 'Abdallah could be sure that France would not attack Transjordan.

Churchill waited until the third meeting with 'Abdallah to make his final crucial proposal: the Amir himself should remain in Transjordan for six months to prepare the way for the appointment, with his consent, of an Arab Governor under the High Commissioner. During that time a British Political Officer would advise the Amir and help him restore order and set the revenues of the area on a proper basis, British officers would help his levies, and Britain would pay a subsidy. No British troops would be sent at that stage but the Air Force would be in constant touch with the territory. The offer was accepted.[29a]

Churchill must have been very pleased with himself after his meetings with 'Abdallah. The negotiating was a very important matter because Transjordan was a keystone in the interlocking arches of his policy, and Churchill trusted only himself in these delicate negotiations, as he had with 'Abdallah's brother in London. What a formidable negotiator he must have been, if in his recollections, greatly distorted by the passage of time, King 'Abdallah could vividly remember the atmosphere of threat if not the exact words Churchill had used.

The same day that he met Amir 'Abdallah, Churchill also received two deputations at Government House. The first one was from the Arab Executive Committee of the Haifa Congress, the body representing the Palestine national movement, and the petition complaining about Samuel and the Zionists was presented by its president, Musa Kazim al-Husayni, asking "in the name of justice and right" for abolishment of the Jewish National Home principle, the creation of a National Government, stoppage of Jewish immigration, annulment of laws and regulations framed after the British occupation, and unification of Palestine with her sister states.[30]

Churchill's reply is an excellent example of the qualities that made him the forceful speaker that he was. His opening statement made it perfectly clear that it was only at the request of the High Commissioner that he agreed to see the Arab deputation as a matter of courtesy and goodwill; it was in no sense a formal conference. His next comment was a point blank accusation of untruthful presentation of many facts, "and I think everyone of you knows in his heart that it must be taken as a partisan statement and one side of the case rather than as a calm judicial summing up of what is best for us all to do in the difficult circumstances in which we find ourselves." He moved on to candidly explain what the situation was: the Jewish National Home was a legal principle ratified by the Allied Powers and it was upon this basis that the mandate would be discharged. But the second part of the Balfour declaration solemnly and explicitly promised the fullest protection of the civil and political rights of the inhabitants of Palestine. If the one promise stood, so did the other. Indignantly, the Colonial Secretary declared, in no uncertain terms, that Britain had a view of its own in this matter and she had a right to such a view.

> Our position in this country is based upon the events of the war, ratified, as they have been, by the treaties signed by the victorious Powers.
> I thought, when listening to your statements, that it seemed that the

Arabs of Palestine have overthrown the Turkish Government. That is the reverse of the true facts. It has been the armies of Britain which have liberated these regions. You had only to look on your road here this afternoon to see the graveyard of over 2,000 British soldiers, and there are many other graveyards, some even larger, that are scattered about this land. The position of Great Britain in Palestine is one of trust, but it is also one of right.[31]

Following his belief in making concessions from a position of strength, Churchill reassured the Arab delegation that it was not Britain's aim to make Palestine into a Jewish state. On the contrary, the British Empire as the greatest of all Muslim states, wished to cooperate with the Arabs and the Palestine administration headed by Samuel endeavored in every way to render impartial justice. It was only on its merits that the Zionist movement could succeed, carrying with it increasing benefits and prosperity to the people of the country as a whole:

> But you will say to me, are we to be led by the hopes of material gain into letting ourselves be dispossessed in our own house by enormous numbers of strangers brought together across the seas from all over the world? My answer is: no, that will not be, that will never be. Jewish immigration into Palestine can only come as it makes a place for itself by legitimate and honourable means; as it provides the means by which it is to be supported.[32]

Here, perhaps unnoticed by Churchill, is the germ of the economic absorptive capacity principle as had been cautiously voiced by Sir Herbert Samuel in his July 1920 statement of policy, later to be expounded in the White Paper of 1922 bearing Churchill's name.[33]

Concluding his long speech, Churchill waxed eloquent, painting a picture of prosperity and religious harmony: "If instead of sharing miseries through quarrels you will share blessings through cooperation, a bright and tranquil future lies before your country. The earth is a generous mother. She will produce in plentiful abundance for all her children if they will but cultivate her soil in justice and in peace."[34]

The Deputation of the Jewish community arrived soon after the departure of the Arab deputation, expressing gratitude to Britain and to Churchill for helping the Zionist cause. Churchill's approach to Zionism fits into his Christian-British view of the world, which is most clearly expressed in an article he wrote for the *Illustrated Sunday Herald* early in 1920.[35] He opened his article with the introductory statement that no one could doubt that fact that the Jews were the most formidable and most remarkable race that had ever appeared in the world, so it followed that the conflict between good and evil was nowhere so intense as in this people. The world owed to the Jews a system of ethics that was "the most precious possession of mankind" on which existing civilization had been built, but the Jews were also in the process of producing another system as malevolent as Christianity was benevolent.

There was at present three main lines of political conception among the Jews. First there were "national" Jews who, while adhering to their religion, regarded themselves as citizens in the fullest sense of the state in which they were dwelling. "This is a worthy conception, and useful in the highest degree." In violent opposition to this were the "International" Jews, atheists, who played an outstanding role in the Bolshevik Revolution and were prominent advocates and leaders of the system of terrorism reigning in Russia.

Zionism offered a third sphere to Jewish political conceptions. A Jewish national home would be beneficial from every point of view, "and would be especially in harmony with the truest interests of the British Empire." The fury with which Trotsky attacked Zionism was most significant for there was beginning a struggle between the two political conceptions for the very soul of the Jewish people. All Jews should combat the Bolshevik conspiracy, declared Churchill, thereby making it clear to the world that the Jewish masses repudiated this movement. At the same time positive and practicable alternatives were needed, and this could be supplied by rapidly building up a Jewish national center in Palestine. Thus one could describe Churchill as a Zionist sympathizer, but it is important to stress that he was one only as long as Zionism was "in harmony with the truest interests of the British Empire." In this Churchill was consistent: the Empire before all else, and this attitude is seen in a terse comment scribbled on a memorandum on Palestine, 18 December: "So far as the security of the Empire is concerned, we are the weaker rather than the stronger, by the occupation of Palestine."[36]

This attitude is also reflected in his reply to the Jewish Deputation, which he told of Britain's two-fold principle, namely establishment of a Jewish National Home, but without prejudice to the existing inhabitants. He was himself perfectly convinced that the cause of Zionism was one which carried with it much that was good for the whole world but the non-Jewish population was alarmed lest it be dispossessed. Therefore he had pointed out to the Arabs that "Zionism can only succeed by a process which confers benefits upon the whole country, and which at each stage provides the means for supporting by industry or agriculture the new-comers who come in."[37]

It was only fair, if he had made a disagreeable statement to the Arabs, to make a disagreeable one to the Jews too, so he warned them that the Jews had to provide him with the means of answering all adverse criticism in London.

> I wish to be able to say that a great event is taking place here, a great event in the world's destiny. It is taking place without injury or injustice to anyone; it is transforming wasteplaces into fertile; it is planting trees and developing agriculture in desert lands; it is making for an increase in wealth and of cultivation; it is making two blades of grass grow where one grew before, and the people of the country who are in a great majority, are deriving great benefit, sharing in the general improvement and advancement.[38]

Churchill clearly counseled prudence and patience, and warned that it was up to them to prove the groundlessness of Arab fears.

The next day Churchill participated in a meeting at Government House to discuss the Palestine and Transjordan defense forces with Churchill ever insistent on the need to reduce expenditure,[39] but nothing was decided and meetings continued on the Hijaz Railway and the Holy Places Commission even after the Colonial Secretary left to attend a reception at the site of the still uncompleted Hebrew University where he was presented with a gift of a scroll of the Law by the Jewish community. His short speech summarized what he had told the Jewish deputation and he concluded that he was going to plant a tree, "and I hope that in its shadow peace and prosperity may once more return to Palestine."

Before leaving Palestine, Churchill also met Pinchas Rutenberg, a Russian-Jewish electrical engineer, who had applied for the concession for electrification of the country and use of the Jordan's waters both for hydro-electric power and for irrigation; the very magnitude and simplicity of the scheme greatly impressed the Colonial Secretary who was thereafter to champion the application.[40] Churchill also tried to settle matters with the

French General Officer Commanding Syria, but the meeting never came about. He did manage to see M. le Caix, one of the French leaders, and explained British policy to him. M. le Caix pressed strongly for the dispatch of British troops to Transjordan, complaining that Britain was not discharging her responsibilities in that region. Churchill accused him of being hostile to Britain, which was strongly denied. Churchill then explained the arrangement with 'Abdallah, which M. le Caix accepted without objection, saying only that he was glad the arrangement was an informal one; should Abdallah maintain order "all would be forgotten and forgiven in six months."[41] Churchill hoped General Gouraud would assist in enabling 'Abdallah to succeed by declaring a general amnesty for the Syrians to synchronize with the British amnesty soon to be announced in Iraq.[42]

Churchill left Jerusalem, his painting completed, 30 March, after visiting the town of Tel-Aviv, the pioneer settlement of Bir Yaakov, and the agricultural colony of Rishon le-Zion. He traveled to London via Alexandria, while the last matters, attended to by the committees meeting in Jerusalem and Cairo were conveyed to him for study and comment on his voyage.

Lawrence later claimed that not only the questions but also the decisions of the Cairo Conference were decided upon in advance in London. "Talk of leaving things to the man on the spot—we left nothing."[43] This is as unfair a claim as is the one that Churchill drank in Lawrence's dream of the Middle East and together they strove to settle all its problems.[44] It is true that the Sharifian solution was Lawrence's, and he suggested it to the Eastern Committee in 1918[45] as the key to a Middle East settlement: 'Abdallah ruling in Baghdad and Lower Mesopotamia, Zayd in Upper Mesopotamia and Mosul, Faysal in Damascus, and Husayn the overall head and religious leader ruling from the Hijaz, to be succeeded by 'Ali, would present a viable confederation bound by blood. But the Sharifian plan was not the only important decision reached at Cairo, nor was Lawrence the only begetter of ideas—Royal Air Force control of Iraq, for example, was just as important to the overall plan, and this was Hugh Tranchard's creation. Churchill himself recorded: "I received always united advice from two of three of the very best men it has ever been my fortune to work with. It would not be just to assign the whole credit for the great success which the new policy secured to Lawrence alone."[46] Successful adoption of the Sharifian plan was in part due to the very weight of the British authorities who supported it, among whom may be included Allenby, Bell, Samuel, Cox, Young, Cornwallis and eventually most members of the Middle East Department. That is not to disclaim the fact that Churchill admired the man. The paragraph continues:

> The wonder was that he was able to sink his personality, to bend his imperious will and pool his knowledge in the common stock. Here is one of the proofs of the greatness of his character and the versatility of his genius. He saw the hope of redeeming in a large measure the promises he had made to the Arab chiefs and of reestablishing a tolerable measure of peace in those wide regions. In that cause he was capable of becoming—I hazard the word—a humdrum official. The effort was not in vain. His purposes prevailed.[47]

It is to be highly doubted if Churchill included himself in the later description of Lawrence, that "he always reigned over those with whom he came in contact. They felt themselves in the presence of an extraordinary being. They felt that his latent reserves of force and willpower were beyond measurement."[48]

But Lawrence was prone to exaggerate and the above claim of having decided everything before the Conference is such an exaggeration. The only things decided upon were the broad intertwining policy outlines: Sharifian setup, R.A.F. control, subsidies to enable drastic military and financial reductions. The vast army of details which were worked out in Cairo at official meetings and in private and informal discussions included Faysal's methods and program for presenting himself as candidate for king of Iraq, the status and defense of Kurdistan, exact troop reduction figures, the disposal of refugees, financial control of Iraq, and what to do with Iraq's railroads. Nothing much was decided on Palestine proper aside from confirming the policy previously adopted and deciding on the composition of the Commission on Holy Places; no final decision was reached on the Palestine defense force. Transjordan was cut off from Palestine, quantitatively limiting the Jewish national home. The question of whose idea this was originally—Lawrence's, Samuel's or Congreve's—is irrelevant because Churchill accepted full responsibility when he telegraphed to Lloyd George to authorize him to meet with 'Abdallah in order to secure settled government and order in Transjordan. Details were also worked out with respect to Middle East Services, subsidies, the cross-desert route, the proposed Anglo-French boundary commission and the Hijaz railroad.

The Conference cannot be dismissed with the claim that it "assembled merely to settle the procedure by which to implement decisions already reached,"[49] as though that were nothing. As Gertrude Bell wrote: "I'll tell you about our Conference. It has been wonderful. We covered more work in a fortnight than has ever before been got through in a year. Mr. Churchill was admirable, most ready to meet everyone halfway and masterly alike in guiding a big political meeting and in conducting the small political committees into which we broke up."[50]

As conferences of the period went, the Cairo Conference was unbelievably short and fruitful. Perhaps this was because of the thorough preparatory work that had been done. Perhaps it was because the delegates were not rival politicians seeking compromises between national and international aspirations, but were governors and their advisers who were summoned to discuss a policy whose larger outlines had been settled in advance by Churchill. If the Conference was not a fresh departure, since its basic policy had either been in effect or under consideration before, it was unprecedented as a forum for evaluating Middle Eastern problems and served to arrest the process of drift and muddle which had characterized British actions since World War I. It seemed, at the time, to form a comprehensible policy set on a firm foundation, and Churchill returned to England satisfied with his artistic prowess for it appeared that his painting was complete and worthy to behold.

CHAPTER 7

Approval of Parliament

The task confronting the Colonial Secretary upon returning from Egypt was the presentation of the Conference's conclusions to the Cabinet and to Parliament for approval. Without this formal endorsement he could not implement the Cairo decisions. He was euphoric about the Conference and his optimism is reflected in his statement to the House of Commons on the afternoon of 14 June 1921. Yet there is another side to the story, because on the morning of 14 June he seriously suggested to the Cabinet that Britain should offer the mandate for Palestine or Iraq to the United States after speaking "with considerable eloquence on the subject of the extent of our burden and expenditure and liability and the meagerness of the advantage to be derived from these mandates."[1] Less than a fortnight earlier he had suggested quitting the two countries, resigning both mandates.[2]

Examination of the source material suggests solutions to this apparent contradiction while illuminating Churchill's activities in the period between his return to London and his Parliamentary presentation. A major clue is the myriad of details with which Churchill busied himself, details normally not handled by a Secretary of State. It is proposed that—in addition to Churchill's penchant for detailed knowledge of the workings of his office—the Colonial Secretary was not going to allow anything to upset his Middle East plans. He had worked hard to develop his policy and to gain support for it from the Middle East experts. A few problems were bound to arise, but since he could neither foresee how numerous they would be nor how large or small, he involved himself in any issue that even hinted at a capability of deterring him from implementing all his work. It is this same determination that pushed Churchill to persevere in his attempt to clear the larger hurdles as well. When confronted with seemingly insurmountable hurdles, his ploy was to circumvent them any way he could, even if it meant a poker-faced request to give up the latest Middle East acquisitions.

The content of Churchill's policy was basically set and we see him, during the months leading up to his first official comprehensive statement on this policy, using a slew of different methods to tie up loose ends. He concurred in actions taken by Cox and Samuel if he considered that these actions forwarded his basic policy or were irrelevant to it. He compromised and even gave in if it made sense to do so, for example, to gain a more important point. But he stubbornly remained unmoved and determined if his plans seem endangered. He oversaw everything and in the end guided his policy over the major hurdle of Parliamentary approval in his own inimitable style.

Most of the loose ends regarding Iraq and Transjordan proved relatively easy to tie up, though at first glance it did not appear so. When Sir Percy Cox returned to Iraq from Cairo, he found himself faced with two potential candidates rivaling Faysal as well as with a potential troublemaker. The shaykh of Muhammarah, an old friend of Great Britain, could not really secure a majority vote and Cox devised a friendly way, concurred in by Churchill, to nip the project in the bud.[3] A more formidable rival was the Naqib of Baghdad, a man of much social and religious prestige, who insisted that he would not support a Sharifian ruler. To satisfy him Cox suggested to Churchill that the latter should reassure the Naqib that Britain would refrain from becoming an active partisan of any individual candidate; Churchill agreed and sent an appropriate telegram.[4] The potential troublemaker was Sayid Talib of Basrah who had a long record as an intriguer.[5] He provided the British with a fortuitous handle to get rid of him by making a seditious and menacing speech on a semi-public occasion. In the interest of law and order the High Commissioner arrested him, 16 April, and requested permission from the Colonial Secretary to deport him to Ceylon.[6] Churchill agreed.[7]

As for Faysal, he was following Churchill's instructions and returned to Hijaz to await the proper time to move into Iraq and present himself as a candidate for its king. In a long telegram to Lawrence,[8] Churchill attempted to tie up the loose ends with regard to Faysal's half dozen outstanding requests. Faysal could be assured, among other things, that in his first public statement in Iraq he would be allowed to say that Britain agreed that after ratification of the constitutional law, modifications in the mandate could be made by negotiation between the Iraqi and British Governments. Lawrence was to explain,

CHAPTER 7 • Approval of Parliament   93

too, that while Britain could not absolutely guarantee that Ibn Sa'ud would not attack the Hijaz, by making him dependent on British financial support Britain hoped the achieve this objective. Churchill also felt that to attach a British official to Faysal at that point would compromise the neutrality assurances; as an alternative, he proposed that Colonel Kinahan Cornwallis, former liaison officer to Faysal, should be sent to Iraq as a member of Cox's own staff to be used again in the same capacity.

The issue of Cornwallis developed into a month-long dispute between Cox and the Middle East Department totally out of proportion to the larger questions still outstanding, because in accepting the Colonial Secretary's reassurances, Faysal made Cornwallis' accompaniment a condition of his going to Iraq. Cox stubbornly refused to accept the proposition that to meet a temporary expedient Cornwallis should be forced on his administration as a permanency.[9] It took all of Churchill's conciliatory abilities to assuage Cox, but he accomplished it and attention could return to Faysal and his schedule for arriving in Iraq. It was agreed that Faysal should leave Jiddah on 15 June, which meant he would arrive in Basrah between 28 June and 3 July, ample time for the Colonial Secretary to make the needed policy announcement to clear the ground for his arrival. Cox had been anxiously awaiting some form of announcement from London confirming the Cairo Conference's recommendations; all he had been able to do until that time was issue a short communiqué on the gradual economies and on the hope for amnesty.

The amnesty issue was still hanging loose because London and Baghdad had to come to an exact agreement as to its scope, for the former wanted the amnesty not to be confined to the 1920 rising but that it should be as comprehensive as possible, a *beau geste* on the part of the British Government.[10] Another cause for delay was the overlapping problem of getting France to agree on a date so that both Mandatories could issue the amnesty statement simultaneously, thus giving the impression to the Arab world that they were working hand in hand. But nothing was heard from General Gouraud throughout April, and the Middle East Department recommended that Britain should wait no longer. Churchill agreed.[11] A month later the scope of the amnesty was completely settled.[12]

A problem that proved harder to solve, because Cox had local interests uppermost in his mind whereas Churchill had the goal of rapid economizing uppermost in his, was troop reduction in northern Iraq. Cox claimed that the proposals for prompt troop reduction made at Cairo were based on the condition that the Turkish menace on the northern frontier came to an end. Listing five incidents of the past month, Cox said that troop evacuation was impossible until Ankara gave proof of a revised attitude.[13] Churchill felt that the incidents listed were not of the nature of an organized attack, the only form that Cairo considered, and therefore he refused to allow any alteration in the garrison reduction plan.[14] But Cox merely repeated himself in the telegram arriving 29 April.[15] After a Group Council discussion a telegram was sent to Cox, with Churchill's consent, informing him that the Foreign Office would try to negotiate with Kemal's government, but in no way would the modification of the evacuation scheme be assented to; Cox must have the levies ready to replace the troops.[16]

Churchill summarized the situation in northern Iraq for the cabinet in a memorandum, 10 May.[17] Pointing out that although the War Office felt troop reductions should cease, the Colonial Secretary did not for he had received assurances from the General-Officer-Commander in Chief, Mesopotamia, that the latter was prepared to reduce the garrison, that he felt no anxiety about Mosul, and that the levies were gradually taking over.[18]

Once and for all the exact method of organizing the levies, paying them, and substituting them for the British garrisons at Kirkuk and Mosul was settled.[19] With this finally cleared up, a minor snag developed over the appointment of the officer to command the levies: the Colonial Secretary had approved appointing General Sadleir Jackson without first consulting Cox. Cox resented this, but Churchill mollified him.[20]

Another difficult issue was financial control of Iraq, and the Colonial Secretary had asked, before going off to Cairo, for a memorandum to be drawn up, in consultation with the Treasury, on this. The memorandum was submitted to him 27 April,[21] and it recognized that direct control of military expenditure could only be exercised by the War Office, although this money was to be repaid from the Vote for Middle East services. It was uneconomical for the Colonial Office to attempt to duplicate the existing War Office machinery. Yet, since the ultimate cost would be upon the Colonial Office, it was for the Colonial Secretary to defend it in Commons. But the Secretary of State could commend his policy to Commons only by reducing expenditure, so he could not accept an arrangement under which the scale of expenditure was determined entirely by the military authorities. Therefore Churchill wanted a financial adviser on the spot with clearly defined functions aimed at speedy and substantial reduction of his charges. He would watch financial policy and would be directly responsible for all expenditure keeping the High Commissioner and thereby the Colonial Secretary informed. It was also suggested to set up an arrangement for regular consultations between the civil and military authority to coordinate policy. Churchill sent this memorandum to Sir Laming Worthington-Evans, the War Secretary, 27 April,[22] with a covering letter claiming that the time had now arrived to decide on procedure.

Needless to say, there was an explosion in the War Office, with everyone minuting his opinion. Worthington Evans finally answered, 6 June,[23] accepting the view that the Colonial Office should have an effective voice in the general scale of military expenditure, and it was for the Colonial Office to settle what it was the War Office had to do. But the War Office was to estimate the military requirements necessary to fulfill these tasks, and if financial or other limitations rendered it impossible to carry out the assignment adequately, the Colonial Office would have to readjust its policy. The War Secretary refused to empower a financial adviser to audit or investigate military expenditure, although the War Office would favor a coordinating body. Major differences of opinion should be settled between the two Secretaries of State or, if necessary, by the Cabinet.

The Colonial Secretary immediately drafted his own reply, but it was not sent because of serious differences within the Department. Colonel Richard Meinertzhagen,[24] Churchill's newly appointed Military Adviser to the Middle East Department, backed the War Office view. It was not up to the Colonial Secretary to decide the strength of garrisons and their dispositions, for this would create a Middle East Empire complete within itself, duplicating the work of another Office. Such a demand would not incline the War Office to concede the Colonial Secretary's second point, financial control. Roland Vernon, the financial adviser, agreed it was bad tactics and the Colonial Office should be content with the right to criticize military expenditure. Young, Lawrence and Shuckburgh agreed.[25] There should be a discussion of the issues but if the Colonial Office put its claim too high at the outset, the War Office would merely come to the discussion in an uncompromising frame of mind. Churchill was convinced by this array of arguments, and wrote to Worthington-Evans in a conciliatory vein, agreeing to talk,[26] thus in effect tying up another loose thread.

There were dozens of other Iraqi loose ends in which Churchill interested himself,[27] and some were intertwined with problems of other areas as well. Confirmation of the aerial cross desert route aimed at linking Iraq with Palestine and Egypt, for example, which was intimately involved in the total picture of the new Transjordan government, proved to be harder to obtain than Churchill imagined. The evening after Churchill returned to London, a Conference of Ministers met in which the Colonial Secretary devoted most of his report to a description of his plans for Transjordan for which he needed their agreement to go ahead.[28] To avoid the necessity of a garrison, 'Abdallah was to have native levies with British officers, cash to pay the levies, political officers to assist him, and three aerodromes for use by the Air Force to visit and support him. Churchill assured the Conference that his proposals really involved diminution of British responsibility. In addition, the establishment of the desert route offered important strategical and political advantages. The Conference agreed that the War Secretary should notify Churchill if he was satisfied that there was no substantial military objection. It sanctioned the use of planes to visit and support 'Abdallah from Ludd, but it felt that the larger question of the use of planes to establish the desert route should be further considered by the Cabinet at a later date.

The War Office, on examining the matter, decided it could not agree to the Air Ministry giving orders to air forces which were directly under the General Office Commanding, Egypt, without reference to the War Office.[29] Eventually a compromise was reached.

No sooner had this been settled than Churchill asked Henry Wilson to help him with the issue of the cross desert route. He was spurred on by a telegram from Lawrence describing the situation in Transjordan as satisfactory, that there was no need for a garrison, and that air flights would be very useful in keeping peace along the frontiers.[30] In addition, a telegram had arrived from Cox saying that the best time for traversing the cross-desert route was slipping away.[31] Churchill sent copies of these telegrams to Wilson, and he tried to convince the C.I.G.S. that a discussion between the War Office, Air Ministry, and himself would suffice to settle the small matter of the cross-desert route reconnaissance.

> The strategic and political advantages are overwhelming. The cost is practically nothing, as it simply means the employment of aeroplanes and motor cars which are now on our constant charge. There is no question of any risk or entanglement. But the linking of Mesopotamia to Palestine and Egypt, enabling the air forces in both theatres to be

available in either in a few hours, offers the prospect of very large economies in the future and is an essential part of my scheme of reduction of expenditures.[32]

But Austin Chamberlain, the Lord Privy Seal, upon discovery that a flight was about to start to reconnoiter the eastern end of the desert route, insisted on a further Conference of Ministers to consider the question again.[33] Churchill defended his actions at that meeting, 19 April, claiming that he had considered the matter one that could have been sanctioned departmentally. At Cairo, all the experts had recommended opening the route at once, and he reiterated all the positive aspects of such a move. The Colonial Secretary's arguments, strongly backed by Trenchard and Young, won over the ministers. Development of the desert air route was to proceed as proposed.

A few knotty items also developed in Transjordan itself. A telegram arrived from Samuel, 21 April, describing his visit to 'Amman.[34] He had discussed with 'Abdallah the size of the local military force: 'Abdallah suggested 4,000 men for internal defense and planes and armored cars to protect against outside incursion but Samuel suggested a 750-man defense force.[35]

This telegram evoked a long note from Churchill to his staff on the misunderstanding prevailing about the use of planes. No one ever intended them to go bombing people to make them pay their taxes; the planes were to win the confidence of the people and bring the political officers into close touch with the people giving a sense of power in reserve. He refused to contemplate more than 750 men, in addition to the 500 civil gendarmes. As for the cost, Churchill's total was 160,000 pounds and felt that 100,000 pounds of it should be raised by local taxation and a contribution from Palestine.[36] 'Abdallah tried again for a 3,000 to 5,000 man gendarmerie,[37] but by the end of May accepted the limit of 750 men, to be led by Lt.-Col. Peake.[38]

If Iraq and Transjordan proved to be relatively easy barriers to clear, that was not the case with Palestine and Turkey which grew into insurmountable ones as did the attempt to obtain confirmation of the mandates by the League of Nations.[39] On 1 May a serious affray broke out between Muslims and Jews in Jaffa necessitating the use of troops, and ending in 250 casualties, 40 fatal.[40] Although Jaffa gradually calmed down, Sir Herbert Samuel, the High Commissioner, decided to take precautions against the spread of disturbances by declaring martial law, requesting no troop withdrawals, asking for ships to be sent to restore confidence, and stopping Jewish immigration.[41] But fighting spread to Petach Tikva, Hedera, Rehovot, and Ramla, where planes and police chased the Arab mobs until gradually things calmed down. Samuel set up a Commission of Enquiry to be headed by Chief Justice Haycroft and wired to London describing his actions.[42] He also dispatched five administrative proposals for Churchill's approval: deportation of all immigrants clearly belonging to a revolutionary organization, temporary suspension of immigration, stricter control of immigration once it was resumed, reconsideration of a Home Force, and early establishment of representative institutions.[43]

Churchill was concerned first and foremost with the added expenses incurred by Samuel's actions. His actions were all geared toward keeping down costs by promoting peace. He shared the High Commissioner's apprehensions that Zionist policy produced a serious unrest among the Arabs, but he felt Britain should persevere. He agreed with Samuel's first three proposals, and telegraphed that Samuel should concentrate upon practical steps only. Before approving the fourth proposal, Churchill wanted Samuel's detailed plans for the defense force.[44]

This telegram crossed one from Samuel repeating his request for approval of his political proposals and asking permission to publish an announcement that at the King's Birthday Assembly, 3 June, he would make "a statement upon certain important constitutional and administrative measures which Government is about to adopt with a view to establishment of greater harmony amongst people."[45] This would induce all sections to adopt a waiting attitude. Churchill concurred and allowed Samuel to announce also that until immigrants in the country were absorbed, immigration would not be reopened; with reopening more stringent measures would be taken to keep out undesirables.[46] Samuel then changed his mind over a defense force plan, suggesting instead a well paid police force and a trained reserve drawn from British officers and non-commissioned officers.[47] The Interdepartmental Middle East Committee met 12 May,[48] and suggested instead an efficient gendarmerie of Jewish and Arab elements, under British command, and responsible to the civil power. In addition, Jewish town guards or rifle clubs for the defense of Jewish colonies should be considered. Churchill agreed with his Department.[49]

But Samuel telegraphed again, 22 May,[50] asking for more precise comments on his proposals. London replied, clearly approving Samuel's suggestions in principle but insisting on the gendarmerie which included an exclusively Jewish police reserve, all to be under one command. Churchill concurred and so the matter rested.

As for Samuel's fifth proposal, representative institutions, Churchill deprecated placing an Advisory Council on an elective basis until the mandate was approved. "To make such a concession under pressure is to rob it of half its value. We must firmly maintain law and order and make concessions on their merits and not under duress."[51] Samuel replied that such an assembly could counteract the strong opposition to the article of the draft mandate establishing a Jewish agency, which was viewed as constituting a partnership between the Zionists and the Government of Palestine to the exclusion of the rest of the population. Perhaps equal recognition could be given to an appropriate body representing the majority group. His pronouncement of 3 June was being anxiously awaited and Samuel urged satisfying the opposition demands as much as possible.[52] But London merely replied that the matter was under discussion.[53]

Before leaving for a visit to Beirut Samuel telegraphed a summary of his proposed 3 June speech for Churchill's concurrence:[54] the first point summarized general progress made; the second stated that the police force was to be improved and this expenditure necessitated postponing the question of the defense force; the third point gave his interpretation of the Balfour Declaration; the fourth stated that immigration had to be proportioned to the employment available and until the situation was reviewed immigration was suspended except for those in transit;[55] the fifth point referred to closer association of the people with the Administration through an Advisory Council and municipal elections would take place at once. Samuel felt it was desirable to mention that there would be a Muslim-Christian consultative body.

Three telegrams went out to Samuel, 2 June, about his impending speech. All was approved, except that the third point necessitated a change on wording to avoid giving the impression that British policy was being altered as a result of disturbances. London refused to set up a Christian-Muslim body because their spheres of representation were the official councils. Churchill tried to ease this refusal by sending a personal and private wire approving Samuel's excellent announcement subject to the small modifications suggested.[56]

Samuel refused to let the matter drop and insisted on having new methods for opposition representatives to see him at regular intervals.[57]

Churchill's secret and personal telegram[58] stated that he was not opposed to a step by step establishment of elective institutions to secure such representation; "I was not of opinion however that the morrow of the Jaffa riots was the best moment for making such a concession," and as soon as disorder was repressed Samuel should seize the opportunity and act. Samuel anticipated this by sending a dispatch[59] to Churchill giving details of his proposed scheme for the election of a representative assembly. The matter was still unsettled as the time drew near for the Secretary of State for the Colonies' policy statement, and despite sending Samuel a telegram conveying his "sincere appreciation of the prompt and able action taken by yourself and the officers serving under you to deal with this difficult situation,"[60] he added a pessimistic note to a military memorandum on Palestine that he was circulating to the Cabinet which summarized his fears.

> There is no doubt we are in a situation of increasing danger which may at any time involve us in serious military embarrassments with consequent heavy expenditure. Besides this, we shall no doubt be exposed to the bitter resentment of the Zionists for not doing more to help their cause and for not protecting them better. With the resources at my disposal I am doing all in my power, but I do not think things are going to get better in this part of the world, but rather worse.[61]

Churchill may have been pessimistic about Palestine but at least he had managed to circumvent the hurdle of combining economizing with a shaky peace and with the principles of the draft mandate for the area. To achieve this he incorporated the economic absorptive capacity principle, proposed by Samuel into his policy. But all his plans, including those for Palestine, rested on the preliminary condition of peace with Turkey, and in this case, despite all the ploys of the Colonial Secretary, the hurdle was not even circumvented.

Churchill still advocated coming to terms with Kemal, and protecting Constantinople and the Straits at all costs. But the issue was now further complicated by the conquests of the Greeks and by the defeats of France and Italy at the hands of the nationalist Turks. France had decided to leave Cilicia altogether and concentrate in Syria, and was trying to make peace with nationalist Turkey along their common border. The British were aware that France held different views on Turkish policy but were determined to try to have the Allies stand united in this sphere. Churchill had to take all these factors into consideration in devising a plan geared towards achieving the goal of peace with Turkey. But all his warnings were to no avail. Greece started her new offensive and Turkey began to move into Ismid, thereby upsetting Churchill's peaceful plans for the Middle East.

Another upset was the postponement of confirmation of the mandates for Palestine and Iraq.[62] At San Remo, in April 1920, the Allied Supreme Council had allocated the mandates and agreed on the clauses of the Ottoman treaty. A few months later the mandatory instruments were framed and awaited confirmation by the League Council. Developments in the Middle East necessitated alterations to some of the clauses, but the delay in confirming the mandates was not because of these alterations. The Americans blocked confirmation for their own ends; they wanted an "open door" policy in the Middle East especially with regard to oil.[63] Of equal importance was the reluctance of France to bind herself to be responsible to the League. France favored regarding the mandates as final documents and as instruments for perpetuating the status quo whereas Britain viewed the draft mandates merely as instruments to enable her to set up the machinery for the expression of representative opinion.[64]

Britain was so interested in having the mandates confirmed because legally the territory was still Turkish, for no peace treaty was yet in effect. To circumvent this, Curzon, Churchill, Balfour, and H. A. L. Fisher, President of the Board of Education serving as one of Britain's representatives at the League, planned to press for the immediate 'provisional' issue of the mandates at the forthcoming meeting of the Council of the League of Nations of 17 June. Churchill was given the job of obtaining Cabinet approval for this step, and he immediately sent identical telegrams to Cox and Samuel[65] to obtain their considered opinions on the effect postponement would have locally. Cox replied[66] that no prejudicial effect would come from ignoring the subject but a rebuff by the League Council would be very bad. Later that evening Samuel's reply arrived.[67] Although he felt postponement would weaken the administration's authority, he agreed that it was better not to press it and have it formally rejected for this would be regarded as reopening the whole question of the future of Palestine.

Churchill also ordered the Middle East Department to draw up a note on the mandates.[68] The Department stated forthrightly that Britain must decide whether she wished to retain the mandates, to what extent international and local opposition should be taken into consideration, what measures would reduce this opposition to a minimum, and whether Britain could afford to take these steps. Having posed the problems, the Department suggested solutions, but when Churchill circulated his memorandum and the telegrams to the Cabinet, 14 June, he rejected his Department's suggestions. Rather, "we should make every effort to secure immediate definition by the Council of the League of Nations of what they regard as a mandate."[69] He felt it was not only American opposition but French reluctance to be responsible to the League that was a root cause of the delay, and in a no-nonsense tone stated:

> I submit that we should without delay inform the French Government officially that unless they co-operate with us in putting the mandates through at the forthcoming session we shall immediately announce that we can wait no longer for the definition by the Council of the League of the conditions under which we are to fulfill the charge entrusted to us by the Principal Allied Powers; ... [and] that unless the mandates go through at the forthcoming session of the Council we will consider ourselves free to establish what relations we think best with the inhabitants of the territories committed to our charge by the San Remo decision.[70]

Perhaps Churchill was over-reacting because Lloyd George had earlier squashed his suggestion of the following through with the Prime Minister's idea of meeting American objections by offering either or both mandates to the United States;[71] on thinking it over Lloyd George had felt that such a statement, without previous reference to the American government, was not the manner in which the subject should be broached, and would only convey the impression that the mandates were useless burdens which Britain wanted to unload.[72] Perhaps Churchill was over-reacting because he had to deliver his statement on the Middle East that afternoon and it rankled that this loose end had not been tied down. He thought that such pressure on France would at least ensure their cooperation in insisting on an immediate definition of the terms of the mandate.

The Cabinet discussed the issue including the Colonial Secretary's proposal to end American opposition by offering them Iraq or Palestine, but finally agreed not to force the matter at the present.[73] As with the Turkish problem, Churchill's advice went unheeded. Despite his frustrations over the major issues of Turkey and mandate confirmation, and despite his pessimism over Palestine, that afternoon Churchill presented an optimistic and eloquent speech in Commons on the Middle East Estimate, a statement he and his staff had been working on for months. He had planned a policy and he wanted to be given a chance to try it out. He could only obtain Parliamentary approval if he presented a positive yet truthful picture. "Churchill's Estimates speeches ... were intricate, comprehensive, and often inspiring, explanations of why economies were needed, and how they could be made."[74]

Immediately upon his return from Cairo, Churchill had noted to Shuckburgh[75] that the first thing to do was to press ahead with the preparation of the Middle Eastern Estimates which should be in an advanced state of preparation by the following week. "It simply means transferring blocks of accounts from War Office, Foreign Office, and Air Ministry Votes to a new Vote and making the alterations involved in the reductions now in progress." Churchill was optimistic enough at that stage to feel that he could assure Parliament that he would be ready to make a statement on his mission to the Middle East and to introduce the Vote early in May.[76] But May came and went without achieving this because of all the loose ends that defied tying up. A final prod was Lloyd George's short note to Churchill, 23 May,[77] asking him to give personal attention to the steps necessary for effecting economies in his Department, which Churchill answered two days later,[78] pointing out that as a result of measures inaugurated in Cairo he hoped to save 5.25 million pounds that year and to reduce expenditure to 9 million pounds the coming year. He hoped that the Prime Minister would consider this a not unsatisfactory response to his order.

Technical details of high importance necessitated conferences with the Treasury, War Office, Air Ministry, and the Cabinet. At the Cabinet of the morning of 31 May,[79] Churchill urgently asked for directions in the preparation of the Middle East Estimates because all the savings he had effected in Cairo had been discounted by Cabinet reductions. He suggested that War Office charges could be compressed for there would be further troop withdrawals, and therefore they should underestimate their charges by the one million pounds he needed. The Cabinet agreed to this. The Cabinet also approved postponing the Estimates vote for a week.[80] With this reprieve to repair his Estimates, Churchill labored rapidly and efficiently. He ordered the overhauling of the financial part of the Estimates in order to be fully prepared for Worthington Evans, who had yet to agree to the one million pound reduction.[81]

He wrote to the War Secretary,[82] detailing the savings he expected to make and explaining that War Office juggling with Middle East expenses to solve its own problems was complicating the issue for the Colonial Office. Worthington Evans finally agreed to reduce his estimate by about one million pounds and Vernon was finally able to send his revised proof to the printer.

A flurry of activity over Turkey, Iraq, Palestine and other areas concerning the Colonial Office preceded the presentation of the Estimates. Cox, for example, telegraphed repeatedly,[83] that it was vital to clear the ground for Faysal by making fuller announcements regarding Iraq. Churchill proceeded with the first suggestion, since the time was right; a special congress was about to meet in Iraq to discuss and express Iraqi views on the form of government which would best suit the needs of the country. He telegraphed to Cox[84] that Reuters would dispatch the necessary communiqué on 13 June, describing that the Hijaz representative had informed the Colonial Office of the special congress, and in response to inquiries from adherents of Faysal "the British Government have stated that they will place no obstacle in the way of his candidature as ruler of Mesopotamia, and if he is chosen he will have their support."

On 14 June Churchill, to be completely prepared for his speech, minuted to Shuckburgh[85] that he wanted "a note in about 3 lines as to Feisel's religious character. Is he a Sunni with Shaih [sic] sympathies, or a Shaih [sic] with Sunni Sympathies, or how does he square it? What is Hussein? Which is the aristocratic high church and which is the low church? ... I always get mixed up between those two." He also wanted the Palestine figures checked by Vernon: "every figure must be checked and ticked." Last, with regard to extra points Cox wished to make, he would try to put in as many as he could but "I cannot fill up my speech with tributing all sorts of people and handing out chits all round for local consumption." The listeners were only interested in how much money was to be taken out of their pockets.

Churchill's speech on the Estimates for the Middle East united into coherent form all the threads he had been involved with individually until then.[86] He took as his starting point Britain's obligations and responsibilities in the area, describing how Britain overran Palestine and Iraq uprooting the Turkish administration and setting up a military rule in its place. A series of promises had been made to the various parties involved, peace treaties had been negotiated and approved by the Cabinet and Parliament solemnly accepting "before the whole world the position of mandatory Power for Palestine and Mesopotamia." Britain had accepted responsibility and must do her duty to discharge it, stressed the Colonial Secretary.

> We are bound to make a sincere, honest, patient, resolute effort to redeem our obligation, and, whether that course be popular or unpopular, I am certain it is the only course which any British Government or British House of Commons will in the end find itself able to pursue. ... But if we are to succeed, if we are to avoid the shame of failure; if we are to bring our enterprise to a satisfactory conclusion, the fundamental condition, the only key, lies in the reduction of expenditure in these two countries to within reasonable and predictable limits.[87]

Before detailing how this was to be achieved, Churchill detoured to describe his role in creating the new Middle East Department, centralizing responsibility for the area under one minister with its own separate Vote; he also summarized the reasons for convening the Cairo conference and stated that the conclusions reached there by the experts were unanimous and would achieve, if successful, "the essential condition of reduction which I set before myself as my paramount object." Moving on to trace the troop reductions since the Armistice and the commensurate cost reductions, Churchill flatly stated that 1921 would cost about 35 million pounds, quickly adding that by 1922 expenses should be down to nine or ten million, "if all went well."

"Let us now see what is the policy and what are the methods by which we hope to achieve this enormous reduction in military strength and in expenditure while at the same time carrying out our undertakings." Turning first to Iraq, the Colonial Secretary described the creation of the provisional Arab government—government with British advice and assistance under the protection of British troops—which he hoped to replace during the summer by an Arab government based on an assembly elected by the people, to install an Arab ruler and to create an Arab army. He hurriedly added that "we have no intention of forcing upon the people of Iraq a ruler who is not of their own choice," yet it was important to choose one suitable to Britain too. He felt it was right to leave such matters entirely in the hands of Sir Percy Cox who "is a great believer in the Arabs; he is devoted to the people of Iraq; he is acquainted with every aspect of Arab politics ..., and I hope that under his guidance the people of Iraq will make a wise and at the same time a free choice." As he had promised Cox, he stated plainly the view of the British Government on this issue: she favored building an Arab state and the best structure around which to build this was the house, family and following of the Sharif of Mecca. "The adherents of the Emir Feisel have sent him an invitation to go to Mesopotamia and present himself to the people and to the assembly which is soon to gather together." Husayn had given his son permission to go, 'Abdallah had renounced his rights there, and Churchill had told Faysal that if he were chosen "he will receive the countenance and support of Great Britain." Faysal was on his way to Iraq. "Our object and our policy is to set up an Arab Government, and to make it take the responsibility, with our aid and our guidance and with an effective measure of our support, until they are strong enough to stand alone, and so as to foster the development of their independence as to permit the steady and speedy diminution of our burden."[88]

This policy was part of a larger Sharifian solution, and Churchill touched on the subsidies to be given to Arab chiefs to keep them under control so as not to upset this solution. He also only touched on the use of the Air Force instead of military force, and on home rule for south Kurdistan which would act as a bulwark against infiltration from Kemalist or Bolshevik sources, before turning to the second important territory under British control: Palestine.

Tackling the main issue right away, Churchill stated that "the cause of unrest in Palestine, and the only cause, arises from the Zionist movement, and from our promises and pledges in regard to it." The promise of a Jewish National Home conflicted with Britain's regular policy of consulting the wishes of the people and giving them representative institutions as soon as they were fit for them, for in this case it would mean an end to any further Jewish immigration. He fully believed, though, that "with patience, coolness, and a little good fortune we may find a way out of" the difficulties.

The Arabs believed they were going to be swamped by immigrants, but such fears were illusory, Churchill claimed, for the Zionists were bound to state their case with the fullest ardor in order to obtain the enthusiasm and support they required. Sir Herbert Samuel, "a skilled, practiced, experienced liberal politician" was in charge, and the Colonial Secretary was giving him every possible measure of confidence and support. By quoting Samuel's 3 June interpretation of "national home" as used in the Balfour Declaration, Churchill firmly set the foundation for the economic absorptive capacity principle. To sweeten this bitter draught to Zionists, Churchill described in glowing terms the Jewish colonies he had visited, declaring that Britain could not allow such effort to be wrecked or all future immigration to be stopped or the British word would no longer hold weight.

> If representative institutions are conceded, as we hope they will be, to the Arabs of Palestine, some definite arrangements will have to be made in the instrument on which those institutions stand, which will safeguard within reasonable limits the immigration of Jews into the country, as they make their own way and create their own means of subsistence. Our task ... will be to persuade one side to concede and the other to forbear, by keeping a reasonable margin of force available in order to ensure the acceptance of the position by both parties.[89]

Transjordan received Churchill's attention next, and he described the chaos that had prevailed until 'Abdallah had come in and Churchill had enlisted his agreement to undertake to maintain order. The indispensable stipulation, that of preventing hostile action against France, was agreed on and with local levies, planes and armored cars the arrangement should be successful. "The Emir Abdullah who is a very agreeable, intelligent, and civilized Arab prince, has maintained an absolutely correct attitude, both towards us and towards the French."

Churchill was concerned over the French attitude and he assured them that the Sharifian solution was the best method of keeping Syria quiet. Referring to major loose ends only briefly, he suggested that Britain and France should act together in the Middle East, and stated that his entire policy was based on a peaceful and lasting settlement with Turkey.

Concluding his hour and a half speech, the Colonial Secretary said:

> I cannot say with certainty that the unknown future which lies before us will enable this policy of reduction and appeasement to be carried out with complete success, but I do believe that the measures which we are taking are well calculated to that end. I have great confidence in the experts and high authorities who have combined in thinking that they are so calculated, and I advise the Committee to give their assent to them and to give us their support in the difficult and delicate process of reduction and conciliation which lies before us, and on which we are already definitely embarking.[90]

The Colonial Secretary sat down amidst much applause. Austen Chamberlain wrote to the Prime Minister, then in Wales: "Winston has had a great success both as to his speech & his policy, & has changed the whole atmosphere of the House on the Middle East question. Send him a line or wire of congratulation."[91] Lloyd George listened to this advice, in response to which he received a note of thanks from Churchill, who was pleased that the French had taken the Faysal issue fairly quietly, but worried about the still dangling items. "I shall require your support in order to realize fully the economies I have in view. If we get through July without trouble in Mesopotamia & if a settlement is reached with Turkey, I shall try to start off another outward move of troops so as to secure an additional saving in the current year."[92]

The Times[93] editorial praised Churchill's plans, but claimed that they were "as speckled with ifs as the leopard with spots."

Nation[94] disagreed that Britain was honor bound to civilize Iraq and make Palestine a Jewish national home, and disparaged Churchill's solution for Iraq claiming the Iraq Assembly "will meet with British battalions sitting around, and British aeroplanes cruising aloft, and Mr. Churchill tells it in advance that if it chooses Emir Feisul we shall be satisfied." *New Statesman*,[95] on the other hand, felt that here was a gleam of hope in this first serious attempt to establish a policy, for "Mr. Churchill at least shows some qualities of decision and imagination, some disposition to face the facts, which have been conspicuously wanting in the pompous rhodomontades of Lord Curzon or the shifty special pleading of the Prime Minister."

CHAPTER 8

Slow Progress

Winston S. Churchill was optimistic about Iraq—despite the unsolved problems of the Turkish treaty and the confirmation of the mandate instruments by the League of Nations—and no longer gave it his undivided attention. His newest challenge was Ireland and gradually Churchill became more and more involved in the attempt to stop the violence and terror there. An Irish treaty excited his imagination and Lloyd George, recognizing Churchill's oratorical power, called on him to defend the Irish policy in Parliament.[1]

Churchill's attention was also diverted from his work by the war memoirs he was writing and by a series of personal tragedies. His mother, Lady Randolph Churchill, died 29 June 1921;[2] two months later his three-year-old daughter, Marigold, fell ill and died. The latter tragedy left his wife Clementine in a melancholic state which worsened as the year drew to a close. She did not have her husband's ability to force herself to forget her troubles through painting and hard work.

Parliament approved Churchill's Middle East policy and he concentrated on its finishing touches. For Iraq the salient points were further troop evacuation thereby reducing expenditures and the enthronement of Faysal to be followed by the formulation of a treaty.[3] Both policy points aimed at saving money thereby meeting the challenge of the "anti-waste" campaign, then at its height, which demanded drastic cuts in government spending,[4] and Churchill played a crucial role in saving his office from these cuts. In the second half of 1921 Churchill was involved mainly in major policy decisions, leaving the daily running of Iraq to his Middle East Department and the High Commissioner. To implement his economizing policies he had to overcome first Faysal's contrariness and then his strong War Office opposition. His tools were mainly telegrams for the former and Cabinet confrontations with the latter. He thought he succeeded in both by the end of the year, but Faysal proved more difficult to maneuver than anyone imagined.

Faysal arrived at Basrah, 24 June. His speech the next day made a "great impression."[5] Cox was satisfied with the Amir's reception in Baghdad, but had to remind Faysal that he had to pose primarily as a candidate of the people with British support and not as a British candidate.[6] Churchill reported the progress of Faysal to the Cabinet and stated that if the situation continued favorably in the next few weeks, he would consult the War Secretary to accelerate troop withdrawal.[7]

The following week the Iraq Council of Ministers passed a unanimous resolution declaring Faysal king of Iraq provided that the government would be a constitutional, representative and democratic one limited by law. Faysal and Cox, however, agreed that there had to be a more specific expression of assent of the people so Cox set up a referendum.[8] By 1 August the results from most places were in and Cox suggested that Faysal's coronation should be 15 August. Since Faysal wanted to make a public announcement defining relations between himself and Great Britain, Britain had to frame lines of policy which would satisfy the general political situation as well as the obligations to the Allies and the League.[9] Churchill reported to the Cabinet the result of the plebiscite and the coronation proposal,[10] and discussed the policy announcement with his department. They agreed that the coronation should take place soon, leaving the date up to Cox, but refused to allow Faysal to issue a statement defining relations between himself and the British Government. These relations would be defined in the Iraqi constitution embodied in an "Organic Law" which was to be drafted in London by a conference of legal advisers, scheduled to meet 15 August through 25 August, and for which the advice and assistance of Sir Edgar Bonham-Carter, late Judicial Secretary of Baghdad, would be available. Cox was reassured that a treaty would come eventually but until then Faysal could not exercise plenary sovereign functions but had to work with the mandate and on Cox's advice.[11]

Faysal's refusal to accept the throne on these conditions spurred the Colonial Secretary to dictate a secret telegram to Cox in addition to an official one.[12] The two are similar in content, giving Cox detailed arguments to present to Faysal, but the personal one is more explicit. Churchill told Cox privately: "You sh[oul]d explain to Feisal that while we have to pay the piper we must expect to be consulted about the tune, whether under Mandatory or Treaty arrangements." If Faysal wished to be a sovereign with plenary powers he had to show that he was capable of maintaining peace and order unaided. This would take some time, wrote Churchill officially, substituting "years" for "time" in his private telegram. True, Britain had promised to convert the mandate into a treaty but this could only be done after Faysal's government was duly constituted and there was someone to contract with. The important thing was the coronation and not upsetting the harmonious march of events in Iraq. Faysal had to be told that Britain regarded his promise to accept the mandatory system subject to treaty modifications as binding, and Britain hoped to make this treaty as soon as possible. Then in the private version Churchill added two strong arguments for Cox to use at his discretion.

> I hope I need not infer from y[ou]r telegram that he is going to play us the same game as he played on the French at Damascus with disastrous results to himself. I cannot believe it, but the French & Gen. Gouraud lose no opportunity at predicting that he will become tool of extremists and will only maintain himself by xenophobia ... . He surely does not want to give the French the joy of saying "We told you so." I am quite sure that if Feisal plays us false & policy founded on him breaks down Br[itish] Gov[ernmen]t will leave him to his fate & withdraw immediately all aid & military force.[13]

Churchill sent a copy of the private telegram to Lloyd George proposing not to trouble the Cabinet as no change in policy was involved.[14] But he did take Faysal's second refusal to accept the mandate with him to the Cabinet Committee meeting which was to discuss the proposed treaty, 19 August.[15] Churchill stated that the time was propitious to place Faysal on the throne and the Committee discussed his accession speech, deciding that Churchill should send off a telegram on the lines suggested by him. Also, a report of political developments in Iraq should be prepared for the League.

Now that he had Cabinet concurrence, Churchill sent the telegram assuring Faysal of British backing and willingness to substitute a treaty for the mandate provided the treaty enabled Britain to fulfill her international obligations. Ignoring Faysal's refusals, Churchill wired that Faysal could therefore frame the Organic Law taking into account the rights and interests of all the people, and establish a judicial system safeguarding foreign interests and religious minorities. His accession speech should refer to all this and, in return, Britain would explain to the League Council why Britain wanted a treaty with Iraq.[16] Faysal needed British support to become king, so he dropped his objections, probably hoping that once in power he would have more leverage to achieve his goals. He was crowned 23 August.

In return, as promised, Churchill drew up a statement on the political developments in Iraq to be presented to the League Council in September, along with the revised mandatory instruments, explaining the Cabinet's decision to carry out the Iraq mandate by means of a treaty. "The march of events was so rapid that it did not admit of their consulting the Council before taking steps of which they were confident that the body would approve, namely the recognition of the sovereign whose recent accession to the throne followed upon the universal demand of the people of the country."[17] Balfour, Britain's representative at the League Council, was to inform the Council of Faysal's speech, emphasizing Faysal's readiness to give written assurances as to the fulfillment of international obligations incurred by Britain, and to point to the organic law which would establish freedom of religion, a judicial system to safeguard foreigners, and equity of commercial dealing with foreign countries. Balfour was to invite the Council to express an opinion on the general lines which the treaty would follow, stressing that a treaty would provide a more satisfactory definition of the relation between Britain and Iraq than any other form of instrument.

Faysal still felt the terms were too vague, and only signed an interim letter safeguarding Britain's international obligations, mandatory obligations, and financial questions.[18] Churchill fully appreciated Faysal's reluctance to commit himself unduly, but "for me to specify in a telegram the exact obligations which we expect him to assist us in fulfilling would be … difficult if not impossible as this would involve lengthy extracts from the various Peace Treaties, the two Anglo-French Agreements, and the draft mandate."[19] The position of Balfour at the League Council would be weaker without Faysal's written assurances, but Britain would present the draft mandates anyway.

Unfortunately, Balfour misunderstood the treaty policy and thought it would be of the ordinary bilateral type in which no third power had any right, and would in effect tear up the mandate.[20] Even after Churchill sent a letter to Balfour, 20 September,[21] explaining that it was not intended to alter the mandate for that would remain Britain's operative document vis-á-vis the League, the misunderstanding remained, and Balfour chose to remain silent so the Council postponed the consideration of the "A" mandates again. Disappointed but undeterred, Churchill ordered his staff to go ahead on their own to formulate a provisional treaty,[22] and explained to Balfour[23] the necessity of making this treaty without delay. It would have been better had the League regularized Britain's position, but he had to continue with practical administrative work and if Britain appeared to depart from the mandate it would only be to reach the goal of Iraqi self-government earlier. "I would add that my advisers have all along represented that very grave inconvenience would be caused by the failure of the League of Nations to regularize matters. I have never fully shared their view, and I think that we now have a good chance of getting through the next year or two on a de facto basis."[24] Churchill's staff agreed that no real harm had been done, for the President of the Council had given a kind of *ad interim* authority by writing a letter that both the Colonial Office's administration and draft mandates were in harmony with the League's Covenant, and this was enough to justify proceeding on their own.[25]

On 19 October Churchill gave Cox the signal to go ahead with the treaty discussions.[26] Hubert Young, then in Baghdad, recommended that the terms of the treaty be based on ten hypotheses:[27] the ultimate policy of Britain was the progressive establishment in partnership with the Arab government of an independent Iraqi state friendly to Britain; Britain expected to fulfill international obligations on the lines of the draft mandate during the mandatory relations; only the High Commissioner was to have control; he would have a staff under his direct orders; the staff would include a second-in-command, a judicial commissioner, a financial commissioner and an officer commanding the garrison; all other British or foreign officials would be servants of the Iraq government; communications between Iraq officials and the High Commissioner's staff would be informal and unofficial; no such would as "Advisor" was to exist; during the mandate the British government would be responsible for the terms of employment of British officials and would compensate them in the event of the termination of the mandate. Churchill approved all the terms relying on Young's expertise.

Hubert Young and R. V. Vernon had been sent by Churchill to Iraq to report on its administrative system[28] and to go carefully into the accounting and auditing systems to simplify them. They were to explain to Cox the organization of the Middle East department with its system of committees and

Group Councils, and to get into personal touch with Cox's British officials to strengthen reciprocal personal interest. Young and Vernon were also to visit Palestine and Egypt to make similar reports. Young and Vernon were also authorized to try to clear up other outstanding issues such as Cox's second in command and the future of Kurdistan. Unfortunately Vernon had a plane accident in Palestine, and Young had to proceed alone to Iraq.

From Baghdad Young wrote an alarming letter to Meinertzhagan[29] advising him to come out at once if there was to be any kind of "good show" by April for no one seemed to know what they were supposed to be doing. He felt there was a ridiculous situation in which the British and Iraqi forces were so independent of each other that their commanders never exchanged views. All was chaotic because there was no coordinated military plan and no one to make one. What was the plan, he asked.

The War Office, Air Ministry, and Foreign Office representatives met those of the Colonial Office to confer on the questions posed by Young, and Churchill approved the decisions.[30] Britain had to retain final responsibility for the security and defense of Iraq but this did not preclude a suitable arrangement under which Faysal would accept responsibility in the first instance; Britain would do its best to repel invasion and disorder but expected cooperation from the Arab army in this; the G.O.C. was the prime military adviser to the High Commissioner but should consult the Inspector of Levies who was to be subordinate to him in case of military operations although subordinate to the High Commissioner for administrative purposes, and the G.O.C. should allow Iraq to assume local responsibility for minor disorders.

This conference with the War Office over coordination of activities in Iraq was fairly minor and peaceful compared to the relations between the two ministries over the major issues of financial control and garrison size. Because they were vital to his financial economizing plans, Churchill took over, trusting no one else with such matters of high importance. He wrote to Worthington Evans, 23 June,[31] continuing the correspondence that had been going on since both had taken their new posts that the concomitant of his undivided responsibility to Parliament for the Middle East had to be full financial control. He insisted on the right to supervise, criticize and disallow any proposed item of expenditure. Churchill was sympathetic to the War Office need of finding employment for as many as possible of the units of the British army, but as he was duty bound to economize and Indian troops were cheaper, he would use the latter. He felt, too, that after consulting the High Commissioners he should be able to tell the War Secretary how many troops were required and what their dispositions should be. "On the other hand, the War Office have a reserved, latent and underlying right and responsibility in regard to the health and safety of British troops." Churchill hoped the two men could discuss these matters and agree upon outstanding differences which could be submitted for Cabinet decision.

Worthington Evans ignored the issue of financial control and concentrated on the future composition of the Iraq garrison trying to get as many British battalions as possible placed there. He tried for seven British and five Indian battalions.[32] But Churchill, who had just received a telegram from Haldane in which he said he could go even lower than a twelve battalion garrison by April 1922, wrote back to the War Office[33] that he could only accept two British and ten Indian battalions as the maximum that the Colonial Office could afford; but if the Army Council was prepared to charge for British battalions in excess of the two the same rate as that of the Indian ones, he would welcome the War Office's suggested number.

The major question the Colonial Office had to decide, Churchill wrote in a long note to Shuckburgh, was whether to go to the Cabinet on the basis of getting the War Office out of Iraq at the beginning of the new financial year. The first step, he decided, was to discuss details with the Air Ministry and see exactly how they proposed to take over control of Iraq. Shuckburgh suggested[34] that as soon as the proposals were in and examined, the War Office should be taken into confidence, showing us that Churchill and his staff were making all these plans in secret.

The detailed Air Ministry report was only part of the ammunition Churchill was building up for his attack on the War Office in the Cabinet. Next the Colonial Secretary noted to Vernon[35] that the latter was to make his own calculations as to how much the Colonial Office ought to pay for Haldane's proposed eight battalion garrison which would remain in Iraq only for six months i.e. from March until October 1922. Vernon had to calculate it all himself because the War Office would simply charge what it liked; Vernon's calculations would serve as the financial basis for Churchill's arguments in the Cabinet. The Colonial Secretary knew by then that there would be no interdepartmental settlement of these costly issues and that the only solution was to go to the Cabinet.

The next day Vernon handed in the memorandum asked for, listing the total cost at over five million pounds.[36] Churchill examined it thoroughly, marking it up with his distinctive red pencil, and three days later wrote a long note to both Vernon and Meinertzhagen questioning almost every figure.[37] Only an absolutely necessary functionary was to remain on the pay list, and if the War Office insisted on a large number, he insisted in return that he would carry on entirely with Indians and the Air Force.

At the same time, Churchill wrote a very secret note to Shuckburgh for comment.[38] Step one, in Iraq was to complete the process of reduction to the twelve battalion scheme by the end of the calendar year, with proportionate reductions enforced on ancillary services, transport and followers. The next step was to open the new financial year, 1 April 1922, on the eight battalion scheme. Step three was to take place on 1 October 1922 when the Air Force would take control and General Haldane would hand over the garrison to General Ironside.

Shuckburgh discussed the plan with Meinertzhagen and Vernon, and minuted in a very secret note that all three fully agreed.[39] The procedure to be followed was to have Trenchard's Air Force scheme accepted in principle by the departments concerned; Churchill could then outline his plan and if there were difficulties he could then go to the Cabinet. Shuckburgh reiterated his warning not to keep the War Office out any longer.

Churchill conferred with Lloyd George[40] on his proposed plan and the Prime Minister agreed generally, even pressing his Colonial Secretary to go much farther, namely to pay Faysal a subsidy and withdraw all the troops from Iraq. This suggestion may have been because of the pressure of the press which was advocating total withdrawal from Iraq and using the money for the slum population instead.[41]

Reporting everything to Cox[42] Churchill reassured the High Commissioner that he would not consent to Lloyd George's plan for the Cairo policy had to be pursued perseveringly. "You will readily understand that these proposals will be hotly contested by the War Office. The economy campaign is pressing them very hard now, and they are desperately anxious to quarter at least seven white battalions in Mesopotamia in order to avoid their possible disbandment. Any such solution will be fatal to Mesopotamian interests."[43]

Churchill was almost ready to face the Cabinet and he completed his draft memorandum on policy and finance in Iraq.[44] He did not begin with a demand for full financial control, but with a statement of the problem, declaring the impossibility of his reconciling War Office financial charges for the Iraq garrison with any of the economizing forecasts he had given to Parliament. He described how he had planned to retain two British battalions only to discover that the War Office wished to retain seven which would mean a cost of over 900 pounds per year for every infantry soldier because of the elaborate staffs and administrative services necessary to control the wellbeing of British troops.

> I cannot in any circumstances face this prospect of anything like it. The kind of organization of the British army which fits it to face a German Army under modern conditions is far too costly for a poor, starving, back-ward, bankrupt country like Mesopotamia. To throw such a weight upon it is to crush it, and if no other way can be found than this of holding the country, we had much better give up the mandate at once.[45]

Having shot down the War Office plan, Churchill next built up his own by describing how the Air Force would work in conjunction with armored cars, trains, gun boats and four battalions of infantry plus local levies and the Arab army. Most important, this was a system which could be maintained within the financial limits Churchill had given to Parliament. All was progressing favorably in Iraq, and Churchill made it perfectly clear that he planned to hold that land not by force but by the acquiescence of the people and their ruler. Only then, having built a rational foundation, did he demand full financial control of Iraq. Churchill spelled out seven specific decisions of policy that he wanted the Cabinet to assent to. In conclusion, to mollify the War Office, he wrote of the debt owed to the War Office for helping the Colonial Office, and "if we desire to part company with the War Office at an early date, it is not because we do not value their loyal and skillful aid, but because we simply cannot afford it."

The concluding remark did not make Churchill's plan any more palatable to the War Office. Wilson described it as a "hot air, Arab, and aeroplane" policy. War Office anger is evident in the answering memorandum drawn up by Worthington Evans,[46] who tersely summarized his objections. First, the military garrison proposed was altogether inadequate. Second, the Air Force, even if allowed a land army and gunboats, was ill equipped for the purpose proposed as it only had punitive weapons. Third, it was undesirable and uneconomical to allow the Air Force to depart from its function as an ancillary force mainly because it would be a wholesale duplication and the War Office would have to lend personnel it could ill afford to do without. Fourth, the estimates of the future cost were illusory. Last, the proposals as to financial and executive control by the Colonial Office of troops of the British Army were unconstitutional and would lead to hopeless confusion.

Churchill tried to get Lloyd George's backing before the latter left for Wales, claiming that he "must be free from the W.O. & able to frame my own Estimates & prescribe what troops if any we are to take from there. Otherwise I c[oul]d not possibly keep my promise to Parliament about reductions, nor c[oul]d I present the Estimates."[47] If his plan, which he enclosed for the Prime Minister to read, succeeded, there would be a considerable advancement in economy, and he confidently expected Lloyd George's support in obtaining the necessary decisions from the Cabinet.

The Cabinet met 18 August[48] to discuss the memoranda of the two Secretaries of State as well as Trenchard's Air Force scheme. After debating the plans, Churchill's laborious preparations paid off for the Cabinet agreed to all of his proposals. Although dissenting, Worthington Evans said he would carry out the decision, but despite this expressed avowal nothing was done. So, Vernon and Young carefully considered what steps to take. They tried first to obtain open War Office concurrence in the retention of only two British battalions. The War Office had not yet informed Haldane of the Cabinet decisions and therefore he would not yet collaborate with Cox in framing proposals for enforcing the decisions. Until that happened the Colonial Office could not discuss with the Finance Department of the War Office the method by which the former was to exercise financial control. To force the War Office's hand, Vernon and Young drafted a telegram to Cox informing him of Cabinet backing and asking him to submit proposals for carrying out the plan; Cox would naturally consult Haldane and if the latter had not yet been instructed by the War Office, Cox would have to telegraph back to inquire what was going on thus forcing the War Office to act.[49] Churchill agreed to this operation, but the results were not as rapid as was hoped.

More than a month passed before the War Office finally made a move. Worthington Evans suggested proceeding by conference instead of by formal letters[50] and the Colonial Office immediately agreed. But, continuing to move at a snail's pace, it was not until 31 October that the preliminary conference met.[51] No decisions were reached and the interdepartmental conference which followed on 3 November[52] was only able to reach general conclusions subject to War and Colonial Office confirmation. There were many other tentative conclusions reached by the conferences between the two ministries,[53] but because Churchill and Worthington Evans did not themselves sit down and confer, the main issues remained unsettled. Until these questions were decided—whether the R.A.F. was going to provide its own administrative services, what was going to be the composition of the infantry portion of the R.A.F. garrison, what was to be their distribution—the War Office could not draw up its estimates and therefore neither could the Colonial Office. It was this inability to complete the estimates that finally pushed Worthington Evans to act, and the two secretaries of state sat down together, 19 December, along with the Secretaries of State for India and for Air, to discuss the problem.[54] The War Office finally agreed in principle to the loan of two British battalions to form part of the Baghdad garrison, and would formulate their minimum conditions and price. In return, the Colonial Secretary agreed to keep up the Kut-Baghdad railroad, if not too costly. It was also decided that the Air Ministry and the War Office would discuss the conditions under which Army personnel would be loaned to the Air Ministry after October 22.

It is amazing that it took this long to settle such important issues. It is not as though the men responsible had to communicate through telegrams and letters; they could have sat down together any day of the week to straighten things out, especially when it was the estimates of each ministry that depended on these solutions. Estimates were important at all times, but even more so during this period, for all services ministries had received a circular letter in May from the Treasury Committee on National Expenditure, better known as the (Sir Eric) Geddes Committee, calling on each department to draw up provisional estimates by the end of July. This was no ordinary committee for its aim was cutting expenditure of the services to the bone, weeding out any excessive or indefensible item. The Geddes Committee was Lloyd George's response to the "anti-waste' campaign of some major London newspapers which threatened the stability of the Government. Geddes was no longer a member of Government and Churchill resented that such a person was given the task of reducing Government spending, for he had no accountability to Parliament.

But the Colonial Office had gone to work, despite Churchill's feelings, and keeping Middle East services separate, had completed the preliminary rough estimates by 22 July.[55] The principal charges were those providing for repayment to the War Office and Air Ministry, but here it was impossible to even frame a provisional estimate until the general question of the Iraq garrison was settled in principle.

The Treasury committee had not been satisfied with the preliminary figures and demanded further details as well as further economies. Long involved memoranda went back and forth, with Churchill little involved, until the Treasury committee sent a list of fifteen questions.[56] Then Churchill attended to matters himself,[57] and his resentment of the committee is clear in his replies. By this time the resentment was not based only on the fact that Geddes was not a member of the Government, but also on the surmise that it was pressure from this committee on the War Office that had caused Worthington Evans to procrastinate and fight the Colonial Office plans as he had. The acrimonious dispute with the War Office was over and Churchill finally had access to all the detailed information he needed to reply to the Geddes Committee, but that did not lessen Churchill's antipathy; it may even have increased it. Churchill's replies are important because they reflect the progress made in economizing on Iraq by the end of 1921.

The Committee, firstly, wanted the Colonial Secretary to inform it of the present position of the Iraq mandate and the extent of the obligations imposed on Britain. Churchill's terse reply was that he had appended the various published documents bearing on this subject, pointing out "that these are essentially matters of policy with which it is understood the Committee is not competent to deal."

The second question dealt with the exact figures to be paid to the army, air force, native levies and railroads, to which Churchill replied he had been working to reduce these figures but he could not, at the present, give any further details. As for the next two queries, whether the Air Force takeover could be effected earlier than October 1922, the Colonial Secretary answered that he too had hoped to do so but after consultation had satisfied himself that it was not possible.

Could the Secretary of State foresee a date at which British liabilities in Iraq would be terminated? The question was one of policy and, referring to the Turkish menace in Mosul, Churchill claimed that he could give no forecast on the interplay of such imponderable factors.

The Committee wished to know Churchill's opinion on the War Office's intention to maintain the British battalions withdrawn from Iraq in the Mediterranean in case of an emergency, thereby not realizing the full saving Churchill intended. Churchill found it difficult to judge "what the action of future British Governments would be in the event of hypothetical and undefined emergencies arising in Mesopotamia," so the Colonial Office was not stipulating for any specific battalions to be held in reserve to proceed to Iraq's aid.

The next three questions were answered by the Colonial Office staff. They involved the Iraq railroads. The staff replied that the Colonial Secretary favored handing the railroads over to the Iraq Government in April 1922 and then leasing the system to a private company; failure to do so would raise a question of high policy because of the high cost, but scrapping the railroads would entail evacuation of Mosul. Valuations were being carried out and the figures would be submitted.

Questions ten through fourteen involved Palestine and will be dealt with later in the proper context. The last one was a request for an explanation of the obligations that necessitated continuing the Arabian subsidies and for how long it was anticipated they would be required. Churchill answered that this formed an essential part of the political processes on which the Iraq garrison reduction had been based. "It will be seen that they do not amount to the cost of a single battalion, whereas as a result of the policy of which they are a part it is expected that thirty-nine or forty battalions will have been removed from Mesopotamia in the course of the current year."

Churchill added that the total reduction effected within the year was not fourteen million pounds as quoted by the Committee but twenty million. But his last paragraph, which jealously guarded his own achievements, was eliminated as an unwise and too personal statement. The replies were sent to the Treasury, 10 January 1922, with a thick pile of enclosures directly relevant to the issues.

It is no wonder that with the pressures of the Geddes Committee, the haggling with the War Office and the rumors of a French-Kemalist treaty that Churchill lost his temper with Faysal. Cox sent telegrams[58] describing Faysal's vehement opposition to France's treaty with Kemal and his strong desire for a definite pronouncement of policy from Britain. Late in September it was learned that France was secretly negotiating with the Kemalists and that France was deliberately attempting to divert Turkish hostility away from Syria to Iraq. A memorandum, drawn up at Churchill's order,[59] declared that "if it was true that in the general agreement which the Prime Minister of France stated had been reached with the Kemalists the French would accord to the Turks facilities for the use of the Cilician section of the Baghdad railroad, this would be deemed "an unfriendly act." France would not do such a thing, noted Churchill. "But clearly the French were negotiating, through M. Franklin Bouillon, a treaty designed not merely to safeguard French interests in Turkey, but to secure these interests wherever necessary at the expense of Great Britain," believing Britain had such an arrangement with the Greeks. France would be only too delighted to have Britain's Sharifian policy fall apart and Churchill felt it was important to open serious discussions with France on this.

The memorandum assembled facts bearing on Britain's grievances towards France. It was circulated before the Cabinet meeting of 1 November[60] but nothing was finalized until the Cabinet meeting of 22 November[61] at which it was agreed to send a note to France on the reprehensible action taken in signing a treaty with Kemal, and to propose to the Allies to invite Kemal to a conference soon.

Faysal's complaints, arriving in the midst of all this high policy decision making, provoked Churchill who angrily wrote a sharp telegram to Cox[62] along with a seething note to Shuckburgh ordering him to send the telegram off. He felt that Faysal was "rather too prone to raise difficult constitutional and foreign questions. He has only just been installed & sh[oul]d devote himself to developing good Government tranquility & prosperity within Iraq instead of constantly seeking to have his position defined." All problems would eventually be settled "but meanwhile why can he not live quietly & do his ordinary practical work as a ruler instead of fretting & fuming." He had to be made aware of the enormous cost and burden Iraq had been and still was to Britain. Churchill was in the midst of the estimates problems and so could quote exact figures of what Iraq was costing, and would be only too delighted to give Faysal satisfactory definitions about his independence and responsibility "if he will show us his capacity to relieve us from our heavy expense. If he takes our money he will have to take our directions." Cox was told to cool Faysal down with such considerations.

Churchill openly wrote to Shuckburgh:

> I am getting tired of all these lengthy telegrams about Feisal and his state of mind. There is too much of it. ... Has he not got some wives to

keep him quiet? ... Whenever Feisal starts talking about Arab aspirations, his sovereign status, and his relations with the French, etc., Cox ought to go into the financial aspect with him and show him that the country on whose throne he has been hoisted is a monstrous burden to the British Exchequer.[63]

As much as Churchill wanted Faysal to stay out of international affairs, he did not dismiss the idea of utilizing him to negotiate unofficially with Mustafa Kemal. Disquieting telegrams about activities of the Turkish Nationalists in the Mosul area had been arriving regularly, as well as the accompanying warning that the Turks could combine with the Bolsheviks to really pose a dangerous threat.[64] It was not until Kemal brilliantly crushed the Greek offensive at Sakarya in September that Churchill felt it again necessary to write a memorandum[65] on the situation that again an opportune time had arrived for making a good settlement between Greece and Turkey.

The brilliant Kemalist action on the battlefield encouraged Cox to reraise the proposition of sending Faysal to informally negotiate with Kemal.[66] Faysal was very much enthused with the idea both for securing his borders and to raise his prestige in the Islamic world.[67] Churchill refused to allow this without Cabinet concurrence, and a further telegram saying that the Turks were raising forces in Kurdistan and the Caucasus to attack Mosul[68] provoked him to push even harder for an early discussion of the issue. Curzon blocked this saying that discussion with the Allies and friendly mediation should be tried once more.[69] Even after the Cabinet decision "in favor of Feisal being empowered to negotiate, subject to certain limitations as to the scope of negotiations, "Curzon held up and had his way. Faysal was forbidden to enter into relations with the Kemalists. Churchill tried this road again anyway, in a modified manner, upon receipt of two more telegrams from Cox, the first of which strongly disagreed that Iraq, especially Mosul, was not an immediate Turkish objective.[70] Cox listed evidence to back this up and Churchill had the telegram printed for Cabinet circulation.

The second telegram, also printed for Cabinet circulation, suggested that, since Faysal could not negotiate openly with the Kemalists, perhaps he could unofficially inquire through his relatives who were with Kemal what the latter's intentions were with regard to Iraq.[71] Along with these two telegrams Churchill also presented to the Cabinet a memorandum[72] drawn up by the Middle East Department on foreign incitement of the Turks to attack Iraq. Faced with this array of documents, the Cabinet, meeting 21 December, agreed to allow private discussions aimed at finding out Kemalist intentions in Iraq.[73]

Curzon may have come out so strongly against Churchill's proposals in this area because he was so annoyed with the latter's actions which impinged on what the Foreign Secretary considered his private domain, Egypt and Persia. It is true that at one time Churchill had tried to get Egypt and Persia within his control but once the Cabinet decision had gone against this, he did not, as some contend,[74] continue to press his claim; rather he set out to protect the interests of the Colonial Office, but being Churchill, he did so with rather more push than Curzon was used to. Egypt was important to him as a communications center for the Middle East and as a central base for airplanes. South Persia was traversed by telegraph lines which were vital in relieving the extraordinarily heavy traffic between London, Karachi and Baghdad; the cost of new cables would exceed the maintenance of the South Persian Rifles, the military force of that area. The question was important enough for Churchill to note[75] that he would be prepared to offer to pay two to three hundred thousand pounds to continue the South Persian Rifles. "I regard this as insurance against disturbances of the oilfields which will react upon our position in Mesopotamia and possibly lead to demands for troops." Shuckburgh added that more important was upkeep of British prestige in the Middle East and prevention of the spread of Bolshevism. This was repeated in a letter to Curzon,[76] in which Churchill carefully wrote, "I do not wish to interfere in matters that are beyond my official concern, but if our whole position in Southern Persia is to collapse and the field is to be left open to the Bolsheviks, the reaction on the Mesopotamian situation can hardly fail to be serious." Threat to the oilfields would call for troop reinforcement ruining his reduction plans.

Sixteen meetings were held by a subcommittee on the protection of South Persian oilfields, and at the end of November its conclusions were submitted, which amounted to asking the Colonial Office to undertake the responsibility for collecting intelligence regarding the safety of the oilfields and to accept the liability for keeping up to date plans for dispatching from Iraq a preliminary defense force in an emergency.[77] Churchill agreed to this on the condition there would be no charges to the Middle East Vote and that troops sent from Iraq would be at once replaced from India at their own expense.[78]

We may conclude that Churchill ventured out into Middle Eastern territories not under his domain only when he felt that Fertile Crescent interests were at stake. Generally, as 1921 drew to a close, he concerned himself with primary policy issues, leaving more and more of the daily running of Iraq to his Middle East Department staff and to the High Commissioner and his staff. Minor issues did arise every so often which were either directed to him for concurrence or upon skimming through the mass of papers as was his wont he chose to comment on or query some. In the latter case the points were usually financial ones. Churchill also commented on isolated issues which interested him, such as setting up a weekly air mail service,[79] and using lachrymatory gas in Iraq: "In my view they are a scientific expedient for sparing life wh[ich] sh[oul]d not be prevented by the prejudices of those who do not think clearly."[80]

Despite the headaches that Iraq posed, Churchill could feel that progress was being made along the path he had set for it. He was optimistic enough not to be very much disturbed by a three-part feature article in *The Times* on Iraq strongly criticizing his policy and advocating immediate withdrawal.[81] The editorial follow up agreed, claiming that the difficulties were so great in Iraq because "far from being prescient (the policy) has been perpetually and narrowly opportunist and consistently short-sighted."[82]

CHAPTER 9

No Progress

The mood of optimism that characterized Churchill's attitude to Iraq at the end of 1921 was not paralleled in his attitude to Palestine. Despite his many declarations of sympathy for Zionism,[1] the impression one gets from reading the material of the second half of 1921 is that Churchill was annoyed with Palestine. His annoyance manifested itself in his relations with the High Commissioner, the Arabs, and the Zionists but mostly in his lack of action. As Colonial Secretary, the very fact that he did little that was concrete about Palestine influenced events and ideas. The question that arises is why Churchill behaved this way. There is no one document one can cite that answers this question. The answer lies in a feeling generated by all the documents relating not only to Palestine but to the Middle East generally. Churchill, the master of argument and cajolery, found himself faced with immovable forces in the shape of the Arabs and Zionists. He could accept such opposition from Englishmen holding views differing from his own. He could accept it from other Europeans. But he could not accept it from peoples of backward areas for which Britain was burdened with the task of bringing into twentieth-century modernity. He perceived the power of nationalism in Ireland, Turkey and Egypt, but rationalized that Ireland was part of Europe, and Turkey and Egypt were peripheral to his tasks as Colonial Secretary. But Palestine and Iraq came directly under his control. Again, he could dismiss the rebellion in Iraq as Bolshevik incited and not a nationalistic uprising, but he could not dismiss so easily the two forms of nationalism developing in Palestine. Churchill's task was economization and this could only take place in a peaceful country. He discovered, after trying to cope with the Zionists and the Palestine Arabs, that doing nothing seemed to bring a semblance of peace. The Zionists and Palestine Arabs began using ploys to attain their goals that presaged their activities for the entire mandate period, the former skirting a Colonial Secretary who was not acting in Zionist interests and appealing to other Cabinet members or to Parliament, the latter adamantly refusing to budge from their initial position. When even face-to-face confrontations did not work, Churchill quickly mastered the varied arts of procrastination, such as deferring action until yet another oral or written report was submitted, ignoring requests for action, or outright refusal to act yet. By the end of the year Palestine, including Transjordan, was in a state of policy drift.

In June, when Churchill spoke so impressively in Parliament, Transjordan seemed to be following the exact plan set for it. Then, without warning, a split grew, both in that country and in London, over the issue of whether or not 'Abdallah should continue to head Transjordan. Provocation of the split was twofold: attacks from Transjordan into the French zone in Syria and negative reports on 'Abdallah's administration. He had not centralized authority, not established security, nor built up a financial regime to Britain's liking, nor even collected taxes. These reports were submitted by General Congreve,[2] G.O.C. Egypt, Sir Geoffrey Salmond,[3] in charge of the Air Force in Transjordan, and Julius Abramson,[4] the Chief British Representative in 'Amman and found sympathetic response and agreement in Gerard Clauson—a Principal of the Middle-East Department—Young and Meinertzhagen. Lawrence, on the other hand, felt that 'Abdallah should continue to be backed, and as long as he could keep peace with his neighbors it did not matter whether or not he ran a good administration. But the peace was broken 23 June by an attack on General Gouraud, the French High Commissioner of Syria, near Kunaytra.

Churchill did not commit himself and wired to Samuel[5] asking for his views on temporarily getting 'Abdallah out of the country so that his Syrian entourage that had been causing all the administrative and military problems could be dismissed; whether or not he was to remain in Transjordan depended on 'Abdallah's wishes. Samuel agreed with Churchill's suggestions and felt that during 'Abdallah's visit to London a new governor should be agreed on too.[6] Lawrence, then on a Middle East tour, added his opinion, that although union with Palestine was Transjordan's best future, in the meantime he deprecated any alteration in the system because it would involve Britain in the responsibility for seeing that effect was given to its decisions and that would mean the expense of military control.[7]

At the end of August there was another attack on the French zone in Syria led by one of 'Abdallah's followers. In answering French accusations[8] Churchill blamed French activities for the initial Arab resentment and defended 'Abdallah's endeavors to prevent such disturbances. Churchill hoped the French would declare an amnesty allowing the Syrian exiles to return home thus greatly reducing Transjordan's difficulties. His note incorporating this answer to the Foreign Office ended on a personal tone to Young who was calling for the removal of 'Abdallah: "I have certainly not decided to remove the Emir Abdullah, but I will discuss with y[ou] tomorrow whether Lawrence sh[oul]d not visit him on his return journey."

Churchill deferred inviting 'Abdallah to London until Samuel, Lawrence and Young had a chance to discuss the question of Transjordan's future.[9] The topic was exhaustively examined in Jerusalem for three days. They decided that if changes were to take place, a new and much stronger chief British representative would be needed, someone of H. St. John B. Philby's caliber. Philby had been serving in Iraq but was removed by Cox a few months earlier because of his open hostility to Faysal. Lawrence was willing to accept the responsibility during the transitional period, and recommended 'Abdallah carrying on for the time being.[10]

Churchill refused to "take Philby in a poke" but wanted to see him in person and find out what his views were. Meanwhile he approved the plan of Lawrence's temporarily taking charge.[11] Again Churchill did not commit himself for or against the Amir, but temporized: "we have got through six months without using any troops and at no g[rea]t expense." Lawrence "recommends Abdullah carrying on. This is my wish too. I do not mean to throw him over easily. He has an impossible task."[12]

Lawrence recommended[13] five other policy steps to the Colonial Secretary, including making a statement explaining that Zionist provisions of the mandate would not apply to Transjordan. In addition, Lawrence also wrote a detailed report[14] criticizing the condition of the armored cars and equipment in Transjordan, but praising Captain Peake's 500 Arab reserves and the Arab administration. He recommended fixing up the cars, the railroads and the roads, while waiting for the reserve force to become strong enough to back up internal reforms. An opposing view was presented by the High Commissioner's Secretariat which felt that Lawrence had been swayed by 'Abdallah and his Syrian followers to form his opinions. They felt that 'Abdallah should be eliminated and a British controlled local government set up because Sharifian rule would mean the severance of Transjordan from Palestine which would be very bad for both.[15]

The Middle East Department split in its views, and Churchill, temporizing again, noted that they should await the receipt of a further dispatch promised by Samuel before making any final decisions[16] Meanwhile Churchill saw Philby and offered him the Transjordan post; the offer was accepted with alacrity.

The confidential five-page report on Transjordan by the High Commissioner arrived in London 8 December.[17] Samuel listed fourteen recommendations, including withdrawal of 'Abdallah and recognition of his brother Zayd as titular head of state with a local leader, Mazhar Arslan, as executive head. Samuel also requested a public statement of policy.

Philby described the conference held in Jerusalem[18]—attended by Samuel, Wyndham Deedes, his Chief Secretary, Ernest Richmond, his Political Assistant Secretary, Ronald Storrs, his adviser, and Abramson, Lawrence and himself—in which Lawrence went through each of Samuel's points. Philby left "with the general impression that no very definite conclusions had been arrived at. It was however satisfactory to know that for the time being at any rate the Amir Abdulla would remain at the head of affairs in Trans-Jordan." Lawrence felt the regime might be given a new lease on life. "This squares with my own prima facie views."

London procrastinated again and decided to await the return of Lawrence and the Cabinet decision on Palestine before deciding what to do with Samuel's fourteen points. Meinertzhagen's description of the lunch conversation Churchill, Frederick Guest—Secretary of State for Air since April—Shuckburgh and he had with Lawrence at the end of December is interesting both for its content and its reflection on the writer:

> I was much struck by the attitude of Winston towards Lawrence, which almost amounted to hero-worship. ... Lawrence had scarce a good word for anyone. He freely criticized Samuel, Cox, Allenby and Congreve, and spoke eulogistically of Feisal and Abdullah. This latter worthless Arab had proved his worthlessness in Transjordan, but Lawrence still sees advantage to us in keeping him on there, drawing a huge salary for doing nothing. I interrupted the conversation by saying I thought Abdullah had better be removed and that we must

administer Transjordania directly, as part of Palestine. Winston and Lawrence would not think of it. ... Winston is quite prepared to spend hundreds of thousands on bolstering up the effete House of Hussayn.[19]

Meinertzhagen's judgments must be taken with a grain of salt for he was a self-avowed Zionist sympathizer, but his feeling that the "atmosphere in the Colonial Office is definitely hebraphobe" is not to be totally discounted, nor is his description that the colonial policy was framed on a "carry-on-somehow" principle.[20]

The "carry-on-somehow" framework for Palestine gradually evolved after Churchill's June speech. Immediately after his triumphal presentation Churchill was active and optimistic about settling the problem of representative institutions, calming Dr. Weizmann's fears, and persuading the Arab delegation to settle their differences with Zionists. As he realized that nothing was working he "carried-on-somehow," refusing to make any statement of policy. Only in the military arena did he exert himself to achieve a settlement; if other points were settled, it seemed to happen almost by accident.

The Arabs demanded representative government and although rejecting the idea earlier, Churchill, on reflection, felt sure the franchise could be devised in such a way as to secure responsible representatives and fair representation of minorities. "But of course the instrument of Government creating the elective institutions must provide for the execution of our pledge to the Zionists. As long as it continues within certain limits immigration laws must be *ultra vires*[21]."

The Group Council met to discuss this as well as the new situation arising out of the Cabinet decision to put off presenting the mandates at the June meeting of the Council of the League of Nations.[22] Their view was that it would be fatal merely to mark time so it was necessary to make it clear that Britain intended to proceed in both Iraq and Palestine with the policy marked out, taking it for granted that the mandatory relation to the two areas would and had to be maintained. The Group Council carefully considered Samuel's electoral law proposals which was based on the Ottoman two-stage system of every 500 primary electors choosing one secondary elector and all secondary electors formed into colleges according to religious communities.[23] Samuel's aim was an elected Advisory Council and the majority of the Group Council agreed with it.

Churchill minuted at length on the Group Council's proposals criticizing the policy proposed because the task of developing representative institutions was basic to the role of a mandatory government.[24] If this complicated electoral law was to be promulgated and elections held and a constituent assembly created, such an assembly would discuss with the Governor the future constitution of the country and make the most extreme demands most of which the Governor would have to reject. Then the assembly would be "dissolved in dudgeon, and what everybody denounces as an inadequate measure of self-government and an unsatisfactory constitution will then have to be put into force in defiance of the constituent assembly and on the mere authority of the Governor." Then the whole elective process would have to be repeated to create the new elective legislative assembly and all those who had opposed Britain most in the earlier assembly would be returned to the new one. "I cannot think of any procedure ... more calculated to produce a steady rise of excitement throughout Palestine culminating in a complete deadlock between the executive and elective institutions."

Churchill recommended a far simpler procedure: the Governor should see Musa Kazim, official head of the Palestine nationalists, and his group to explain that Britain wished to give them some elective institutions at once but before that there had to be an understanding about Jewish immigration. Since Britain insisted on continuing immigration within the narrow limits recently defined, how would Musa Kazim safeguard Britain from not being interfered with by the elective body.

> On this Musa Kazim & Co. will probably say, What sort of electoral body are you going to give us, and what will be its power? Here the Governor must be ready to state in outline the sort of elective assembly he has in view, what its powers and functions will be, and what subjects will be definitely *ultra vires*. As a result of these pourparlers, it is to be hoped that Musa Kazim and his committee, for the sake of getting its own representative institutions, will accept the offer on the basis that immigration within the limits indicated will be definitely outside their scope, and that their legislation tending to prevent it will *ipso facto* be invalid, i.e., without the veto of the Governor.[25]

Churchill felt this bargaining process should be tried in the first instance for at least they would know more what the situation was; then a constitution could be promulgated, elections held and assembly convened. "In any case this procedure avoids the folly of going out of our way to procure a hungry lion and then walking up to him with a plate of raw beef to see how much he would like to take."

Samuel was telegraphed[26] to inform the Muslim-Christian delegation that was preparing to leave for London, that Churchill was working on a scheme of popular representation but that nothing could interfere with the Jewish national home policy. If the delegation chose to go to London anyway, all right, but they would not be dealt with formally.

Samuel conveyed Churchill's message but the delegation decided to go to London and left 19 July. Samuel believed they were well disposed and did not really expect an end to the Balfour Declaration though they would ask for it. But if no accommodation were reached and they returned embittered, there could be great trouble, Samuel reminded Churchill, and the success of the latter's efforts would determine Palestine's fate.[27]

Meanwhile Dr. Chaim Weizmann returned from a trip to the United States and was busy meeting the leaders of the Dominions gathered in London for the Imperial Conference. He was summoned by Churchill but at first refused to go "on the ground that I could not discuss with him profitably the situation, because I knew the sort of declarations he would give. Unless Mr. Churchill is prepared to grant us definite concessions, it is of no use discussing academic declarations of sympathy."[28] Churchill called Weizmann again and the two met for an hour and a half. Weizmann pointed out the vicious circle into which the attitude of the Palestine Administration and the Government was placing the Zionists, for on the one hand they complained about Zionism being a burden on the British taxpayer, and on the other, when the Zionists desired to lighten the burden by developing Palestine they refused to allow this for fear of an Arab outbreak. "I think Mr. Churchill saw the strength of this argument and after a long discussion he has agreed to my demand that a conference should be called ... [to] consider our demands ... and a definite policy of political action should be established and initiated in Palestine."[29]

The conference took place, 22 July,[30] in Balfour's house and was attended by Lloyd George, Balfour, Churchill, Hankey, and Weizmann. Weizmann began by reporting on his visit to the United States, saying that Samuel's 3 June speech vitiated all developments in Palestine because it precluded mass immigration and therefore was a negation of the Balfour

Declaration, which meant an ultimate Jewish majority. Churchill demurred at Weizmann's interpretation of the speech, taking the official view that there was a difficult situation there owing to the Balfour Declaration, which was opposed by the Arabs, by nine-tenths of the British officials on the spot, and by some of the Jews of Palestine; it was a poor country in which destitute emigrants could not be dumped. Weizmann refuted this and directed the conversation to the representative government project, asking why this was contemplated. Churchill's reply was because it was being forwarded in Transjordan and Iraq, but Weizmann rejected this reply claiming it a farce. When Lloyd George agreed, and told Churchill not to give representative government to Palestine, the Colonial Secretary "sulkily" remarked that the question would have to be brought up before the Cabinet. Weizmann pressed his point even further demanding to know whether or not Britain cared about what happened in Palestine. Lloyd George replied: "Frankly speaking you want to know whether we are going to keep our pledges?" Weizmann nodded, adding he would also like to know how Britain proposed to do it. Both Lloyd George and Balfour retorted that they always meant a Jewish state, but Churchill said nothing. Neither did he agree with Weizmann's statement that the Zionists were not an economic burden on Britain. Discussion turned toward related matters and Churchill asked what would satisfy Weizmann in the way of immigration; Weizmann could not formulate it in numbers but in conditions, e.g. the granting of the large Rutenberg concession, as discussed below. Discussion then moved to the defense of Palestine, and ended after one and a half hours. Weizmann was directed to write down his desiderata for Churchill.

The conference marked a small turning point. Churchill in effect had to give up his plans for a representative legislature and devise one that would be advisory only or be so composed as to present no necessity for overruling its decisions. It also marked the final push necessary to get the economic development plans for Palestine into motion. Weizmann listed the Rutenberg concession as one of his desiderata, and wrote that he was very optimistic about an impending amelioration of the situation in Palestine.[31]

Rutenberg's hydro-electric scheme was a main pivot of the Zionist program and the Middle East Department regarded its early initiation as a potent factor towards the successful development of Palestine for it would bring in money, industrial development and large employment. Technically it passed all reviews, but politically there were a few snags and therefore it was not until September that matter finally came to a head. The concessions were divided under two headings, the Auja concession which granted directly to Rutenberg the exclusive right of producing electrical energy by means of water power within the district of Jaffa for a period of 32 years, and the Jordan concession which would confer on the company an exclusive right for the generation of electrical energy by means of water power throughout the whole of Palestine, exclusive of Jaffa, for a period of 70 years. Describing the concessions in detail, Shuckburgh asked the Colonial Secretary's approval on signing the Auja concession which Samuel had already approved and submitting the Jordan concession to the Treasury for concurrence if Samuel agreed to it.[32] But before submitting this note to Churchill a telegram arrived from Samuel showing his reluctance to agree to the Jordan concession until the Arabs agreed to it as well as reluctance on certain technical grounds namely, electrification of the railroad, purchase by the Government of current, and the lease of 50,000 dunams.[33] Young felt that they should proceed boldly, without obtaining Arab consent, and he and Vernon should take the agreement in its final form to press it on Samuel in person.[34] Shuckburgh agreed and, since Churchill was in Scotland where he was staying after the death of his daughter, sent a telegram off to Samuel informing him of the uselessness of trying to get any Arab approval. He asked if Samuel agreed to sign it if the three points of difficulty were left out, and to publish it to see what its reception would be.[35] Shuckburgh kept Churchill informed[36] and wired that Rutenberg had agreed to waive the points Samuel objected to; they would be dealt with in subordinate agreements. The main document did not actually grant a concession but merely undertook that one should be granted within two years of its signature, thus providing ample time to review Arab representations. Shuckburgh assured Churchill that Rutenberg was fully alive to the necessity of treating Arab interests sympathetically and realized that without Arab cooperation his plans could not succeed; the Under-Secretary wanted Churchill's authorization to proceed at once with the conclusion of the agreement if Samuel's reply was favorable.

Samuel replied that it was not clear how the agreement could be signed and yet still be contingent on the attitude of the Arabs being satisfactory; if this point were met he would concur in the signature of the agreement.[37] Shuckburgh felt that this difficulty could be overcome if Rutenberg could be induced to state in writing that in practice it would be quite impossible for him to give effect to his project unless he could carry local opinion with him.[38] Rutenberg did so,[39] and copies of all these documents were forwarded to Churchill along with Shuckburgh's urgent minute that there was no reason why the main agreement should not be signed forthwith.[40] The urgency was because of the imminent departure of Young, Vernon and Rutenberg for Palestine. Churchill wired back, "Rutenberg concession proceed as you propose."[41] Action was taken at once and Samuel was duly informed.[42]

There was good reason for the Department's reluctance to approach the Arabs then in London for approval of the Rutenberg concessions. In complete contradiction to Samuel's optimistic prognostication that the Muslim-Christian delegation would not really insist on abrogation of the Balfour Declaration, and to Churchill's equally optimistic feelings expressed at the conference of 22 July that discussions between Weizmann and the Arab delegation would solve all outstanding problems, the delegation, from the day of its arrival, 28 July, refused to discuss anything but the Balfour Declaration. The Department prepared a memorandum for the Colonial Secretary discussing the attitude to be adopted towards them, i.e. that they were to be informally received, the series of public announcements defining British policy in Palestine was to be read to them with the emphasis on equal weight being given to both parts of the Balfour Declaration, and they were to be invited to formulate any concrete proposals.[43]

Vernon and Young met the Muslim-Christian delegation, 11 August, and for three hours discussed their complaints and demands. Young was pleased that he succeeded in modifying their views but added that they would probably swing back to their demand to abrogate the Balfour Declaration and to set up an elected government by the next day. He was optimistic enough to conclude his minute describing the meeting and the earlier one of 10 August between the delegation and the Archbishop of Canterbury, that he was "convinced that they could be induced to cooperate with us, provided that the constitution is framed on really liberal lines and that the Representative Assembly is recognized as having the right to criticize the administration officially if it appears to be departing in any way from the second clause of the Balfour Declaration."[44]

The next day the delegation met with the Colonial Secretary. Churchill flatly stated that he had no authority to alter basic British policy. But as its execution and administration was in his hands the Arabs could have an elective assembly if it would be framed properly. However, the delegation insisted on its basic demands, namely, National Government, abolition of the Jewish National Home principle, and no Jewish immigration, and refused to meet Weizmann and the Zionists. Churchill ended the interview saying he would see them again only if they met the Zionists to try to draw up a working arrangement. "After I have seen you again, if I find you are really making an effort to come to an agreement, I will endeavor to persuade the Prime Minister to receive you."[45] But the delegation refused to be bribed and would not meet the Zionists.

Despite this Churchill met them again 22 August,[46] and again Churchill stated point blank that the British Government meant to carry out the Balfour Declaration. He had no power to repudiate it, and this had to be accepted by the delegation whose job it was to see to the carrying out of the clauses that protected the Arabs and to find some basis for a friendly arrangement for the next few years. So the delegation moved to its next demand, true representation and not merely a legislative assembly. However Churchill insisted that this could not be allowed as the government it would create would at once tear up the Balfour Declaration and stop Jewish immigration; it was Britain's intention to bring Jews in. The next tactic was to attack the Jewish activities in Palestine saying that Arab interests were not safeguarded, an accusation which Churchill denied, retorting at length that there was room for everyone and when the electric and water works were completed there would be work for everybody. The British government would give them an instrument creating a Council and an Assembly that would enable the Arabs to improve their country and would enable the Arabs to take their seats at the council table and put the cause of the Arabs officially. Churchill sympathized with both sides and wanted them both to live in peace, appealing,

> ... throw in your lot with us. Work with us hand in hand. Reassure your people. Bring them along. Take up your share in the government of the country. Associate yourself with the British Government. Give the Jews their chance to come and develop the country, and if it does not work and does not answer, you will have a great chance and plenty of time to show the whole world that it has not answered and to make your complaint.[47]

He repeated himself three times and in short easily understandable sentences to be sure he put his main points across. But "he feared they would still swim round and round in a circle, saying that they wanted a National

Government and to get rid of the Balfour Declaration." Stressing again and again that there were two sides to the problem, he asked the delegation to come the next day to discuss the particular institutions that were proposed which would at least give the Arabs influence if not control. Churchill also voiced a not-so-veiled threat, before concluding, that force was at Britain's disposal but he would have no need to use it as he was sure agreement could be reached.

Unfortunately Churchill's fear that they would swim in circles was a more valid prediction than his hope of reaching an agreement. Musa Kazim al Husayni sent a note regretting they could not modify their differences because the executive body proposed by Young was not in the people's hands nor was the legislative body truly representative.[48] Churchill therefore agreed to wire Samuel to go ahead with the draft constitution on his own with the Muslim-Christian Consultative Committee. But Musa Kazim told this Committee not to attend Samuel's meetings in an attempt to force Britain's hand in London. Shuckburgh was furious and wanted to write them a stiff reprimand but was overruled by Sir James Masterton Smith, Churchill's Permanent Under-Secretary of State, who had been told by the Colonial Secretary that he wished to see the delegation again after hearing from Samuel.[49]

Such dilatory action was not the case with the issue of defense, the one exception to the inaction of the second half of 1921. A good deal of discussion had turned on this issue at the meeting of 22 July,[50] Before this meeting Churchill had already given up his plan for a trained Jewish police reserve, bowing to the combined opposition of Samuel and his Middle East Department.[51] Instead, he saw the value of a mobile, disciplined and well-trained gendarmerie of about 500 men, a plan with which Weizmann fully agreed.

The Palestine garrison drew Churchill's attention for this was an issue which was both familiar to him, and, because of the enormous sums of money involved, important to him. In late August he informed Young[52] that he proposed to follow the same line in Palestine as had been recently approved for Iraq, namely to claim entire financial control from 1 October, and to make his own arrangements for raising the necessary forces to keep the country quiet. He would decline to employ any British units or to have the forces connected with Egypt in any way; instead he planned to use Indian units, the local gendarmerie, the Air Force, and a reserve force of Jews to defend their colonies.

Churchill noted his tentative ideas for the specific breakdown of the Palestine garrison, adding that all Indian troops were to be non-Muslim, and asking for tables to be drawn up comparing the approximate costs.[53] Minutes went back and forth with Churchill digging to the very root of the cost of each item, changing his garrison plan according to what was reported back to him. Meanwhile he tried to get Lloyd George's backing for his new idea, writing that "the fact remains that Palestine simply cannot afford to pay for troops on the War Office scale. It is not giving us a fair chance to carry out our pledges to lay this burden upon the country. ... The War Office continue to think in Brigades, Divisions, Columns of troops, Lines of Communication, etc. What is wanted in Palestine is primarily an operation of police."[54] He hoped for the Prime Minister's support in his plan to get rid of the British troops altogether thereby saving over a million pounds.

Churchill planned to bring the new program before the Cabinet in late September, but the Cabinet paper was not finalized until mid-November and, as with Iraq, the conferences with the War Office and Cabinet did not take place until mid-December. Samuel was informed in a personal and secret telegram of Churchill's program, 12 November,[55] in which the Colonial Secretary asked for every possible assistance in getting matters into his hands first because "many of the British Military authorities are undoubtedly hostile to the Zionist policy, and reports of friction and lack of sympathy are continually reaching me," and second because of the inordinate expense of the present garrison.

Some outstanding examples of the "lack of sympathy" on the part of the military were the letters on the futility of the Zionist policy sent by Congreve to London,[56] as well as the letter he sent to the Palestine troops openly stating that whilst the army was not supposed to have politics, "in the case of Palestine these sympathies are rather obviously with the Arabs, who have hitherto appeared to the disinterested observer to have been the victims of an unjust policy, forced upon them by the British Government."[57] The Department was unanimous in its feeling that the military was anti-Zionist, and this last letter, which was very strongly protested against by Sir Alfred Mond, Minister of Health,[58] was used by Churchill to prove this point at the crucial Conference of Ministers of 21 December.

Samuel fully endorsed Churchill's military policy and telegraphed encouraging news about the shaping up of the gendarmerie.[59] Churchill was finally ready to present his plan to the War Office, and sent a copy to

Worthington Evans early in December so that he could consider it before the formal meeting. Churchill's memorandum was concise and to the point.[60] He detailed the present garrison of Palestine, showing that it totaled 13,287 men at a cost of 3.5 million pounds. "I consider that this is more than we can afford. I invite the Cabinet to transfer the military control of Palestine to the Colonial Office." His substitute garrison was then listed as well as the 700-man Palestine gendarmerie of British nationality[61] which would be under the civil administration, "& would animate and dominate the local gendarmerie and make it an effective instrument." Over 1.5 million pounds would be saved immediately.

The Army Council examined the memorandum and Henry Wilson deprecated the British gendarmerie idea.[62] But at the conference of 19 December[63] attended by Churchill, Montagu, Worthington Evans, Guest and their assistants, the War Office accepted Churchill's proposals for Palestine in principle and the change would take affect in April 1922. The Colonial Office agreed to take the responsibility for the Kantara-Rafa railroad but Churchill insisted that Samuel had to pay for it. Meinertzhagen described the meeting, and felt that "Winston was head and shoulders above the rest in ability and his superior intellect dominated the conference."[64]

The Conference of Ministers meeting two days later was told of the agreement reached on the 19th and approved Churchill's proposal for garrisoning Palestine.[65] This enabled him to answer the Geddes Committee questions on Palestine querying the cost of the garrison as well as its size and British obligations there, and asking for economizing measures. Churchill drew the attention of the Committee to the new policy soon to be carried out, but reminded them that Britain was committed to the Zionist policy which "is of course extremely unpopular with the vast majority of the local inhabitants" and he was doing his best to reconcile the conflicting views and aspirations of the Arabs and Jews. "It is a very delicate and difficult task requiring time and patience."[66]

Time was just what Samuel kept urging they did not have, and patience was something Churchill was rapidly running out of. Samuel kept writing that even with military policy solved, the basic need was that of clear political policy. "Winston is inclined to pay more attention to reconstituting the Palestine Garrison than to remedying the political situation. ... If one is living on a volcano, it is better to remove the volcano than to make preparations to deal with it when it exploded."[67]

The political status of Palestine was still not regularized by a formal document. The mandate idea of embodying the Palestine constitution in an instrument was still to be settled and a Conference of Legal Advisers was set up in London in July to do just that. Young and Vernon were to bring the drafts out to Palestine and Iraq.

It was in the wake of the Jaffa riots, the suspended immigration, Samuel's 3 June speech and Churchill's speech in Commons, that Weizmann had made his strong appeal to the Prime Minister, Churchill and Balfour, 22 July, fearing the form the constitution would take. Weizmann's nine suggestions for action to restore faith in British Administration that he submitted to Churchill included energetically punishing those guilty of the riots, reparation to the sufferers, protection of the Jewish colonies, replacing the police force with a small neutral constabulary, having anti-Zionists resign their posts, cutting the Palestine garrison off from Egypt, asking the Zionist Organization to advise and cooperate with the Government on immigration, granting the Rutenberg concession, and having the Zionist Organization comment on the organic law or constitution.[68]

Young agreed with Weizmann that what was needed was action, not words, and at a Group Council he presented his suggested actions which were the same as Weizmann's with some slight variations. He did not include Weizmann's idea that the Zionist Organization should comment on the organic law, but did suggest combining Weizmann's tactics with the establishment of an Advisory Council on an elective basis and the strict limitation of immigration to the numbers which could really be absorbed into the population.[69] Meinertzhagen—unlike Weizmann who agreed in order to secure his own points—disagreed with the Advisory Council idea and strongly advocated allowing the Zionist colonies to arm themselves by the legalization of the gun-running which was being successfully carried out.[70]

Shuckburgh endorsed Young's eight points and suggested the time had come to submit them to the Cabinet to settle policy once and for all.[71] Before drawing up the memorandum, Young asked Churchill to give him "an indication whether you agree with the general line of policy" for only then could it be submitted to the Cabinet.[72] Churchill's response was a red scribble, "Let me see y[ou]r paper in print." Young had it ready 11 August, and Churchill wrote his own introduction to the memorandum, one that was not very encouraging nor optimistic.[73] "The situation in Palestine causes me perplexity and anxiety," he began. "The whole country is in a ferment. The

Zionist policy is profoundly unpopular with all except the Zionists." Both sides were arming. Elective institutions were refused in the interests of the Zionist policy" and the high cost of the garrison "is almost wholly due to our Zionist policy." Meanwhile even the Zionists were discontented at the lack of progress and the "chilling disapprobation" of the British officials and the military.

His note never states whether he concurred in the policy in the memorandum and the feeling that comes across is that Churchill had reached the end of his tether and was ready to back out of the Balfour Declaration if the Cabinet so decided. "It seems to me that the whole situation should be reviewed by the Cabinet. I have done and am doing my best to give effect to the pledge given to the Zionists by Mr. Balfour on behalf of the War Cabinet and by the Prime Minister at the San Remo Conference. I am prepared to continue in this course, if it is the settled resolve of the Cabinet."[74] Perhaps the complications of Palestine were becoming too much for the Colonial Secretary who had thought that once he would determine the plan for the territory nothing really drastic could go wrong. Perhaps he was bored with the whole issue, considering it a nuisance, and more interested in Iraq, Ireland and the Dominions. Whatever the cause, Churchill did not press the case very strongly at the Cabinet and discussion was adjourned ostensibly because of the absence of Balfour.[75]

Likewise, Churchill did not authorize Weizmann to make any fresh declaration of policy ensuring adequate protection for the Jewish colonies on behalf of the British Government at the Carlsbad Zionist Congress and merely sanctioned his publicizing a very innocuous telegram: "Please convey to Congress the cordial and good wishes of His Majesty's Government who are confident that success will crown your efforts to re-establish Palestine as a flourishing and prosperous country where Jew and Arab alike shall combine to secure this common good."[76] Churchill also ignored Samuel's telegrams[77] begging for action on two main fronts: first, the necessity of securing a settlement on the question of the mandate for until then elections could not take place, nor could the Holy Places Commission be appointed, nor could there be government loans, currency or mineral resource development; second, the need for obtaining from the Zionists an open declaration that they backed the new definition of the Balfour Declaration and that their purpose was not to establish a Jewish state but a commonwealth. It was equally necessary for the Arabs to stop demanding the cancellation of the Balfour

Declaration and stoppage of Jewish immigration. Such action would defuse the "uneasy political situation" in Palestine, according to Samuel.

Churchill may have ignored Samuel in retaliation for the High Commissioner's ignoring Churchill's orders with regard to the report of the Commission of Enquiry into the Jaffa riots which was completed and printed in September.[78] The report blamed the riots and subsequent acts of violence on the feeling of discontent with and hostility to the Jews because of political and economic causes connected with immigration and Zionist policy. Racial strife was begun by the Arabs and they were the aggressors, though the outbreak was not premeditated. The raids on the Jewish agricultural colonies arose from the excitement produced by reports of Jews killing Arabs in Jaffa, and the military intervened successfully.

The High Commissioner sent in reports of losses suffered by the Jewish colonies and although favored exacting reparation from the Arab villages, was averse to forcing the Jaffa Arabs to pay compensation.[79] The Middle East Department felt it was worth taking the chance of another outbreak in Jaffa and enforce the levy in order to restore British prestige by proving that there was security, the rudimentary factor of good government. Even Churchill agreed that all concerned should bear the burden.[80] Samuel drew up a plan for collecting the fines from the four villages involved but reiterated his opposition to collecting the fine from Jaffa,[81] to which Churchill remarked "Sir Herbert Samuel should be held stiffly up to the enforcement of the fines on Jaffa."[82] The operations in the villages were completely successful and all the fines were paid, but Samuel ignored Churchill's directive partly because he felt it was impossible to devise direct measures for Jaffa and partly because he felt that such action could endanger Jaffa's sanctioning of the Rutenberg Auja scheme which was much more important than the compensation. Churchill's final word to Samuel was, "My views in regard to Jaffa remain unaltered but I will not press them further in view of your very strong opinion."[83]

Churchill was momentarily jolted out of his lethargy by the violence in Jerusalem on the anniversary of the Balfour Declaration, and he called the Zionists and Arab delegation to a joint conference to meet on 16 November. A few hours before the meeting was scheduled to begin, Churchill backed out pleading illness, after flatly refusing Meinertzhagen's request to make a public declaration of policy in favor of the Jewish National Home; he suggested no alternative beyond encouraging the Arabs and Zionists to come to terms with each other.[84]

The dispute over Jewish immigration continued to the end of the year because it was one of the matters that Churchill wanted discussed by the Arabs and Zionists. Weizmann had come to an agreement with the Colonial Office in October on how the new rationing system was to be worked, how to ensure that the immigrants were politically, socially, technically and physically qualified, as well as the exact numbers it was hoped to introduce into Palestine.[85] On 25 November the Colonial Office also agreed to reestablish the "certificate system" whereby any Jew in possession of a Zionist Organization certificate stating that work was available for him in Palestine would be admitted into that country. This system had been suspended by Samuel, and the new decision delighted Weizmann, but was not enough to counterbalance his depression over the lack of a clear-cut overall policy, for in the end this concession might amount to nothing.

Not even the gloomy reports on the political situation arriving from Palestine nor Weizmann's strong protest to Shuckburgh against Congreve's letter to his officers nor the stalemate in Zionist-Arab talks of 29 November[86] gave Churchill the needed impetus to make a statement of policy to both the Zionist Organization and the Arab Delegation. The only thing upon which the Zionists, Arabs and Palestine administration could agree was that the major initiative for defining policy had to come from London, but London and Churchill seemed to favor inaction and so 1921 drifted to a close, in an atmosphere antipodal to the euphoric excitement with which the year had opened.

CHAPTER 10

Iraq: From Stalemate to Solution

The issues of concern to the Colonial Secretary at the beginning of 1922 were many. He was very involved, during January and February, in modifying the Geddes Committee report and worked hard at preventing the disappearance of the Air Ministry, one of the Committee's recommendations. He was very involved in politics and was a major advocate of maintaining the Coalition Government instead of separating the Liberals from the Conservatives. When the Soviet Government approached Britain for economic aid and as a result Lloyd George planned to meet the Soviets in Genoa towards the end of April, Churchill, always anti-Bolshevik, renewed his campaign. The issue of overriding concern, however, was Ireland. With the signing of the Irish Treaty at the end of 1921, Ulster and the Irish Free State became Churchill's responsibility. He worked all year drafting an agreement between the North and the South trying to reconcile the conflicting passions.[1]

Iraq was relegated to second place on Churchill's busy agenda, for the Colonial Secretary was content to leave the detailed negotiation of the Iraq Treaty in the hands of Sir Percy Cox and the changeover to Air Force control of Iraq in the hands of Sir Hugh Trenchard. He kept a watchful eye over expenditure issues but only took the reins back into his own hands when a crisis developed with Faysal during the summer over mandatory control. The crisis built up slowly, as each of Faysal's moves was parried by Churchill via telegram until Faysal made his main attack in August. This so enraged the

Colonial Secretary that he counterattacked, using the ultimate weapon of deposition. It was a fluke of luck that Faysal remained king of Iraq.

Expenditure issues all related to the War Secretary's obstreperousness. Despite all the Cabinet decisions of 1921, Worthington Evans wanted to remove all British units from Iraq at the time of the changeover to Air Force control, as well as armored car companies and ancillary services;[2] he also wanted to withdraw to Basrah immediately. This would ruin Churchill's Iraq Estimates completely[3] as well as endanger Mosul.[4] Again, the two Secretaries of State faced each other at a Conference of Ministers, and again the two repeated their points of view.[5] Churchill's new argument was that it would be a pity to run the risk of losing Mosul by an immediate troop withdrawal just when the Allies were about to confer in Paris on a Greco-Turkish treaty; if the result of the Paris conference was satisfactory the danger of Turkish attacks on Mosul would be removed and the Arab army and levies would have time to develop.

The ministers discussed the two sides and reaffirmed their decisions that two British and four Indian battalions should remain in Iraq at Colonial Office expense; part of the armored car company and garrison should remain at Mosul until the conclusion of the Paris conference when the matter would be reconsidered.

With Cabinet backing reconfirmed, Churchill turned his attention to Parliament. He needed its sanction for the supplementary sum of 1.7 million pounds for Middle East Services, mainly to repay India for soldiers used in Iraq and to cover that country's deficit in its civil budget. With his tremendous powers of persuasion at work, he convinced the House of Commons to agree to his request.[6] During his speech, Churchill described Faysal as "a man of very commanding personality with great gifts of courtesy and address and with a charming manner." Yet a few weeks later he described him as "most unreasonable" and by the end of the summer Churchill seriously considered deposing him.

In tracing the events leading up to this crisis the question arises: how can one explain Faysal's behavior? The answer seems to lie in his personality, for most people who knew him agreed that he was a weak man. "In order therefore to govern his new state he had recourse to the shifts and contrivances which weak men, placed in positions of power, have to use: deceit, double-dealing, complicated intrigues, ambiguous advances and still more ambiguous retreats."[7] Faysal found himself trying to balance between his British mentors and his subjects. He owed his throne to Britain and he could not yet dispense with their military support. On the other hand, to build up moral support and a strong following in the Arabs, he had to oppose the British by joining forces with the nationalists. He hoped by joining with the nationalists to win concessions from Britain which would give Iraq real independence and place more power in his hands.[8]

The year started out promisingly with the final draft of the treaty, negotiated by Cox and Faysal, ready for consideration by 10 January.[9] Everything was agreed on except one article, Article 5, which related to the method by which Britain was to exercise control over the foreign relations of Iraq. Churchill and his staff submitted the entire treaty to the Cabinet for their assent along with the request to settle the differences regarding Article 5.[10] His memorandum explained the situation and presented the three versions of the article in dispute: Faysal and Cox wanted Iraq to have the "right" of foreign representation, and in states where Iraq had no representatives her interests would be entrusted to Britain; the Foreign Office wanted Faysal to have an agent in London but elsewhere to be represented by Britain; the Colonial Office agreed with Faysal's version but without the "right" demanded i.e., foreign representation had to be agreed upon by the contracting parties.[11]

The Cabinet met, 21 February, to discuss whether or not to give general authority to Churchill to proceed with the treaty, and to rule on the wording for Article 5. Lloyd George, Balfour, and Curzon opposed granting Feysal's demand each for his own reasons,[12] and the Cabinet voted for the Foreign Office version until Iraq was firmly established. Churchill was empowered to ask the High Commissioner how important the matter was to the maintenance of Faysal's prestige; subject to this, the Colonial Secretary was authorized to proceed with the negotiation of the treaty. Perhaps to sweeten this defeat, Lloyd George declared that the Cabinet should congratulate the Colonial Secretary on the change he had effected in Iraq. "It was due to his sagacity and courage that a policy had been evolved which had made it possible for us to hold it." Otherwise Iraq would probably have been lost to Britain.[13]

Churchill telegraphed to Cox[14] who answered that yes, Faysal's prestige would be affected.[15] But now, in addition to his demand regarding foreign representation, Faysal felt that it was far more important for Britain to insert a clause into the Preamble of the treaty formally abrogating the mandate. Faysal threatened to drop negotiations altogether if this was refused. Churchill conferred with his Iraq advisers as well as with Balfour and Fisher, Britain's representative at the League, on how to deal with this development and drafted a long telegram to Cox[16] giving rational reasons for refusing the king's demand. It was impossible to agree to Faysal's demand because of the insuperable international difficulties it would raise. The right to conclude the treaty with Faysal was given to Britain only by the existence of the mandate and so, if the mandate disappeared, Iraq would revert to the status of a conquered Ottoman territory whose ultimate disposal could be determined only by an agreement between all the Allied Powers. All legal claims to Britain's special position in Iraq, on which the whole policy of the treaty depended, would have to be forfeited. Cox was to make all this clear to Faysal, and the king had to choose between the alternative of Britain dropping the treaty negotiations if Faysal adhered to his present position thus indefinitely postponing the regularization of Iraq's status, and the alternative of placing Iraq's political rights on the firm foundation of a guarantee of the League of Nations by dropping his demand. A third alternative existed, that of British evacuation, a possibility Churchill considered scarcely credible at this time yet did not entirely dismiss from his mind.

Churchill decided to send Lawrence out to Baghdad to make the situation plain to the king, setting great store on Lawrence's personal influence. But Lawrence felt very strongly that his mission would have little chance of success unless he were able to tell Faysal that his wishes with regard to foreign representation would be met.[17] Churchill agreed to raise the topic of the Iraq treaty again in the Cabinet before the Prime Minister and the Foreign Secretary left for the conference soon to be held in Genoa.[18] But before the Cabinet could meet to rediscuss the foreign representation article and the new difficulty raised by Faysal[19] three telegrams arrived from the High Commissioner which added more fuel to the slowly growing crisis. The first[20] stated that Faysal and the Naqib were staunch to the principle of exclusive relations and a treaty with Britain, but the real stumbling block was the name and theory of "mandate,"[21] for Faysal felt the Constituent Assembly would repudiate him if he signed the treaty as it stood. Such arguments were mere excuses, for the nationalists would oppose this system no matter what the name. The deadlock remained. In addition, Cox turned down Churchill's suggestion that Lawrence should come to Baghdad, claiming that not only would he not have any influence but he would weaken Cox's position in other matters.[22] The most ominous telegram was the one describing Faysal's dismissal of five of his ministers without consulting Cox.[23] The excuse the king used was lack of action on their part in dealing with a raid by Ibn Sa'ud's followers on the Arabian border, but the real reason was his dissatisfaction with his Cabinet because it would not agree to increase the military budget.

Churchill discussed all these Iraq issues at the Cabinet meeting of 4 April.[24] He favored going to the League, and asking their approval to temporarily postpone the conclusion of the treaty. But the Cabinet, including a very reluctant Foreign Secretary, preferred the second course suggested by Churchill, i.e. telegraphing Cox that the Cabinet was prepared to amend the foreign representation article to the Colonial Office version, but was not prepared to formally abrogate the mandate, and unless Faysal actively cooperated, Britain would have to contemplate evacuation.

The Colonial Secretary telegraphed as directed, adding a few items on his own which neutralized the Cabinet decision: first, Cox was not to tell Faysal anything of this until further word came from Churchill; second, Churchill wanted to know if it was possible to leave the whole matter in suspense for a few months.[25] Cox replied the next day that although he preferred to defer communicating the Cabinet's conclusions to Faysal until after the gathering of religious leaders at Karbala was over, both he and Faysal viewed indefinite suspension of matters with misgiving.[26] The meeting at Karbala was ostensibly to discuss defense against Ibn Sa'ud, but in reality was a gathering of the nationalists to organize action.[27] Churchill, on the advice of his staff, agreed to wait until the Karbala meeting was over before communicating with Faysal. The Conference gave Britain a formal resolution of loyalty and support, reported Cox on 15 April,[28] adding that because he felt the main difficulty lay in the terminology of the treaty, perhaps he and Faysal should come to London.

After consulting his staff, the Foreign Office and Fisher, the Secretary of State refused permission to come to London,[29] and enclosed his draft message to Faysal again containing rational arguments in an attempt to convince the king. Again he clearly spelled out the reasons why Britain could not abrogate the mandate, but he also defined the meaning and purpose of the mandate as that of regulating and restricting the action of Britain while safeguarding the interests of Iraq. The treaty could only be on the basis of the mandate, and as soon as Iraq became strong enough to stand alone, without Britain having to spend large sums helping in its defense and maintenance of order, Britain would be in the position to state that her task was fulfilled. The king had the choice of accepting British guidance whilst requiring British aid, or of continuing on the present indeterminate basis, or—and he had only to say so—of asking Britain to leave. Churchill concluded by adding that Britain would be only too glad to be rid of the burden of Iraq. He was safe in making this offer, for Faysal knew he could not remain king in Iraq without British backing.

Cox was pleased with the draft, although he could not understand why Churchill favored temporizing. He suggested that the announcement should be made public in the House of Commons as a question and answer instead of in a personal message to the king.[30]

In a newsy letter to Curzon, who was very ill, Churchill, himself bedridden because of a heavy fall from a horse ("I've been like a beetle on its back for the last five days") wrote of the Iraq situation, revealing his reasons for temporizing: "Feisal is most unreasonable. ... He asked for the Treaty. It has been so shaped as to give him the fullest measure of satisfaction. If now he declines to sign, I propose to leave matters in an undefined and indeterminate condition and see what happens next. I would rather get through these dangerous months before presenting what I expect will be the inevitable ultimatum."[31]

Despite his desire to procrastinate, Churchill telegraphed to Cox a few days later that he would not delay beyond the following week if Cox thought that the psychological moment had come for bringing matters to a head.[32] By the following week he decided against any public announcement, especially in Commons, for he felt that any hint to the British public that negotiations were breaking down would revive strong public opposition to spending any money in Iraq. He therefore told Cox to use the issuance of a public statement as a threat to Faysal and returned to urging the settling of the treaty's outstanding points.[33]

For over a month telegrams went back and forth modifying the wording of the treaty. It seemed that Faysal was listening to reason and would not press for abrogation of the mandate, provided that Britain agreed to the textual modifications he demanded. Churchill ordered discussions with the Foreign Office to amend the treaty again and on 15 June the Colonial Secretary was presented with four telegrams to Cox for his authorization. The first two telegrams dealt with details of wording, the third gave Cox permission to sign the treaty even before receiving the complete English text from London, and the last, a personal message to Faysal, encouraged the king not merely to accept the treaty for himself but to use every effort to carry the country with him when the National Assembly met to discuss it.[34]

Initialing the draft telegram, Churchill probably felt great relief, believing that this was the end of the fencing match and now normal relations between the two countries could commence. He was pleased with the news from Cox that both Faysal and the Iraq Council accepted the treaty terms,[35] as well as with the news that the notables and shaykhs were prepared to form a strong combination, once the treaty was out, to secure the election of suitable candidates to the national congress.[36] Unfortunately the Colonial Secretary's optimistic relief was short lived. Faysal merely shifted his focus from the treaty itself to the resolution to be made by himself or by his Council in publishing the treaty. This new tactic was spelled out in Cox's telegram of 9 July.[37] Faysal agreed in principle to support the treaty, but because there was an articulate element in Iraq which resented the mandate, they had to be given hope of an early escape from it, and the best step to achieve this would be via announcements by both the Colonial Secretary and the King. Cox suggested the wording for Churchill's announcement assuring the people of Iraq that Britain would fully cooperate in gaining Iraqi admittance to the League of Nations before which Iraq could plead her own cause.

Churchill wired back that the proposed announcement was already in Article 6 of the treaty and was made even clearer in Article 18.[38] This crossed the High Commissioner's telegram which gave the exact wording of the Council's resolution for Churchill's consideration. The resolution, instigated by Faysal, accepted the treaty as the sole document defining the relations between Iraq and Britain and requested the High Commissioner to make it known to the British Government the repugnance felt by the Iraq Government at the mandatory idea; the Iraq Government begged Britain to appeal to the League to abandon or reconsider their mandatory policy.[39] Not all the ministers accepted this resolution, including the Naqib, because signing the resolution in effect admitted that there still was a mandate.[40]

Cox suspected that Faysal was playing for time in the belief that the League Council would deal with the mandate question in a way that Faysal could take advantage of. Therefore he recommended that Faysal be telegraphed that the League would not be discussing the Iraq mandate.[41] The Secretary of State did so,[42] adding in a private and personal telegram that the British public would not support Faysal's plan for abrogation of the mandate but would feel that he was repeating in Iraq the same unreasonable behavior that led to his expulsion from Syria.[43]

Faysal parried and defended his resolution proposal in the same rational manner Churchill was using. He claimed that if the treaty were concluded without any reservation publicly recorded by himself or the Government of Iraq which would leave the door open for an appeal against the mandate, Iraq would be stopped from freeing herself. Iraq would then turn upon him. Somehow it had to be made plain to the people that the door of escape from the mandatory position was conclusion of the treaty and that the people could rely on him to pursue the matter constitutionally before the League.[44]

To break the deadlock, Cox felt that perhaps he and Faysal should fly to London where agreement could be reached by personal discussion.[45] At first Churchill was ready to agree to Faysal's announcement provided that a parallel one be issued by Cox to the effect that the British Government remained mandate-bound, thus ending the matter and precluding the proposed trip to London. But when the Foreign Office raised grave objections to this course of action in that it could raise suspicions that the British Government had concurred in Faysal's announcement, Churchill decided to agree to Cox's proposed trip to London in early September.[46]

Faysal, however refused to come to London unless he was assured of a successful solution to the mandate problem with permission to announce in Iraq that Britain conceded the principle of emancipation from the mandate and the object of the London visit was to settle procedure.[47] Cox wired that Faysal feared that he would be asked to resign and the two men had discussed a possible solution to the impasse: the text of the treaty should be published in Iraq with an announcement explaining Britain's inability to escape from the mandate question, asking the people through the elected Assembly to decide whether they would accept the treaty or not; if not, Britain would evacuate immediately.[48] The High Commissioner kept pressing for some announcement from London before 23 August, the anniversary of Faysal's coronation, because that would be a logical time for all the extremists to demonstrate.

Churchill was then in France so Shuckburgh met with Young, Lawrence, Vernon and Meinertzhagen to discuss the next move. Young drew up a memorandum which summarized the latest events and stated the Department's proposed plan of action.[49] The Department opposed Cox's plan for it would give the impression in Iraq that it was up to the people to decide between

Faysal and Britain. Such was not the case because no change in policy was contemplated and if Faysal refused to come to London, the Colonial Office was bound to go on anyway. The first step, wrote Young, was to proceed with the election of the representative body and only when this Constituent Assembly approved the treaty would the British Government sign it.

The papers went off to Churchill for a decision and Masterton Smith telegraphed to Cox explaining the reason for the delay and hoping that a further five or six days would not endanger matters.[50] Cox answered immediately, 17 August, that the tension was at the breaking point and any delay would bring unfavorable developments; he and Faysal were ready to sign the treaty with a resolution of non-acceptance of the mandate attached.[51] Cox knew this was not a good solution, but he trusted the good sense of the majority to suppress extremist action.

Meanwhile, in France, Churchill was ignorant of Cox's latest telegram and considered the issue as he thought it stood, deciding that there was not the slightest reason for hurry on his part since he could not possibly make such a vital policy decision without referring to the Cabinet which had separated until September.[52] He hoped Cox would not be "disheartened or get tired of playing a long game."

Cox's tense telegram of 17 August was forwarded to Churchill with the Department's endorsement of Cox's suggested action. But Churchill refused to be swayed,[53] repeating that a Cabinet decision was required and meanwhile the responsibility rested on Faysal for preventing violence, consequences of which would be most disastrous to Iraq.

The situation in Iraq was tense partly because of Faysal's intriguing with the nationalists to throw the provinces into turmoil. He even approved nationalist denunciations of his own cabinet. When the cabinet demanded that the king should show that it could rely on his support and confidence, Faysal replied ambiguously that he saw no reason to change his policy.[54] The cabinet, except for the Prime Minister, thereupon resigned.

The crisis grew. Faysal's next step was to get his Prime Minister, the Naqib, also to resign, hoping that by getting rid of these moderates he could scare London into accepting the demands. Faysal tricked the Naqib into resigning saying that immediately upon doing so the king would ask the Naqib to form a new Cabinet. But when the Naqib did as suggested, Faysal merely accepted the resignation and moved to his next step: he informed Cox that should there be an outbreak, the king disclaimed any responsibility. Cox should either assume the conduct of administration or give Faysal a free hand to direct affairs. Cox saw that as a bluff to free himself from liability to Britain, for each had his own sphere of responsibility.[55]

Churchill sent these telegrams on to the Prime Minister with a letter requesting either a Cabinet or a meeting of Ministers. The Colonial Secretary now contemplated very serious action. "Feisal is playing a very low & treacherous game with us. ... Questions of deposition and/or evacuation will have to be considered. I think there is no doubt Cox can keep order in Baghdad. Feisal seems determined to justify every word Gouraud ever said about him."[56]

Churchill was not the only one to be disappointed in Faysal. Cox sent a very disillusioned telegram,[57] that although he realized the humiliation involved in acknowledging the failure of the Faysal policy and the subsequent need to totally recast Britain's entire Arabian policy, he had to tell his chief of his disappointment. Faysal, according to Cox, was charming and kind, but was morally weak and unstable, a subtle and accomplished schemer and a bad judge of men. In administrative areas immune from Faysal's meddling the administration ran smoothly with cooperation, but not in areas near Faysal. Sadly, Cox ended his telegram: "He [Faysal] was not and will not make good."

Cox's telegram was provoked by what had happened on 23 August, the first anniversary of Faysal's accession, when Cox had gone to offer his congratulations to the king. Leaders of the two extreme nationalist parties had been purposely given appointments just before Cox and had prolonged their visit so as to be present when the High Commissioner arrived. They were in the midst of making anti-British speeches to the cheering crowd below the royal apartments during Cox's visit. Cox demanded an apology from the king and the arrest of those responsible for the affair.

Cox's telegram probably served to further confirm Churchill's plan of action which he spelled out in a four part telegram.[58] Churchill presumed Cox was strong enough to repress disorder in the Baghdad area, and gave Cox permission—but only in the last resort—to place armed British guards around Faysal's residence on the pretext of protecting him but in fact to prevent him from escaping from Baghdad for the purpose of starting a revolt in another part of the country. Cox was to confer with the General Officer Commanding to decide on any troop or levy movements necessary, but Churchill did not yet feel it was time to inform the War Office and Air Ministry of these plans.

He told Cox, as part of his tactics to bring Faysal into line, to inform Faysal openly that the only certainty emerging from a catastrophe if Faysal provoked it was that the principal weight of it would fall on himself personally for he would be exiled and ruined. This ultimatum was strengthened by a long personal message to Faysal pointing out the ramifying misfortunes his action might bring i.e. it was only Britain's hand that was restraining Ibn Sa'ud from attacking the Hijaz. "I trust," warned the Colonial Secretary, "that a careful consideration of these grave matters may enable Your Majesty to tread the path of safety. That path can easily be discovered. It consists simply in following in these critical weeks with great fidelity the advice tendered by Sir Percy Cox. ..." Pending the Assembly decision on the treaty he would have to be guided by Cox on the selection of his Ministry. Meanwhile Churchill would bring the situation before the Cabinet.

The fourth section, added by Young, and approved by Churchill, shows that this was no mere bluff. The Colonial Secretary asked Cox if he would be prepared to revert to the pre-Faysal temporary government led by the Naqib and hold elections that way? This would entail the deposition and deportation of Faysal, which would make a hero and martyr of him among his adherents, "but he would be a hero and a martyr on his way to Ceylon." Faysal's removal would be shown as proof that the whole policy had failed and would greatly increase the demand for evacuation. But even evacuation was preferable to going on with Faysal after they had definitely reached the conclusion that "this man, who was put in to help us and who owes everything to us, is himself continually counterworking us, persecuting and provoking our friends and supporters in the country, and adding to our difficulties in every way."

On 25 August Winston Churchill ordered Young to send off all four drafts unless he had some serious observation to make; if so he was to telephone at seven. A hairbreadth away from possible deposition and deportation, Faysal came down with an attack of appendicitis, and the telegrams were held off.

Cox saw Faysal before his operation but the king refused to arrest the leaders of the extremists responsible for the demonstration of 23 August. As there was no government and the king was incapacitated, Cox acted on his own, arresting some extremist leaders and exiling others, and made a public announcement explaining why he was acting alone, telling the people it was their duty to wait patiently.[59] Cox telegraphed[60] that his announcement had

had an excellent effect. Now it was up to Cox and Churchill to decide on the line to take with Faysal. To make his moves appear constitutional, it was essential that they be ratified by the king, so Cox felt that Faysal should be told that if he dissociated himself from the High Commissioner's action and refused to publicly endorse it either the king or Cox would have to retire. The public was not aware of Faysal's non-cooperation and an announcement telling them to rely on Britain's friendship and to be patient until he and the cabinet about to form would find a happy solution to all the problems would rally the community to moderate lines. The king would have to give assurances that he would abstain from interference in internal administration that was not his business, as well as follow Cox's guidance in selection of a new cabinet. Cox felt that Faysal's illness had given Britain the opportunity to repatch the situation for him in spite of himself and was optimistic about being able to make something of him yet. Churchill approved Cox's action, and told him to propose a plan to reinstate a moderate Ministry under the Naqib.[61]

The Cabinet unexpectedly convened in the late afternoon, 28 August, at the Prime Minister's home to discuss reparations and unemployment, and the Colonial Secretary interjected the issue of Iraq, summarizing the events to date. They took note of Churchill's intention to bring the whole question of British policy towards Iraq before the Cabinet in early September and meanwhile approved Cox's actions as well as proposed actions.[62] Churchill relayed this news to Cox praising the High Commissioner for the skill and firmness with which he was handling a difficult situation.[63]

The next day Churchill again wired[64] to Cox, suggesting steps the High Commissioner should take; the most important was inducing the Naqib to form a moderate government to carry on the routine work of administration. Churchill was prepared to recommend to the Cabinet the following week to publish the treaty and to take steps to convene the Constituent Assembly which would decide whether to accept the treaty as it stood on condition that either the Naqib or Cox stated that the treaty itself provided for Iraq's escape from the mandate by admission to membership of the League and that this could not take place until a constitution was established and frontiers defined. So, queried Churchill, could they not proceed with or without Faysal's consent while he was still out of action? Then he would have to face the alternatives of supporting Cox and the Naqib or being deposed. Echoing the telegrams not sent because of Faysal's opportune appendicitis attack, Churchill added: "It should, I think, be made clear to him [Faysal] that we will not allow our whole policy to be wrecked by his obstinacy. Nor should he suppose that he will be allowed freely to retire to the Hedjaz. We have not brought him to Iraq to play the autocrat, but to settle down into a sober constitutional monarch, friendly to us."[65]

Churchill's next telegram[66] bluntly stated that everything turned on Faysal's answer. He repeated his strongest threat, namely the fall of the entire Sharifian house if Faysal refused to identify himself with Cox's moves. The Colonial Secretary must have really been thoroughly disgusted with Faysal's actions to be willing to give up his Sharifian policy.

This disgust is reflected in the letter Churchill wrote to Lloyd George, 1 September,[67] voicing his deep concern about Iraq. The first paragraph is a list of complaints showing why the Iraq situation was becoming so impossible: the Turkish menace was worse; "Feisal is playing the fool, if not the knave"; his incompetent Arab officials were not only disturbing some of the provinces but they were also failing to collect the revenue; Britain had overpaid 200,000 pounds the previous year and as Iraq would certainly not repay the money, this entailed a Supplementary Estimate, and a further deficit was nearly certain as well. The need to maintain troops in consequence of the Ankara quarrel had upset all his troop relief plans too. Everyone was shouting for evacuation of Iraq, and "in my own heart I do not see what we are getting out of it. ... Altogether I am getting to the end of my resources."

The time had come, continued Churchill, to put a different ultimatum brutally to Faysal and the Constituent Assembly "that unless they beg us to stay and to stay on our own terms in regard to efficient control" Britain will evacuate. That would be a solution. Churchill turned to the Prime Minister for definite guidance as to what he wished and was prepared to do.

Before receiving the Prime Minister's reply a few more telegrams went back and forth between London and Baghdad. Cox's telegram of 31 August[68] did not do much to dispel the Colonial Secretary's gloomy anticipatory feelings. The Naqib was averse to resuming duties at Cox's request because he felt that the king was in good health and the arrangement would flout Faysal as well as prejudice the Naqib's future usefulness by putting Faysal permanently against him. Cox agreed with this. Meanwhile, Colonel Cornwallis was doing much on his own initiative to clear out unsuitable employees.

He and Cornwallis would be guided by Churchill's telegram indicating the arguments to be used with Faysal but Cox would not visit the king for another week, giving Churchill the time needed to ask for Cabinet guidance.

Churchill had reached the end of his tether with Iraq and in his answering telegram[69] he clearly enumerated what Cox should demand from Faysal, concluding with the two ultimatums although the second was not yet concurred in by the Prime Minister. Only if Faysal acted satisfactorily would the British Cabinet assent to the treaty; if not, the Cabinet would be free either to remove Faysal or to quit Iraq. Meanwhile, "it seems to me important that you should see Feisal at the earliest moment."

Lloyd George's reply to Churchill's harried letter arrived before there was any reply from Cox on his impending interview with Faysal.[70] The Colonial Secretary probably felt irritated when he started to read the Prime Minister's calm letter, the first two-thirds of which was a history of how Britain got into Iraq during the war. Finally reaching the present situation, Lloyd George remarked that it was "disappointing that Feisal has responded so badly to your excellent efforts to make him self-supporting" but no effective case could be made against Britain "if we stand together and meet criticism courageously." The main item that would bother the Prime Minister should Britain withdraw, was the possibility that Iraq was rich in oil. Finally, in the last sentence, Lloyd George wrote something which Churchill could lean on: "On general principles, I am against a policy of scuttle, in Iraq or elsewhere, and should like you to put all the alternatives, as you see them, before the Cabinet on Thursday."[71]

Now that he had the Prime Minister's viewpoint and Cox's increasingly optimistic telegrams, Churchill dropped his plans to jettison Iraq and hoped for a positive outcome of the crisis. His reply to Lloyd George reflects his renewed optimism.[72] He summarized the latest events in Iraq defending his decision to withdraw troops in the north for "I did not feel that I could run the risk of a minor military disaster at the same time that we were making a *coup d'état* and facing a crisis in Baghdad itself." Cox had successfully dealt with the crisis and was about to come to a clear understanding with Faysal. Since he had not yet heard from Cox, Churchill did not think that the issue should yet be presented to the Cabinet for decision. The Colonial Secretary concluded: "Like you, I am very much against a policy of scuttle and after your clear expression of opinion you may be sure I shall do all in my power to avoid it."[73]

On 6 September Cornwallis saw Faysal and the king said he would have no difficulty in endorsing the High Commissioner's action and in principle he was prepared to accept reasonable safeguards for his conduct provided they did not destroy his prestige. The Naqib said that a favorable reply from Britain to the mandate and the treaty would meet with cordial response all over Iraq.[74] This was the news Churchill was hoping for and he sent a congratulatory telegram to Cox immediately, telling him that he could now bring the whole issue to Faysal. Churchill would wait to hear the result of this discussion before asking for a Cabinet decision.[75]

Cox met with Faysal for two hours, 10 September.[76] Faysal was amenable on essentials. He agreed to write a letter thanking Cox in general terms for the effective measures taken to maintain law and order, thus pleasing both Cox and Churchill. But the rest of Faysal's statements did not please Churchill for the king tried a new ploy. Faysal agreed to invite the Naqib to form a new Cabinet in consultation with Cox but only after Britain announced her policy; if Britain published the treaty accompanied by Churchill's announcement about the mandate ending once Iraq joined the League, Faysal would immediately announce his acceptance and would authorize the Naqib to sign as well as to form a Cabinet; once the treaty was signed, the Constituent Assembly formed and the Organic Law framed, then Faysal would act as a limited constitutional monarch but not until then.

Churchill sent a heated reply to Faysal's proposals.[77] He had not at all meant to make the formation of Faysal's cabinet contingent on Britain's agreeing to the treaty. The king had no right to continue ruling without a responsible Ministry. Moreover he was to be guided by Cox's advice in choosing all ministers until Iraq became a League member. Faysal should summon the Naqib at once to form a Ministry and that body should consider the treaty questions, not the king alone. Only then would he, Churchill, be ready to submit to the Cabinet the proposals for the treaty settlement. "I must be able to assure the Cabinet that Feisal has come into line, and that he is supported by the Naqib and his Cabinet, and in adopting the treaty settlement as defined they will be taking a course which will secure immediate and responsible support in Iraq."[78] The next question was whether to settle and sign the treaty with Faysal and the Cabinet or whether they should merely declare themselves in favor of it and wait until the Constituent Assembly was formed to sign the treaty. Churchill favored the lengthier second course.

Cox agreed with Churchill's demands except that he felt it was urgent to sign the treaty at once in view of recent Turkish successes.[79] He met Faysal, 18 September, and the king finally realized that he was up against an adamant Colonial Secretary and there was no more negotiatory reply but merely an agreement on his part to call on the Naqib for form a Cabinet at once.[80] Churchill congratulated Cox on the results he had achieved and was now awaiting the news that the Naqib's government was complete and ready to support the treaty before going to the British Cabinet.[81] This assurance arrived, 25 September,[82] and Cox suggested that Churchill should telegraph both the Cabinet approval and the exact text of the proposed announcement, then the Naqib and Cox would sign the treaty, and only then would the public receive the communiqué in the form of a treaty as just signed, a "fait accompli." Churchill agreed to these tactics and the matter was finally presented to the British Cabinet, 5 October, and their authorization sought for Cox to sign the treaty. Churchill argued that the treaty would enable Faysal to unite the Arabs against Turkish attack quickly reassuring the Cabinet that the treaty did not commit Britain to giving any definite military or financial assistance to Iraq. His most conclusive argument in favor of the treaty was that costs in Iraq would be reduced from eight to four million pounds as compared with the 32 million pounds Iraq cost two years earlier. The Cabinet agreed to approve the proposed treaty as well as the text of Cox's announcement, and authorized the High Commissioner to sign on His Majesty's behalf.[83]

Cox was telegraphed accordingly but told not to publish anything in Iraq until Curzon informed Britain's allies as well as the League Council.[84] The treaty was signed 10 October 1922[85] and Faysal swore a most solemn oath of friendship and loyalty. Authorization for publication of the treaty came a few days later along with telegrams of appreciation and congratulations to both Cox and Faysal.[86] A major goal had been attained.

As for outstanding questions, no action was taken, neither in civil matters nor military matters, because of the British-Turkish confrontation at the Dardanelles. Perhaps because of larger issues at stake in Turkey, military command over Iraq passed peacefully from War Office to Air Ministry control 1 October as planned.

CHAPTER 11

Policy for Palestine

Palestine too was relegated to a place of secondary importance on the Colonial Secretary's busy schedule during 1922. He was content to leave affairs in the capable hands of Sir Herbert Samuel and the Middle East Department. They were the ones who worked out the statement of policy on Palestine known as the Churchill White Paper; Churchill merely initialed each item as it was presented to him for concurrence. As in Iraq, he was involved in matters of economy, and the interest he had in Transjordan is easily understandable for it fit into this category.

The major active role that Churchill played was that of defender of the Balfour Declaration. There was growing hostility to Zionism in Britain during 1922 and criticism mounted in both Houses of Parliament. Churchill's brilliant speeches in Commons as well as his verbal and written rebuttals succeeded in reaffirming the Balfour Declaration as a basic feature of British policy. This also ensured its inclusion in the mandatory instrument, provisionally approved by the League of Nations in July 1922.

At the start of the year Churchill took care of as many economizing matters as he could, in preparation for his presentation of the Middle East Estimates in early March. He sanctioned the military amalgamation of Transjordan and Palestine while keeping the two administrations separate.[1] He agreed that it was more efficient that the Air Ministry and not the War Office should act as the Colonial Office's military agent in Palestine, as in Iraq, despite the fact that the Air Force would only consist of one or two squadrons;[2] but an army officer and not an air officer would command the Palestine troops.

CHAPTER 11 • Policy for Palestine | 161

Churchill insisted that the gendarmerie be under civil control for that way he could recover a proportion of the cost from Palestine. He ordered the raising of the Palestine British gendarmerie,[3] after approving the detailed estimate of Major-General Tudor, Commander of the Irish 'Black and Tans' Constabulary. The communiqué to the press announcing the gendarmerie scheme culminated months of negotiation to attain the goal of cost reduction plus safety.[4]

Next, Churchill tried to get Samuel to agree to pay for this new gendarmerie.[5] Samuel pointed out that the revenues of Palestine could not bear this cost and that the country was living from hand to mouth. Churchill had agreed to include this cost in Middle East Estimates in the form of a grant-in-aid from Imperial revenues, but was "strongly impressed on further reflection with the difficulty of inducing Parliament to accept this." There was growing hostility in both Houses to Zionist policy in Palestine, the Colonial Secretary telegraphed to the High Commissioner, which made it increasingly difficult to meet arguments against spending money there on an unpopular policy. He, therefore, was asking Samuel to reconsider whether Palestine could pay for the gendarmerie.

Samuel fully appreciated Churchill's position but was absolutely devoid of funds to meet this charge. Should he try to reallocate funds to pay the British troops, policy in Palestine would definitely fail.[6]

With the deadline for the Estimates drawing closer, Churchill tried again to force Samuel to agree to bear the charge for the gendarmerie.[7] But at the same time he noted to his staff that until this burden was transferred, "provision *must* be included in our votes wh[ich] sh[oul]d be increased accordingly."[8]

Pushed into a corner, Samuel fought back. He indignantly telegraphed that the Palestine Government had never asked for a British gendarmerie nor for a grant-in-aid and he resented the misrepresentation of the situation. Furthermore, even if he suppressed the entire health, education, agriculture, and antiquities costs of Palestine, the money would not only total the cost of the gendarmerie but the deed would destroy the regime of Government.[9]

Both Vernon and Shuckburgh felt that the Colonial Office should maintain the position in principle that Palestine had to ultimately find the money for the force, but to ask the High Commissioner to find the money from the first was an impossible burden.[10] Churchill thought better of the matter and wired that he was very obliged to Samuel for the way in which Samuel had always tried to meet him in these matters.[11]

Churchill turned to other ways to economize. He combined the position of General Officer Commanding with that of the civilian post of Director of Public Security putting them in the hands of General Tudor.[12] He then placed the military garrison under a Colonel Commandant of the Indian Army, pleasing the Secretary of State for India while at the same time saving money.[13]

A few small but important items that needed Churchill's decisions were the date the remainder of the British garrison in Palestine could be released and the date of the Royal Air Force takeover.[14] The first of April was the date set for the latter and the former was staggered from April through June.[15] The Interdepartmental Conference on Palestine settled all points on the transfer of material and personnel.[16] Churchill was ready to present the estimates on Palestine.

In the first months of the New Year Churchill made some decisions on Transjordan as well, all with his goal of economizing constantly before him. He did wish to see 'Abdallah settle himself firmly in the Transjordanian saddle even if it meant the possibility of Palestinian Arabs wanting him to be their king in the future.[17] He would also not allow Zionists in there for the present. "I do not want to change Abdulla or the policy followed during the last 9 months. ..."[18]

He also gave permission to aid Transjordan gain control of the desert around Wadi Sirhan bordering Iraq and Arabia to protect the Baghdad air route.[19] As a first step he allowed Philby, now Chief British Representative in Transjordan, to visit the area to establish relations with the local shaykhs but noted that "we do not want to extend our commitments in this area at the present time.[20]

Therefore when speaking on Transjordan before Parliament, Churchill could report that 'Abdallah was doing so well that Britain had no troops there at all. But Transjordan was of minor interest; the focal point in his presentation of 9 March was Palestine.[21] Churchill centered attention on the drop in expenditure and the prediction of even further reductions. Then he added, at the behest of his Middle East Department, a declaration of policy. There was a difficult situation in Palestine, said the Colonial Secretary, because of British pledges to carry out Zionist policy which included Jewish immigration. "I am bound to retain in the hands of the Imperial Government the power to carry out those pledges."[22] As a policy statement this was much too general; what was required was a statement clear-cut and yet flexible enough to work.

CHAPTER 11 • Policy for Palestine   163

Churchill was not interested in working out such a policy statement. He had tried to bring the Arab delegation to see Britain's point of view and had failed. In early February he had presented them with the draft constitution "which they have taken off to mumble over." His Middle East Department had drawn it up and it embodied the principle of indirect election of a Legislative Council. Ignoring Churchill's admonition that the document was confidential, they handed a copy to the editor of the *Morning Post*, a newspaper known to be anti-Zionist. Shuckburgh was incensed over this and drafted a letter to the delegation, which was approved by Churchill, telling them plainly that unless a satisfactory explanation could be given for this breach of faith, the Colonial Office would have no further dealings with them.[23]

The Arab delegation disclaimed showing any documents to the editor of the *Morning Post*, a disclaimer which was indignantly seconded by the editor. The Colonial Office had no alternative but to accept this as literally accurate but made it quite clear that the office was not fully satisfied with the explanations.[24]

What may have convinced Churchill that he would have nothing more to do with the delegation was their formal reply to the proposed Palestine Order in Council, 21 February.[25] The Arab delegation refused point blank to accept any constitution which would fall short of giving the Palestinian people full control of their own affairs, for to do so would mean agreeing to an instrument which probably would be "used to smother their national life under a flood of alien immigration." Then, the delegation enumerated each of the articles of the proposed constitution which they found to be wholly unsatisfactory and why, beginning with the preamble which contained the unacceptable Balfour Declaration. Instead they requested that the constitution for Palestine should safeguard the civil, political and economic interests of the people, provide for the creation of a national independent government in accordance with the League's Covenant, safeguard the legal rights of foreigners, guarantee religious equality to all peoples, guarantee rights of minorities, and guarantee the rights of the assisting power. The delegation appealed to the justice and sense of fair play of the British Government to consider their reply with sympathy since the delegation's chief object was to lay the foundation for a stable government in Palestine.

Upon receipt of this letter, a Group Council met in the Colonial Office to consider a draft reply. The draft finally submitted to Masterton Smith and Churchill was a detailed one "not because it is likely to have any great effect on the minds of the Delegation, but because the correspondence will doubtless be published…, and it is desirable that we should have a good answer to show to the world."[26] Shuckburgh apprised his chiefs of his opinion that he had little hope of inducing the Arabs to modify their proposals. "Experience has shown that we never get any further with them and that after hours of discussion they merely fall back into their original position, from which nothing can dislodge them. I anticipate a contentious reply to our letter."[27]

Shuckburgh added that they had not yet had a reply from the Zionist Organization about the proposed constitution, but he understood from Dr. Weizmann that the reply would be generally favorable. The reply to the Arab delegation was necessarily prepared with one eye on the Jews "who would cry out at once if they thought we had gone too far in the direction of placating the Arabs."[28] It was not easy, he concluded, to strike exactly the right note between conciliation and firmness, but that is what the Council had attempted to do.

Both Masterton Smith and Churchill thought the draft letter a very good one, and it was sent off to the Arab delegation, 1 March.[29] It explained the reasons why the British Government proposed to adhere to the policy of a national home for the Jewish people and outlined the extent to which they were prepared to meet the Arab delegation's objections to what the Arabs anticipated would be the effects of this policy. There was no question of repudiating the Balfour Declaration, which anteceded the League's Covenant, therefore the British Government could not endorse their request for national government for this would preclude the fulfillment of the pledge to the Jewish people; but the Government readily endorsed the five other requests.

There would be no flood of Jewish immigration, for Jews could immigrate only within the limits fixed by numbers and the interests of the Palestine population. Immigration was such a vital issue that the Colonial Secretary wanted it reserved from discussion by the Legislative Council and decided by the High Commissioner in Council, after reference to His Majesty's Government. An immigration board could be formed as an advisory panel, and the delegation was asked for its opinion on this suggestion.

The remaining half of the letter deals with the specific points raised in the letter sent by the Arab delegation, and it concludes with the hope that this reply would show that sympathetic consideration was being given to their point of view.

About a fortnight later the Arab delegation sent its reply.[30] It was a repetition of their old demand for the rescission of the Balfour Declaration reiterating each and every point it had been making ever since arriving in London. As for the proposed advisory board on immigration, because the Zionist Organization would also have a point of view that would be considered, the delegation felt that only the creation of a national government could safeguard Arab interests. In a long concluding section the delegation again appealed to British justice and deeply regretted that it seemed so irresponsive to the Secretary of State's continued courtesy in considering their representations. But, the delegation desired to remind the Secretary of State that the cause entrusted to them was nothing less than the salvation of their small country "which has been handed down to us by our fathers and forefathers from time immemorial, from the aggression of the alien Jews." There was no point in entering into detailed discussions on the Constitution since the foundation on which these details were built was a subject of disagreement.

Shuckburgh minuted[31] that that was exactly what he had expected the delegation to reply and he strongly doubted that any amount of argument would move them from this position. He was prepared to close the correspondence at the juncture but for one very important objection: Easter, the season of domestic ferment in Palestine, was coming up and it was hoped that by keeping the delegation in play a while longer things would stay quiet. Therefore he submitted a draft reply to the delegation leaving "unnoticed some of the more crudely absurd arguments." The one point that could not be passed unnoticed, according to him, was the old argument that Palestine was one of the countries promised the Sharif in 1915 by Sir Henry McMahon. Masterson Smith passed the draft letter along to Churchill for official sanction, and the letter was sent off 11 April.[32]

This relatively short letter tersely reiterated His Majesty's Government's intention to fulfill its pledges, including the Balfour Declaration, and equally tersely rejected the delegation's interpretation of the Husayn-McMahon letters. The Colonial Secretary was disappointed that the delegation should decline to cooperate with him in seeking a practical solution to the second half of the Balfour Declaration, and failed to see what advantage they expected to derive from such a purely negative attitude. But Britain would not be diverted from the line of action she conceived to "be in the best interests of the people of Palestine as a whole."[33]

As for the control of immigration the new suggestion was to set up a Standing Committee of the Legislative Council comprised of half the total number of elected members under the Chief Secretary,[34] and acting in an advisory capacity. Mr. Churchill invited the delegation to discuss details of the scheme, for he would feel regret if they should leave England without accomplishing any constructive work.

Sir Herbert Samuel arrived in England just then. He came to confer with the Colonial Secretary on finances[35] and to clear up points upon which public misconception existed.[36] He had many discussions both with the Arab delegation and the Zionist authorities in London, and met often with Shuckburgh on the question of the next step to be taken by the Colonial Office. Samuel's view was that although the local situation was outwardly calm, the undercurrent of political unrest was unabated, and that until a political settlement could be reached satisfying the reasonable claims of all parties, Britain could not count on continued immunity from disturbance. He was particularly apprehensive of what might ensue should the Arab delegation return empty handed and convinced that they had nothing more to expect from the British Government.[37]

From his interview with the Arab delegation, Samuel derived the impression that they would not press their three main demands i.e. abrogation of the Balfour Declaration, representative government, and control over immigration, if they could be given some clear assurance that the policy of the British Government was not directed towards the accomplishment of the ends desired by the more extreme Zionist elements or towards the extinction of Arab culture and political rights in Palestine. He felt that the time had come to make a public pronouncement which would definitely put both parties in their proper place and make it clear to both what Britain's intentions were. He proposed to draw up, in consultation with the Middle East Department, a statement of policy covering all the points at issue. He proposed to show the statement informally to both parties and to do his best to get them to accept it in advance. If he succeeded, the statement would then be sent to them officially for formal acceptance; if not, then the statement would be published and the Arabs given to understand that that was the Department's last word.

Samuel dictated a preliminary draft of the policy statement as well as a draft covering letter to the Zionist Organization. Shuckburgh worked with Samuel on the final drafts, and the two men were sure both that the Zionists would accept the statement and that the Arab delegation would not.[38] But the statement would present the latter with the opportunity of returning to Palestine not entirely empty handed, ostensibly to refer the issue back to the Muslim-Christian Society itself, to whom the Delegation was responsible.[39]

Shuckburgh asked Churchill to authorize Samuel to approach both the Zionists and Arabs informally with a view to securing their acceptance of the draft statement of policy drawn up by Samuel. Very early orders were solicited as Samuel was anxious to leave England at the end of the following week.[40] Authorization was given and Weizmann was immediately sent a copy with the admonition to treat the issue as very confidential partly because he had been sent a copy before one was sent to the Arabs.[41]

Samuel handed a copy of the draft statement to the Arab delegation 30 May, and the official letter to the Zionist Organization went off 3 June. Shuckburgh showed the draft to Weizmann who happened to drop by to see him the same afternoon, and Weizmann assured Shuckburgh that the Colonial Office should receive a reply intimating Zionist acceptance. "He was on the whole in good spirits, and is taking his basin of gruel with a better grace than I expected."[42] He was referring to the sections of the policy statement that displeased and disappointed the Zionists.

The covering letter to the Zionist Organization is a mere paragraph introducing the statement of policy, and asking the Zionist Organization to declare identity of aim with the British Government's policy.[43] The policy statement, purporting to have been written by the Colonial Secretary in consultation with the High Commissioner, and therefore called the Churchill White Paper, claims to summarize the essential parts of the correspondence that had already taken place between the Arab delegation and the Colonial Office.

Turning first to the Arabs, the statement declared that Arab apprehensions in Palestine were based on exaggerated interpretations of the meaning of the Balfour Declaration. The British Government had no aim to create a wholly Jewish Palestine nor had it ever contemplated the disappearance or subordination of the Arab population, language or culture in Palestine.

The Jewish population, on the other hand, was apprehensive that Britain may depart from the policy embodied in the Balfour Declaration. These fears were unfounded. After a brief description of the accomplishments of the Jewish community to date, the question raised by so many different people is openly asked: what is meant by the development of the

Jewish National Home in Palestine? "... it may be answered that it is not the imposition of a Jewish nationality upon the inhabitants of Palestine as a whole, but the further development of the existing Jewish community, with the assistance of Jews in other parts of the world, in order that it may become a center in which the Jewish people as a whole, may take, on grounds of religion and race, an interest and a pride."[44] But to achieve this, it was essential that the Jewish people should know that it was in Palestine as of right and should be internationally guaranteed and recognized to rest on ancient historic connection.

To fulfill the policy of developing a Jewish National Home it was necessary that the Jews should be able to increase their number by immigration. "This immigration cannot be so great in volume as to exceed whatever may be the economic capacity of the country at the time to absorb new arrivals."[45] The immigrants could not be a burden on the Palestinians as a whole, nor should they deprive any section of its employment. Politically undesirable persons would be excluded. It was intended to set up a special committee in Palestine consisting of members of the new elected Legislative Council to confer with the Administration on matters relating to the regulation of immigration.

Another point needing clarification was the Arab claim that Palestine was included in McMahon's promise to Husayn of an independent Arab state, a claim Britain firmly denied. Nevertheless, it was Britain's intention to foster self-government in Palestine, but gradually. The first step was establishing the nominated Advisory Council. It was now time for the second step, establishing a Legislative Council containing a large proportion of members elected on a wide franchise. Before further self-government was extended, and the Assembly placed in control over the Executive, some time should elapse to enable the institutions to become well established and to gain experience.

A policy on these lines, the gradual attainment of self-government coupled with religious liberty, was most commendable and was the best basis upon which to build the spirit of cooperation so necessary for future progress.

Subsequent to approving both the draft and the procedure drawn up by Samuel and the Middle East Department, Churchill instructed Shuckburgh to send the statement and plan of action to Lord Balfour for his opinion. The Department planned that as soon as the official reply was received from the Zionist Organization, they would write officially to the Arab delegation enclosing a copy of the correspondence with the Zionists, and saying that they propose to publish the document immediately. After an interval of forty-eight hours the papers would be published.[46] Balfour approved both the communication and the proposed procedure.[47] The short formal letter from the Zionist Organization intimating acceptance of the policy terms arrived. It was written after a special meeting of the Zionist Executive to deal with the matter at which meeting a resolution was passed assuring His Majesty's Government that the activities of the Zionist Organization would be conducted in conformity with the policy set forth in the statement of 3 June.[48] The letter, signed by Weizmann, further observed with satisfaction the reaffirmation of the Balfour Declaration and the need for immigration. It was agreed that immigration should be determined by the economic absorptive capacity of Palestine, and Weizmann strongly affirmed proceeding in harmonious cooperation, hoping that the policy "may mark the opening of a new era of peaceful progress."[49]

It remained only to write formally to the Arab delegation. Both Samuel and Shuckburgh felt that the Arabs need not be asked to reply for it certainly would be unfavorable. The delegation could then gracefully return to Palestine. They also agreed that the publication should take the form of a Parliamentary White Paper rather than of a mere communication of documents to the press.[50]

For some reason, the letter of 17 June from the Arab delegation did not arrive at the Colonial Office until after 20 June. It is a very long one, conveying their comments and criticisms on the proposed statement of policy.[51] It is "a rechauffe" of all the old arguments that have been used against us ever since they came to England, and amounts in effect to a definite refusal to accept the new statement as a basis of argument."[52] At first the Department advised against including the letter in the White Paper, and merely asked for approval of the revised draft letter to the delegation. Churchill approved the draft and the text of the White Paper, and a few days later approved Shuckburgh's reconsideration to include the Arab delegation's last letter for if it were left out the argument would run that they dared not publish it because its arguments were irrefutable.[53]

Two more short items are included in the White Paper. The first is the Colonial Office's reply to the Arab delegation enclosing the correspondence with the Zionist Organization, stating that the Zionists accepted the policy as laid down in the British statement.[54] It was hoped that this fresh definition of policy should finally allay all Arab apprehensions, and the delegation was informed that all the correspondence was being laid before Parliament, the League Council, as well as the Officer Administering the Government of Palestine

The Officer Administering the Government of Palestine, Sir Wyndham Deedes, received a telegram in the name of the Colonial Secretary summarizing the official statement of policy and giving him permission to publish it on 3 July.[55] This is the last item included in the White Paper which was formally laid before Parliament on Saturday, 1 July 1922.

The event that knocked Churchill out of his passive role was the passage in the House of Lords of a resolution against the Balfour Declaration, 21 June.[56] The anti-Zionists mustered their forces, particularly to denounce the Rutenberg concession which they saw as the beginning of Jewish domination in Palestine, because they knew that the Colonial Office Vote was to take place shortly. That was to be the occasion for the Commons to approve Britain's Palestine policy.

Churchill could not immediately make a statement in Commons to remove the impression this resolution made, because the next day Sir Henry Wilson was murdered and Parliament was closed. The resolution of the Lords was dangerous for Palestine policy and Churchill knew that he would have to ask for a vote of confidence from the House of Commons specifically upholding the Balfour Declaration.

Churchill finally rose in the House of Commons to defend his Palestine policy, 4 July.[57] He was addressing a Parliament that was wavering in its backing of the 1917 pledge to the Zionists, so he opened by placing the major issues before the House immediately, and made an "amusing and clever speech ... a gala debate."[58] First, were they to keep the 1917 pledge, and, second, were the measures being taken by the Colonial Office to fulfill that pledge reasonable and proper measures. Parliament was committed to the 1917 pledge, Churchill stated unequivocally, and to those opposed to this policy he directed his fire:

> You have no right to say this kind of thing as individuals; you have not right to support public declarations made in the name of your country in the crisis and the heat of the War, and then afterwards, when all is cold and prosaic, to turn around and attack the Minister of the Department which is faithfully and laboriously endeavoring to

translate these perfervid enthusiasms into the sober, concrete facts of day-to-day administration. I say, in all consistency and reasonable fair play, this does not justify the House of Commons at this stage in repudiating the general Zionist policy.[59]

Having admonished the house, he turned to the second issue: whether the measures being taken by the Colonial Office to fulfill the pledge to secure the establishment of the Jewish National Home were reasonable and proper measures. The prime focus of attention was the proposed Rutenberg concession. The previous autumn the Colonial Office had signed an agreement with Rutenberg undertaking, subject to the fulfillment of certain conditions in the interval, to grant him a concession for his hydro-electrical scheme within a period of two years. Rutenberg was pressing the Colonial Office to agree in principle to the electrification of the Jaffa-Jerusalem railroad line. The Crown Agents and their engineering advisers approved and suggested informing Rutenberg of this. The Middle East Department favored the concession because it was always trying to divert the attention of the Zionists from political to industrial activities, and preaching to them that their best chance of reconciling the Arabs to the Zionist policy was to show them the practical advantages accruing to the country from Zionist enterprise. The Rutenberg concession fulfilled all this."[60]

"What better steps could we take ... than to interest Zionists in the creation of this new Palestinian world which, without injustice to a single individual, without taking away one scrap of what was there before, would endow the whole country with the assurance of a greater prosperity and the means of a higher economic and social life?" queried the Colonial Secretary of the Commons. The Rutenberg concession followed regular Colonial Office procedure and was scrutinized by the agents and engineers. Also, no one else applied for the concession. Coming to the crux of the issue, Churchill faced his audience.

> I come to Mr. Rutenberg himself. He is a Jew. I cannot deny that. I do not see why that should be a cause of reproach, at any rate on the part of those who have hitherto supported Zionist policy. It is hard enough ... to make a New Zion, but if, over the portals of the new Jerusalem, you are going to inscribe the legend, "No Israelite need apply," then I hope the House will permit me to confine my attention exclusively to Irish matters.[61]

Furthermore, Rutenberg was not a Bolshevik, and Churchill had proof that Rutenberg had been kicked out of Russia by the Bolsheviks.[62]

Churchill felt that he had to ask for the vote on the Colonial Office estimates to be taken as a vote of confidence for the Palestine mandate "because we cannot carry out our pledges to the Zionists ... unless we are permitted to use Jews, and use Jews freely within what limits are proper, to develop new sources of wealth in Palestine."[63] He did not think the supplementary estimate, approximately 308,000 pounds, was too much for Britain to pay for the control of Palestine and for keeping the word she gave before all the nations of the world.

Churchill received his vote of confidence, 292–35, much to the dismay of *The Times* which was strongly against the Rutenberg concession. The editor complained that the Colonial Secretary obtained his desired goal by the "simple expedient of giving the Commons the heartiest laugh they have had for many a long day."[64]

Because Commons approved Churchill's statement that the Balfour Declaration was an indivisible part of the Palestine mandate, the Arab delegation was ordered to return home at once. The Middle East Department thought it would be good for Churchill to see them one more time but the Colonial Secretary refused and delegated the duty to an assistant.[65]

When it came to dealing with a memorial signed by members of both Houses and forwarded by Lord Islington, a leading anti-Zionist, to postpone the Palestine mandate from coming before the League,[66] Churchill did not delegate anyone else to deal with matter. Churchill rejected the request because the overwhelming majority of Commons confirmed his policy. Such activities encouraged the Arab delegation to maintain an attitude of uncompromising obstinacy, and the memorial would be circulated within Palestine as proof that Parliament did not support the Palestine policy and violent effort could therefore change it. Should there be an outbreak, Islington and his colleagues would be responsible, claimed Churchill.[67]

Churchill defended his strong stance to Balfour by claiming that it was quite possible there would be bloodshed in the near future, in which case his opponents would say, 'See what comes of your Zionist Policy.' He would like to be able to reply 'Did I not warn you of the consequences of your meddling?'[68]

Islington replied that this was constitutional criticism and he took strong exception to Churchill's placing future bloodshed in Palestine on them. Automatic fidelity to the Coalition Government was not the acid test of patriotism.[69]

Further criticism came from Lord Sydenham, another leading anti-Zionist, who asked if Churchill really wished him to believe that criticism of Government policy made the critics responsible for disasters which could follow.[70] Churchill replied by asking how he had managed the political somersault from favoring the Balfour Declaration to opposing it.[71] Sydenham explained how,[72] but Churchill wrote that the most important reason had been omitted; it was popular to be pro-Zionist in 1917 and now it was a laborious task to give honorable effect to that pledge.[73] Each refused to accept what the other wrote.

Such bickering was of relative unimportance compared to the inter-governmental squabbling that at more than one point almost prevented the Palestine mandate from being considered by the League of Nations. America would not approve the Palestine mandate unless it was embodied in a treaty that would ensure American privileges there.[74] Italy was against the League Council appointing the Palestine Holy Places Commission and its chairman.[75] The Vatican was against Britain's plan of having non-Christians form the majority of the membership of the Holy Places Commission.

The Colonial Office tried to clear up all these objections as quickly as possible because the Middle East Department and Herbert Samuel felt that formal approval by the League of Nations of the Palestine mandate would put the Office in a much stronger position vis-á-vis the anti-Zionist critics, end all uncertainty and morally sanction Britain's administration there. Churchill felt that formal League approval of the Palestine mandate made no difference to the administration of Palestine,[76] but followed his advisors' line anyway.

Churchill agreed to America's demand for a treaty on Palestine provided it contained a recital of the mandate in the form finally approved by the League and he approved the draft asking the Foreign Office to go ahead. Just by starting negotiations it was hoped to obtain from the United States some statement that would satisfy the League Council that there was no American objection to the terms of the Palestine mandate.[77] The scheme worked.

As for the Vatican's objections to the plan for the Commission, a telegram to Balfour in Churchill's name gave him a free hand to devise a plan that would satisfy all parties.[78] Even though the Vatican was not a League member, it was very powerful in that it could make use of representatives of minor Catholic powers to stultify all of Britain's efforts. Colonial and Foreign Office representatives met with Count de Salis, the Vatican representative, in London during June, and the result was a new form for Article 14 of the mandate,[79] which the Pope obliquely referred to with favor during Samuel's interview with him in Rome, 6 July.[80]

There remained the objections of Italy. Informal discussions with the Italian representative at the end of June, initiated under the oral instructions of the Colonial Secretary, as well as a formal conversation held in Balfour's room 3 July, removed these objections.[81] Britain would not obstruct Italian enterprise in Palestinian public works and would give diplomatic support to Italy's claims for economic concessions in Asia Minor, but Churchill absolutely refused to influence the British members of the Holy Places Commission in favor of Italy's interests.[82] Italy finally agreed to approve the mandates for Palestine and Iraq.

Young and Shuckburgh attended the secret meeting of the Council of the League of Nations on the morning of 19 July at which the question of the mandates for Syria and Palestine finally came up. But because the proceedings took a rather unexpected turn,[83] it was not until 22 July that the Council reconvened, and, after six hours of discussion finally approved both the Palestine and Syrian mandates subject to some minor changes. Then 24 July, a public meeting was held to announce these decisions.[84] Weizmann immediately wrote a short congratulatory letter to Churchill, in which said:

> To you personally, as well as to those who have been associated with you at the Colonial Office, we tender our most grateful thanks. Zionists throughout the world deeply appreciate the unfailing sympathy you have consistently shown towards their legitimate aspirations and the great part you have played in securing for the Jewish people the opportunity of rebuilding its national home in peaceful co-operation with all sections of the inhabitants of Palestine.[85]

Knowing how well Weizmann knew the inner workings of the Colonial Office, this letter might have been written a bit tongue in cheek. He knew that throughout 1922 Churchill had only been intimately concerned with the military and monetary aspects of Palestine policy and had left most everything else to his Middle East Department and Sir Herbert Samuel. He also could not have been too happy that the economic absorptive capacity idea had become formal British policy for as it was worded, there was no clear indication of how it would be defined nor to what uses it would be put. Yet it was a logical thing to write, for 1922 was a culmination of Churchill's earlier plans for Palestine; he had designed the machine and set it going and felt that he could leave it to others to tend. Also, it was Churchill who had stood up and defended the Palestine policy in Parliament and obtained the much-needed vote of confidence. More important nothing the Middle East Department wanted to do could be done without the Colonial Secretary's, albeit at times offhanded, initialed sanction. So, Weizmann's letter of thanks was appropriate.

The mandatory instrument legalized the Jewish National Home. It also recognized the separation of Transjordan from Palestine. Raids by Ibn Sa'ud's followers caused a brief crisis over Transjordan for 'Abdallah wanted permission to retake the oasis of Jauf.[86] When this permission was refused the Amir decided that he would rather not remain in Transjordan than not be able to protect his tribes from the Sa'udis. This withdrawal would necessitate a more expensive provision for the area as well as injure Arab opinion, therefore Samuel urged that 'Abdallah and Philby be asked to come to London for discussions on this as well as the status and finances of Transjordan.[87]

"Major Young," minuted the Colonial Secretary. "Please let me have your comments on this, bearing in mind that I was very averse to your telegram preventing Abdulla from coming to London as arranged. I had particularly looked forward to his visit here, and I blame myself for having allowed myself to be dissuaded."[88]

Churchill was referring to a long series of telegrams from the start of the year from Samuel urging Churchill to invite 'Abdallah to come to England. The Middle East Department, especially Young, who was acting for Shuckburgh because the latter was on sick leave, had been against such an invitation, and Churchill had given in.[89]

Now, with the arrival of Samuel's latest telegram, Churchill blew up at Young. He did not care whether Philby accompanied the Amir or not provided that Samuel was confident that the affairs of Transjordan would not suffer in the interval. Samuel could provide a telegraphic report on the financial arrangements connected with the territory to be used in discussion with the Amir. "I think it is a very serious thing to treat with indifference the strong desire of a cautious man like Sir Herbert Samuel to have this nest of disturbance suppressed."[90] General Tudor should be asked for a military report in consultation with the air authorities and with 'Abdallah's authorities as to whether Jauf could be occupied without Britain getting deeply entangled. The Colonial Secretary proposed to telegraph accordingly and overly politely concluded his minute to Young: "Pray let me have your comments so that I may settle the matter on my return this afternoon."[91]

The comments were ready as requested. Young defended his advice not to occupy Jauf because it was opposed by Air Marshall Trenchard. As for refusal to grant any more money to 'Abdallah and insistence on cutting his grant-in-aid down to 50,000 pounds the coming year, Young was merely following the Colonial Secretary's instructions. Churchill immediately noted in the margin in red: "I don't wish to cut Transjordania down next year. A little over-draft might be permitted."[92] On 'Abdallah's visit to London, Young wrote that he had always understood that Churchill' intention for 'Abdallah's personal visit was social, to keep him happy. What Philby was proposing through Samuel was tantamount to transferring the administration of Transjordan temporarily to London, over the head of the High Commissioner. Two other reasons rendered the moment inopportune for the visit: the recrudescence of Ibn Sa'ud's advance and the possibility that matters may not be successfully arranged with Faysal in Iraq. "It would be most inconvenient for one brother to be in London if for any reason the other was at the same time taking up an openly hostile line in Iraq," concluded the defense.[93]

Churchill sent a personal and secret telegram to Samuel the next day. As soon as Samuel would reply to the dispatch about finances, Churchill would decide on the definite date of 'Abdallah's visit provided Samuel reassured the Colonial Secretary about the imminence of the Ibn Sa'ud menace. Samuel also had to reassure him that the absence of both 'Abdallah and Philby at the same time would not be too serious to handle. As for the occupation of Jauf, Samuel was to ask Tudor to consult with Air and local Arab authorities and then report whether the military advantages were proportional to the effort involved and that Britain would not be checked or entangled.[94]

Samuel answered the next day reassuring the Colonial Secretary as requested and promising a dispatch about Transjordanian finances in next week's bag; he was sure that all outstanding matters would be adequately discussed in the conference in London.[95] The invitation to 'Abdallah was despatched, arrangements were made for financing his stay at the Carlton Hotel with his entourage, and for meeting him with royal carriage and a guard of honor.[96] The few last minute snags were straightened out,[97] and the Amir arrived 13 October. But before 'Abdallah could meet with the Colonial Secretary a massive upheaval in the British Government took place and Churchill was out of power.

The Coalition Government of David Lloyd George did not fall because of one blow, but because of an intricate intertwining of situations and events.[98] Some leading factors causing this downfall included the personality and devious methods of the Prime Minister himself. Another contributing factor was the fact that Lloyd George relied heavily on a few Conservative ministers to keep that party in line, especially on Andrew Bonar Law the Conservative leader; but Bonar Law resigned his office early in 1921 because of ill health and was replaced by Austen Chamberlain. Chamberlain was an ineffective leader who in the end united the Conservatives against himself and the coalition. In addition, there was a split within the Liberal party itself over the leadership of Lloyd George and Herbert H. Asquith, dating back to 1916 when Lloyd George replaced Asquith as prime minister; this split distracted Liberals from determining future policies.

Another factor contributing to the fall of the Government was the opposition and criticism of the press. Lloyd George offended the most important single journalist Lord Northcliffe who began a crusade against the Prime Minister's policies in *The Times* and the *Daily Mail*; his brother, Lord Roterhmere, and his papers, the *Daily Mirror* and the *Sunday Pictorial* did the same. They were joined by Lord Beaverbrook, the proprietor of the *Daily Express*. This accounted for over half the London daily circulation.[99]

Against this background a series of events occurred which gradually built up a body of Conservative Members of Parliament which opposed one or two aspects of government policy or party leadership until in October 1922 a peak was reached and the majority voted against the Coalition. The Irish treaty was a main source of discontent and caused the secession of a sizable fragment of the Conservative party from the Coalition, to form the core of the "Diehard" group. Then came the crisis over an election in January 1922 which would have forced the Conservatives to commit themselves for or against permanent coalition.

Important too were two serious blows to Lloyd George's foreign policy. The first was the failure of the Genoa Conference which the Prime Minister had called in an attempt to get an all-Europe non-aggression pact; this would have involved recognizing the Soviet Government. But the signing of the

Treaty of Rapallo by Russia and Germany as well as French antagonism frustrated these hopes.

The second blow to Lloyd George's foreign policy was the Greek rout in Asia Minor. In July 1922 Greek and Turkish forces were fairly evenly balanced in Asia Minor though the Greek lines were overextended. King Constantine decided to retire from the forward position and consolidate around Smyrna. Before doing so he diverted some of his force to Constantinople in a vain attempt to take over that city. This Greek diversion weakened Greek lines around Smyrna and Kemal's forces resumed their offensive there. By the end of August Greek withdrawal had become a rout ruining Lloyd George's pro-Greek policy and leading to the Chanak crisis which was in effect the final straw causing Lloyd George's downfall.[100]

Churchill's role was a major one, but center stage was held by Lloyd George himself. The most important contribution that Churchill made was ending his opposition to the Prime Minister's Turkish policy. By siding with Lloyd George, these two masters of persuasion carried the Cabinet along with them to what many contemporaries believed was the brink of war. There are times when the threat of force can avert a major war and in the case of Chanak this brinkmanship worked. But Chanak also served as a catalyst for the Conservatives who gathered in the Carlton Club, 19 October, to discuss whether to back Lloyd George's actions and the Coalition Government; the vote was overwhelmingly against such a stand and the Prime Minister had to resign, carrying his Government down with him. Again actions with regard to the Middle East affected Churchill's career for not only did he lose his ministerial office but in the November elections he lost his seat in Parliament as well.

CHAPTER 12

The Shaping of the Middle East

Can one person influence the course of history? After reading the facts about four years of Winston S. Churchill's long career, one would have to conclude that—given the limitations of his entering onto a scene already in play and the limitations connected with his offices—the answer for this particular person is in the affirmative. His fertile and creative mind grasped the problems presented to him in all their aspects, he milked dry the theories of all his advisers, combined their advice with his own experience and ideas, and formulated his policy. Policy formulation is important but it is not enough; it is but a beginning. Enactment must follow or the policy will forever remain in the realm of theory. Churchill's contribution to Fertile Crescent policy was important both for its formulation and for its enactment. The policy he developed can be summarized succinctly in a few sentences but his activities to enact it can and do fill a book. I have attempted to trace both aspects of Churchill's contribution to the shaping of the Middle East.

When, in 1919, the Prime Minister appointed him Secretary of State for War and Air, Churchill's instructions called for rapid demobilization and strict economizing. The Middle East was only one of the world areas under his responsibility, but gradually, as the year unfolded, the War Secretary realized that he had to develop a new policy for it. Such a policy had to take into account the two ingredients of demobilization and economizing plus an ingredient thrust upon him from the outside: Bolshevism. Churchill was an imperialist and saw the British Empire as the greatest and most effective international organization in history. Imperial greatness was the enduring reality to him and he saw Bolshevism as a menace to this, especially in the Middle East. By 1920 he found himself caught between his duties as War Secretary and his duties to himself to uphold his imperial beliefs.

To meet these challenges, Churchill developed a Middle East policy with the War Office which included the use of a combination of airplanes, armored cars, police forces, small garrisons and subsidies. But when he tried to implement this innovative policy he met frustration no matter which way he turned. No one Government office controlled the Middle East and each of the three offices that had a say—the Foreign, India, and War Offices—was out to protect its own interests. Disgusted by the lack of progress, Churchill used his persuasive powers to convince the Cabinet to create a Middle East Department as part of the Colonial Office. His activities with regard to the Middle East were part of the reason he was asked to become Secretary of State for the Colonies.

Churchill, as Colonial Secretary, set his new house in order and rounded out his policy for the Middle East centered on the Fertile Crescent. He added a new and crucial item to the plan worked out earlier as War Secretary: sponsoring the Sharifians. Once his policy outlines were prepared, Churchill conferred in Cairo early in 1921 with all the Middle East experts to fill in the details. He gave the conference its direction and had to convince the Prime Minister via telegram to confirm the decisions made in Cairo. Faysal had agreed to become king of Iraq after Churchill negotiated with him in London; the conference sanctioned the choice. To get 'Abdallah to agree to become custodian of Transjordan, a decision reached earlier in London, Churchill traveled to Jerusalem to negotiate with him as well. He too agreed and the first step in severing Transjordan from Palestine was complete.

The euphoria of the Cairo Conference was followed by months of humdrum and detailed work overcoming as many problems as possible before Churchill presented the Cairo decisions to Parliament for approval. Churchill was not going to let anything stand in the way of this opportunity to try out his new policy, and his Parliamentary presentation was one of his best. Churchill felt, after attaining Parliamentary sanction, that he could move on to new spheres and leave the Fertile Crescent in the competent hands of his Department and the High Commissioners. His interest in economizing remained, but whereas Iraq slowly progressed along the path set for it, Palestine bogged down in nationalist strife. Churchill was forced to make some plan changes because of Zionist pressure and an unyielding Arab delegation. He tried to keep peace by doing nothing and 1921 drifted to a close.

Ireland was the focal point of Churchill's attention in 1922 but his was drawn back into the Fertile Crescent arena when Faysal refused to sign the Iraq treaty. The Colonial Secretary, after sparring with Faysal long distance, decided to depose the king and was in the midst of preparations to do so when Faysal came down with appendicitis. This opportune illness in effect saved the situation and Faysal conceded defeat by signing the desired treaty.

Churchill was also drawn back into Palestine issues for anti-Zionism was on the rise in Britain. He played a passive role in drawing up the new policy statement on Palestine, but even a passive role for a man in his position had an effect and the "economic absorptive capacity" principle became a fundamental part of Palestine policy. His active role was that of defender of the Balfour Declaration and his speeches in Parliament ensured that it remained a basic part of British policy as well as an integral part of the mandatory instrument for that area.

During these four years a new force built up in the Middle East which, at the end of 1922, Churchill viewed as a challenge to the British Empire. The nationalist Turks led by Mustafa Kemal smashed the Greek forces in Asia Minor and advanced to the Straits and Constantinople. Churchill felt that should the Turks cross into Europe Britain would lose all the gains of World War I. He stood by Lloyd George in a bellicose response and though the brinkmanship worked and Kemal stopped his forward surge, the warlike activities of the two ministers contributed to the downfall of the Coalition Government. Churchill lost his ministerial post and then his seat in Parliament.

The story of these four years is presented in detail so as to enable the reader to feel how Churchill worked to attain his goals and also to feel his frustrations when he seemed to get nowhere. People in high office develop their own methods to get what they want and Churchill was a master at this. His tactics were many: he built up an arsenal of reliable data and memoranda, he then used this arsenal to convince those men whose supportive opinions he needed and only then did he approach the high level decision makers. At times he used a personal approach to Cabinet members or to Lloyd George, but his most effective tactic was his oral appeals to Parliament. Churchill's maneuverings can serve as an example of how a person in high government position in any country participates in the decision making process and how such work can in turn influence such a person's career.

The story contains many echoes of the modern Middle East situation. There are the frustrations of the big powers trying to cope with the various nationalisms of the area—Arab, Israeli, Turkish, Greek—while attempting to stay out of any military involvement. Economizing efforts have strong echoes in the present day as do intergovernmental and intragovernmental joustings, with each government or department out for its own ends. A strong echo too is the present day individual who is trying to shape Middle East policy.

Churchill helped mold the Fertile Crescent at a time when it was at its most malleable. He helped lay the foundations for the kingdom of Iraq, the Amirate of Transjordan, Palestine policy, Air Force control, and the Middle East Department of the Colonial Office, aside from a myriad of smaller items. He really did think that what he was doing was best for Great Britain in the first instance, and for the Fertile Crescent in the second instance. If history judges otherwise it is through the knowledge and wisdom attained with hindsight. The policy Churchill developed and enacted did bring a semblance of peace and development to the Fertile Crescent for a while: in Palestine—with one or two exceptions—until 1936 when the Arabs rose in rebellion; in Iraq—again with some exceptions—until 1932 when Iraq stood ostensibly as an independent state and member of the League of Nations. The Amirate of Transjordan continued to be shaped by British advisers and became the Kingdom of Jordan in 1950 with the Sharifian line still in existence. Reliance on modern technology as a means of reducing dependence on expensive manpower became accepted British policy throughout the empire. On the other hand, the policy developed and enacted by Churchill introduced anti-British sentiment as a fundamental principle of Iraqi politics, laid the groundwork for the further paring down of the Balfour Declaration in Palestine, and created what many consider to be an artificial unviable state in Transjordan. The only aspect of Churchill's to come through almost unscathed was the economy effected by reliance on modern technology to control the vast reaches of the British Empire. Whether for good or ill, Winston S. Churchill, as an individual, did help shape the contours of the Middle East. His activities reacted on his own career and the experiences probably carried over to the next time he was in a position to help shape such policy, as Prime Minister of Great Britain.

Endnotes

Chapter 1

1. A. G. Gardiner, *Prophets, Priests and Kings* (London: 1914), 231.
2. Stephen Roskill, *Hankey: Man of Secrets* (London: 1970), Vol. I, 185.
3. D. Lloyd George, *War Memoirs* (Boston: 1933), Vol. 3, 27.
4. Ralph G. Martin, *Jennie: The Life of Lady Randolph Churchill* (Englewood Cliffs, N. J.: 1971), vol. 2, 69.
5. A. G. Gardiner, *op.cit*, 231.

Chapter 2

1. Elie Kedourie, *England and the Middle East, the Destruction of the Ottoman Empire 1914–1921* (London: 1956), 22.
2. H. F. Frischwasser-Ra'anan, *The Frontiers of a Nation* (London: 1955), ch. 2.
3. For text, see J.C. Hurewitz, *Diplomacy in the Near and Middle East, a Documentary Record, 1914–1956* (New York: 1956), vol. 2, 7–11. (Hereafter cited as *Diplomacy*); Briton Busch, *Britain, India, and the Arabs, 1914–1921* (Los Angeles: 1971), 66–67.
4. For text, see Hurewitz, *Diplomacy*, vol. 2, 11–12.
5. Isaiah Friedman, *The Question of Palestine, 1914–1918; British-Jewish-Arab Relations* (London: 1973), 15.
6. Friedman, *op. cit.*, 19–21, praises the report as one of acute political thinking; Busch, *op. cit.*, 48, describes it as vague and idealistic and states that it did not take into account the claims of other powers.
7. Frischwasser-Ra'anan, *op. cit.*, ch. 3; George Antonius, *The Arab Awakening* (New York: 1939), ch. 13; P. C. Hanna, *British Policy in Palestine* (Washington, D. C.: 1942), ch. 2; Jukka Nevakivi, *Britain, France and the Arab Middle East 1914–1920* (London: 1969), ch. 2; Friedman, *op. cit.*, x.
8. For text, see Hurewitz, *Diplomacy*, vol. 2, 18–22; Busch, *op. cit.*, 81–88; Friedman, *op. cit.*, ch. 7.
9. Kedourie, *op. cit.*, 41; Kedourie lists other reasons for secrecy, including incompatibility with the new principle of self-determination, and shielding the Sharif from accusations of being a traitor to Islam for choosing to conspire with Christian states against a Muslim state. See also Friedman, *op. cit.*, 107–9; Busch, *op. cit.*, 81–88; Nevakivi, *op. cit.*, ch. 2; Antonius, *op. cit.*, ch. 13.
10. For text, see Hurewitz, *Diplomacy*, vol. 2, 23–25.
11. Kedourie, *op. cit.*, 33; for India's point of view, see Busch, *op. cit.*, 71–78.

12 For text, see Hurewitz, *Diplomacy*, vol. 2, 13–17; for details on the Husayn-McMahon Correspondence, see Antonius, *op. cit.*, chs. 7–12; Hanna, *op. cit.*, ch. 2; Esco Foundation, *Palestine: a study of Jewish, Arab, and British policies* (New Haven: 1947), vol. 1, 63–70; Ronald Storrs, *Memoirs* (New York: 1937), ch. 8; Friedman, *op. cit.*, ch. 6.
13 The most detailed books are Leonard Stein, *The Balfour Declaration* (New York: 1961), and Friedman, *op. cit.*; for text, see Hurewitz, *Diplomacy*, vol. 2, 25–26; see also Hanna, *op. cit.*, 30–38; C. Weizmann, *Trial and Error* (Philadelphia: 1949), chs. 14–18; Esco, *op. cit.*, vol. 1, 74–118.
14 Busch, *op. cit.*, ch. 3.
15 For text, see Hurewitz, *Diplomacy*, vol. 2, 36–37.
16 Frischwasser-Ra'anan, *op. cit.*, ch. 4.
17 Nevakivi, *op. cit.*, 77.
18 For India's role in the formation of Britain's policy toward the Arab Middle East in the era of World War I, see Busch, *op. cit.*
19 Busch, *op. cit.*, 205; he also describes Sykes' impassioned appeals on the need for coordination.
20 Curzon Papers, Box on Middle East, India Records Office, London, F/11/8, F/12/1.
21 The Arab Bureau was established in 1916 in Cairo to coordinate Middle Eastern policies. Busch, *op. cit.*, 99–109.
22 For texts, see Hurewitz, *Diplomacy*, vol. 2, 28–30; see also Antonius, *op. cit.*, ch. 13; Hanna, *op. cit.*, chs. 2, 3; P. W. Ireland, *Iraq: A Study in Political Development* (London: 1937), chs. 7–9; Busch, *op. cit.*, 194, 198–99.
23 For detailed analyses, see Kedourie, *op. cit.*, chs. 2, 3, 5; Busch, *op. cit.*, 188–214.
24 Busch, *op. cit.*, 277–85.
25 Frischwasser-Ra'anan, *op. cit.*, 297–300; Nevakivi, *op. cit.*, 91–92.
26 For text, see Hurewitz, *Diplomacy*, vol. 2, 50–59; see also Nevakivi, *op. cit.*, chs. 6, 7; Busch, *op. cit.*, 303–9.
27 Max Beloff, *Imperial Sunset* (New York: 1970), vol. 1, 287–98.
28 For text, see Hurewitz, *Diplomacy*, vol. 2, 66–74; Kedourie, *op. cit.*, 143–45; Busch, *op. cit.*, 309–16.
29 For texts, see Hurewitz, *Diplomacy*, vol. 2, 62–64; see also Nevakivi, *op. cit.*, 167–70.
30 Busch, *op. cit.*, 316–21.
31 Summary of proceedings, 17 September 1919, Cabinet papers, series 21, file 153 (hereafter only the numbers will be used), Public Record Office, London; also discussion by the Five at Paris on 15 September 1919, see Woodward and Butler, *Documents on British Foreign Policy 1919–1939* (London: 1952), vol. 1, 685–701.
32 Kedourie, *op. cit.*, 185.
33 13 September 1919, Cabinet papers, series 21, file 153; War Office Papers, 32/5730.
34 See note 31.
35 Busch, *op. cit.*, 350–54.
36 Nevakivi, *op. cit.*, ch. 9.
37 Cabinet 16 (1920), 23 March 1920, Cabinet papers, 23/20.
38 For text see Hurewitz, *Diplomacy*, vol. 2, 75–77; see Nevakivi, *op. cit.*, 148–155, chs. 11, 12; Busch, *op. cit.*, 375–88.
39 For text see Hurewitz, *Diplomacy*, vol. 2, 81–87.
40 A. J. P. Taylor, *English History 1914–1945* (Oxford: 1965), ch. 4.
41 Idem.

Chapter 3

1. Churchill—Lloyd George, 10 January 1919, Churchill Papers (hereafter Ch.P.) 2/105.
2. *The Times*, 18 July 1917; Sara Reguer, "Churchill's Role in the Dardanelles Campaign," *British Army Review*, Dec. 1994, No. 108, 70–80; some of the best books on Lloyd George are Lord Beaverbrook, *The Decline and Fall of Lloyd George* (London: 1963); Michael Kinnear, *The Fall of Lord George: The Political Crisis of 1922* (Toronto: 1973); Donald McCormick, *The Mask of Merlin: A Critical Study of David Lloyd George* (London: 1963); Frank Owen, *Tempestuous Journey: Lloyd George, His Life and Times* (London: 1954).
3. The War Office is the department of the civil government which administers the military forces of the Crown. The Secretary of State has general control and all departments report to him through a member of his War Council. In Churchill's time, 1919–20, this Council was composed of himself and seven others. Four were military men: the Chief of the Imperial General Staff who was the advisor on military policy, the Adjutant-General Staff who ran personnel, the Quarter-Master General who had charge of housing and maintaining the army, and the Master-General of the Ordinance, in charge of stores and material. Two were political members: the Parliamentary Under-Secretary of State and the Financial Secretary. The last Council member was the permanent Under-Secretary of State who was the coordinating link between the Secretary of State and the War Office. Hampden Gorden, *The War Office* (London: 1935), 4–9.
4. Memorandum by Churchill, 19 January 1919, Lloyd George Papers (hereafter L.G.P.) F/8/3/3, Beaverbrook Library, London: see also C.L. Mowat, *Britain between the Wars, 1918–1940* (Chicago: 1955), 22–23.
5. Memorandum by Churchill, 19 January 1919, L.G.P. F/8/3/3.
6. Churchill—Lloyd George, 27 January 1919, Ch.P. 16/3.
7. 28 January 1919, Cabinet Papers (hereafter CAB) 23/9, Public Record Office, London; for more details on demobilization see Martin Gilbert, *Winston S. Churchill: The Stricken World* (Boston: 1975), chap. 10. Churchill's activities took place against the backdrop of the Paris Peace Conference and Anglo-French sparring over the massive problems to be solved, including the Arab question. See Nevakivi, *op. cit.*, chs. 6, 7; A. Klieman, *Foundations of British Policy in the Arab World: The Cairo Conference of 1921* (Baltimore: 1970), ch. 2.
8. Memorandum by Churchill, January 1919, Ch.P. 16/20.
9. Diary of Mrs. Speirs, 24 January 1919, Ch.P.
10. 17 March 1919, CAB 23/15.
11. Churchill—Lloyd George, 14 March 1919, Ch.P. 16/21.
12. Churchill—Lloyd George, 9 April 1919, Ch.P. 16/6.
13. 29 May 1919, Parliamentary Debates.
14. One of the most detailed descriptions of Churchill and Bolshevism is to be found in Gilbert, *op. cit.*, chapters 12–22, 24, 25, 43.
15. Eastern Report no. cxii, 20 March 1919, cited in Ivar Spector, *The Soviet Union and the Muslim World, 1917–1956* (Washington: 1956), 20.
16. For details, see Spector, *op. cit.* It is amazing to note that some scholars relegate this most important factor to a mere paragraph or so. Cf. Klieman, *op. cit.*, 25; Nevakivi, *op. cit.*, 176.
17. 12 January 1919, Ch.P. 16/1; Churchill—Long, 18 January 1919, Ch.P. 16/3; Long—Prime Minister, 1 February 1919, L.G.P. F/33/2/8.
18. Churchill—Long, 8 February 1919, Ch.P. 16/1.

19 Churchill—Birkenhead, March 1919, Ch.P. 16/5; for details on the Air Ministry, see Gilbert, *op. cit.*, chap. 11.
20 Churchill—Lloyd George, September 1919, Ch.P. 16/11. This arrived on the Prime Minister's desk just at the time that Lloyd George was ready to try and heal the breach in Britain's relations with France which had reached a low point in May 1919 when the two premiers had almost come to blows. Nevakivi, *op. cit.*, ch. 8; Busch, *op. cit.*, 346–55.
21 Churchill—Lloyd George, 1 May 1919, Ch.P. 16/7.
22 So much has been written on Mesopotamia that a selected list of recommended references will have to suffice: A.J. Barker, *The Bastard War: The Mesopotamian Campaign of 1914–1918* (New York: 1967); Lady Bell, ed., *The Letters of Gertrude Bell* (London: 1927); Elizabeth Burgoyne, *Gertrude Bell: From Her Personal Papers, 1914–1926* (London: 1961), 2 vol.; Briton Busch, *op. cit.*; Henry A. Foster, *The Making of Modern Iraq* (Oklahoma: 1935); M.A. Fitzsimons, *Empire by Treaty: Britain and the Middle East in the Twentieth Century* (Indiana: 1964); Philip Graves, *The Life of Sir Percy Cox* (London: 1938); Philip W. Ireland, *'Iraq: A Study of Political Development* (London: 1937); Elie Kedourie, *op. cit.*; Stephen H. Longrigg, *'Iraq, 1900 to 1950: A Political, Social, and Economic History* (London: 1953); John Marlowe, *Late Victorian; The Life of Sir Arnold Talbot Wilson* (London: 1967); Elizabeth Monroe, *Britain's Moment in the Middle East 1917–1956* (Baltimore: 1963); Jukka Nevakivi, *op. cit.*; Sir A. T. Wilson, *Mesopotamia 1917–1920: A Clash of Loyalties* (London: 1931).
23 Churchill—Lloyd George, September 1919, Ch.P. 16/11.
24 Churchill—Lloyd George, 6 September 1919, Ch.P. 16/11.
25 Idem.
26 Secretary of State for War (hereafter S/SW)—General Officer Commanding Mesopotamia (hereafter GOC, Mes), 9 September 1919, War Office Papers (hereafter WO) 32/3514, Public Record Office, London.
27 Churchill—Secretary, Chief of Imperial General Staff (hereafter CIGS), Adjutant General (hereafter AG), 6 August 1919, WO 32/3510.
28 GOC Mes—S/SW, 12 September 1919, received 20 September, WO 32/3514.
29 S/SW—GOC mes, 25 September 1919, WO 32/3514, 5227.
30 S/SW—Marsh, 30 August 1919, WO 32/5227.
31 GOC Mes—S/SW, 6 October 1919, WO 32/3514.
32 "The Garrison of Mesopotamia," 15 October 1919, WO 32/5225. Churchill could use such direct methods in dealing with military personnel in Iraq. But the head of the civil administration was under the direct control of the India Office and was involved in a protracted clash with London over Iraq policy, thereby indirectly contributing to Churchill's problems with this area. See Busch, *op. cit.*, 356, 363–64, 368–69; Longrigg, *op. cit.*, 114–21.
33 11 January 1919, WO 106/55.
34 19 March 1919, Foreign Office Papers (hereafter FO) 371/4142, Public Record Office, London.
35 WO—US/S FO, 4 July 1919, WO 32/5223; 21 July, 28 July 1919, WO 32/5223; Director of Military Operations (hereafter DMO)—Dmov, 21 August 1919, WO 32/5223; 2 September 1919, WO 32/5223.
36 9 September 1919, WO 32/5223.
37 9 September 1919, WO 32/5223.
38 10 September 1919, WO 32/5223.

39 Churchill—Private Office, 9 September 1919, WO 32/5225.
40 12 November 1919, WO 32/5225.
41 16 April 1919, WO 32/5222. For analyses of Wilson's administration in Iraq during 1919, see Busch, *op. cit.*, 274–76, 280, 293–94, 201–3, 355–70; Klieman, *op. cit.*, 53–55; Longrigg, *op. cit.*, 112–14; Marlowe, *op. cit.*, ch. 9; Kedourie, *England and the Middle East*, 176–97; Ireland, *op. cit.*, ch. 10. For Wilson's viewpoint, see *Mesopotamia*, chs. 5, 6, 7, 9.
42 16 April 1919, WO 32/522.
43 4 May 1919, WO 32/5222.
44 S/Sw—Deputy Chief of Imperial General Staff (hereafter DCIGS), 14 May 1919, WO 32/5222.
45 Idem.
46 DMO—DCIGS, 14 May 1919, WO 32/5222.
47 S/SW—DCIGS, DMO, 17 May 1919, WO 32/5222.
48 Churchill—Bonar Law, 24 April 1919, Bonar Law papers 97/2/15; Churchill—Lloyd George, 21 May 1919, Ch.P.; Churchill—Seely, 5 March 1919, Ch.P. 16/5; Churchill—Lloyd George, 1 May 1919, Ch.P. 16/7; Churchill—Austen Chamberlain, 22 June 1919, Ch.P. 16/8.
49 25 November 1919, CAB 23/18. Main landing grounds were to be Cairo, Basra and Karachi; intermediate landing grounds for refueling were to be Damascus, Baghdad, Bushire, Bundarabbas and Charbar; emergency landing grounds were to be Ramleh, Tadmor, Abukemal, Hit, Ramadieh, Sheiksaid, and Amara. FO 371/4228.
50 Churchill—Balfour, 12 August 1919, Ch.P. 16/10; Balfour Papers 49694, British Museum, London.
51 Idem. There was a great public pressure for reduction of expenditure because public funds were deteriorating; this led to an accelerated push for further demobilization. See Busch, *op. cit.*, 347; Nevakivi, *op. cit.*, 185.
52 14 August 1919, CAB 23/11. Palestine was still under military administration in 1919, and therefore was a direct charge of the War Office. For details on this administration, see Esco, *op. cit.*, Vol. 1, 127–34.
53 Balfour—Churchill, 17 August 1919, Ch.P. 16/10; Balfour Papers, 49694.
54 Churchill—Balfour, 2 August 1919, Ch.P. 16/10. Lloyd George decided the time was ripe to end the Anglo-French impasse over the Middle East and the two countries arrived at a provisional agreement, 13 September 1919, calling for the evacuation of British troops from Syria and Cilicia. See Nevakivi, *op. cit.*, ch. 9; Busch, *op. cit.*, 349–55.
55 16 September 1919, WO 32/3514; Churchill—Wilson, 17 September 1919, Ch.P. 16/11.
56 Wilson—Churchill, 18 September 1919, Ch.P. 16/11.
57 Lloyd George—Churchill, 22 September 1919, Ch.P. 16/11.
58 Idem.
59 Churchill—Lloyd George, 22 September 1919, Ch.P. 16/11.
60 Idem.
61 Churchill—CIGS, AG, 23 September 1919, WO 32/3514.
62 Supra, note 29.
63 Churchill—CIGS, AG, Quartermaster General (hereafter QMG), September 1919, WO 32/5227
64 Civil Commissioner, Baghdad—S/S India—Churchill, 29 September 1919, WO 32/5227.
65 GOC Mes—S/SW, received 7 October 1919, WO 32/5227.

66 Idem. It was A.T. Wilson who constantly stressed that Faysal was intriguing in Iraq and Wilson firmly refused to allow the return of Faysal's Iraqi officers. Busch, *op. cit.*, 321–24, 368–69; Kedourie vindicates Wilson's fears of Sharifian activity, see *England and the Middle East*, ch. 7.
67 Churchill—Prime Minister, 7 October 1919, WO 32/3514; also an earlier version, not sent, 25 September 1919, Ch.P. 16/11.
68 Idem.
69 8 October 1919, WO 32/3514.
70 8 October 1919, WO 32/3514, 5225.
71 Hankey—Churchill, 8 October 1919, WO 32/5780, FO 371/4183.
72 WO—Allenby, 9 October 1919, WO 32/5730, FO 371/4183.
73 General Headquarters Egypt (hereafter GHQ)—WO, 22 October 1919, WO 32/5730; Churchill—CIGS, 22 October 1919, WO 32/5730; WO—GHQ Egypt, 23 October 1919, WO 32/5730.
74 WO—GHQ Egypt, 25 October 1919, WO 32/5730.
75 Milne—WO, 20 October 1919, WO 32/5733.
76 25 October 1919, Ch.P. 16/18. For details on Churchill and Turkey in 1919-1920, see Gilbert, *op. cit.*, ch. 27.
77 25 October 1919, Ch.P. 16/18.
78 Report to WO, 18 November 1919, FO 371/4261.
79 "Izvestiya Kommunisticheskoi Partii," 22 November 1919, CAB 21/177.
80 Quoted in Spector, *op. cit.*, 18
81 Meeting of 10 December 1919, CAB 21/203.

Chapter 4

1 5 January 1920, CAB 23/20.
2 5 January 1920, *The Times*.
3 Idem.
4 Churchill note for Cabinet meeting, 6 January 1920, Ch. P. 16/51.
5 Idem.
6 Wilson—Secretary of State, 2 January 1920, WO 32/5735; 15 March 1920, WO 32/5736.
7 Cabinet 1 (20), 6 January 1920, CAB 23/20.
8 Army Estimates, 1920–21, 7 February 1920, WO 32/5227.
9 Army Estimates, 1920–21, 7 February 1920, WO 32/5227. On Churchill and the Arab Middle East, 1920, see Gilbert, *op. cit.*, ch. 28.
10 9 February 1920, CAB 23/20.
11 The War Office was surveying the Mesopotamian oilfields and was planning a pipe and railway line across the British sphere of influence to the Mediterranean. Conference of Ministers, 23 January 1920, CAB 23/20.
12 DMO— CIGS, 9 February 1920, WO 32/5227; this view was based partly on information supplied by the India Office, e.g. Viceroy-Secretary of the State for India, 1 January 1920, LGP, F/206/4/8.
13 18 February 1920, WO 32/5227.
14 Speech to constituents at Dundee, 14 February 1920, *The Times*.

15 Churchill—Chief of Air Staff (hereafter CAS), 29 February 1920, FO 371/5076. For personal issues and interservice problems, see A. Boyle, *Trenchard* (New York: 1962).
16 Churchill—Secretary, CIGS, DCIGS, AG, QMG, FM, 5 March 1920, WO 32/5280.
17 March 1920, WO 32/5280.
18 Churchill—Secretary, AFS, AG, 16 April 1920, WO 32/5280.
19 Churchill—AG, DCIGS, 5 March 1920; DCIGS—Secretary of State, 26 March 1920, WO 32/5227.
20 Allenby—FO, 7 March 1920, WO 106/195. See also Busch, *op. cit.*, 375–77; Klieman, *op. cit.*, 46–47; Nevakivi, *op. cit.*, 209–19; for the impact on Iraq, see Wilson, *Mesopotamia*, 227–38.
21 WO—General Officer Commander-in-Chief (hereafter GOCinC) Mesopotamia, Egypt, India, 13 March 1920, WO 106/195.
22 Churchill—Haldane, 1 April 1920, Haldane Papers, copies in Ch.P. For Wilson's reactions to Haldane, see *Mesopotamia*, 270–75.
23 Churchill—DMO, 10 April 1920, WO 32/5806.
24 DMO—DCIGS, 15 April 1920, WO 32/5806.
25 Secretary of State—Haldane, drawn up 22 April, sent 25 April 1920, WO 32/5227.
26 AG—Secretary of State, 23 April 1920, WO 32/5227.
27 23 April 1920, WO 32/5227.
28 For proceedings of the Conference of San Remo, see Woodward & Butler, *Documents on British Foreign Policy 1919–1939* (London: 1952), First Series, Vol. 8, ch. 1; for Wilson's reactions to San Remo, see *Mesopotamia*, ch. 11; see also Nevakivi, *op. cit.*, ch. 12; Busch, *op. cit.*, 375–77, 387–88.
29 "Mesopotamian Expenditure," 1 May 1920, Cab 24/106.
30 General Staff note, 5 May 1920, WO 32/5227; LGP, F/205/6/1.
31 Cab 24 (20), 5 May 1920, CAB 23/21.
32 Memorandum by CIGS, 6 May 1920, WO 32/5281.
33 6 May 1920, WO 32/5281.
34 Idem. For A. T. Wilson's views on Churchill's plans, see *Mesopotamia*, 238–40.
35 Innumerable books have been written on Palestine; some of the best are: Fannie Fern Andrews, *The Holy Land under Mandate* (Boston: 1931), 2 vol.; Nevill Barbour, *Nisi Dominus, A Survey of the Palestine Controversy* (London: 1946); Norman Bentwich, *My 77 Years* (Philadelphia: 1961); John Bowle, *Viscount Samuel, A Biography* (London: 1957); Aharon Cohen, *Israel and the Arab World* (New York: 1970); Esco Foundation for Palestine, *Palestine: A Study of Jewish, Arab, and British Policies* (New Haven: 1947), 2 vol.; T. R. Feiwel, *No Ease in Zion* (London: 1938); H. F. Frischwasser-Ra'anan, *Frontiers of a Nation* (London: 1955); Philip Graves, *Palestine, the Land of Three Faiths* (London: 1923); Sami Hadawi, *Bitter Harvest: Palestine between 1914 and 1967* (1967); Ben Halpern, *The Idea of the Jewish State* (Cambridge, Mass.: 1961); Paul L. Hanna, *British Policy in Palestine* (Washington, D. C.: 1942); J.C. Hurewitz, *The Struggle for Palestine* (New York: 1950); Albert M. Hyamson, *Palestine under the Mandate, 1920–1948* (London: 1950); Barnard Joseph, *Ha-Shilton Ha-Briti Be-Eretz Yisrael* (Jerusalem: 1948); N. Katzburg, *Mishtar Ha-Mandat be-Eretz Yisrael* (Tel Aviv: 1967–68); Eli Kedourie, *England and the Middle East: The Destruction of the Ottoman Empire 1914–1921* (London: 1956); Ernest Main, *Palestine at the Crossroads* (New York: 1937); Richard Meinertzhagen, *Middle East Diary, 1917–1956* (New York: 1960); Jukka Nevakivi, *Britain, France and*

the Arab Middle East 1914–1920 (London: 1969); Chaim Weizmann, *Trial and Error* (Philadelphia: 1949), 2 vol.

36 7 June 1920, FO 371/5203. For the appointment of Samuel as High Commissioner, see Bowle, *op. cit.*, 189–95; Kedourie, *The Chatham House Version*, 52–53; Esco, *op. cit.*, Vol. 1, 259–63, 325–26; Klieman, *op. cit.*, 63–64; Feiwel, *op. cit.*, 113–14.
37 Churchill—Lloyd George, 13 June 1920, Ch.P. 16/47.
38 Memorandum by secretary of State for War to Cabinet, 8 June 1920, WO 106/196.
39 26 April 1920 in Richard Meinertzhagen, *Middle East Diary* (New York: 1960), 81. For details on the riots, see Esco, *op. cit.*, 132–33; Klieman, *op. cit.*, 62–68; Hanna, *op. cit.*, 43–44. Kedourie claims that these riots were an urgent reason for Samuel's conciliation policy; see the *Chatham House Version*, 58.
40 May 1920, FO 371/5118, 5119.
41 Cab 23 (20), 22 April 1920, CAB 23/1.
42 29 April 1920, Parliamentary Debates, Commons.
43 4 May 1920, Parliamentary Debates, Commons.
44 Weizmann—Eder, 8 June 1920, Weizmann Archives, Jerusalem.
45 Samuel—FO, 15 July 1920, WO 32/9614.
46 Churchill—Henry Wilson, 31 July 1920, WO 32/9614.
47 "Military Liabilities of the Empire," 27 July 1920, WO WO 32/5745.
48 CIGS—Secretary of State, 30 July 1920, WO 32/5745.
49 Some recommended books on Transjordan are King Abdullah, *Memoirs* (New York: 1950); Esco, *op. cit.*; John Bagot Glubb, *Syria, Lebanon, Jordan* (New York: 1967); James Morris, *The Hashemite Kings* (New York: 1959); Raphael Patai, *The Kingdom of Jordan* (Princeton: 1958); Benjamin Shwadran, *Jordan, A State of Tension* (New York: 1959); B. U. Touken, *A Short History of Trans-Jordan* (London: 1945).
50 Minute by Young, 29 July 1920, FO 371/5121. See Bowle, *op. cit.*, 204–8; Klieman, *op. cit.*, 68–69, 72. For description of anarchic situation, see Kirkbride, *A Crackle of Thorns* (London: 1956, ch. 3; Morris, *op. cit.*, 87–88.
51 GHQ Egypt—WO, 4 August 1920, FO 371/5121.
52 FO—Samuel, 11 August 1920, FO 371/5121; also 7 August 1920, WO 106/198; also WO-FO, 22 November 1920, FO 371/5289; WO-FO, 28 December 1920, WO 32/5770.
53 WO—FO, 31 August 1920, FO 371/5257.
54 FO—WO, 12 August 1920, FO 371/5257.
55 Interdepartmental Committee on Palestine, 10 August, 17 August, 20 August, 24 August, 25 August, 27 August, 31 August, 3 September, 7 September, 10 September, 12 October, 26 October 1920, FO 371/5277.
56 For details see Busch, *op. cit.*; Longrigg, *op. cit.*; Marlow, *op. cit.*; Wilson, *Mesopotamia*; Ireland, *op. cit.*
57 Churchill—Lloyd George, 13 June 1920, Ch.P. 16/47.
58 Idem. A.T. Wilson acted on his own to counteract any rumors of British withdrawal from Mosul and announced the formation of a Legislative Assembly including representatives from Mosul despite the fact that London had rejected this plan. Busch, *op. cit.*, 391–97, 404; Ireland, *op. cit.*, 200 ff; Wilson, *Mesopotamia*, 242 ff; Marlow, *op. cit.*, 187 ff.
59 Conference of Ministers, 17 June 1920, CAB 23/22.
60 Conference of Ministers, 18 June 1920, CAB 23/21, 22.
61 Churchill—CIGS, AG, CAS, 18 June 1029, WO 32/5227

62 GOC Mes—Wo, 21 June 1920, WO 32/5227. Sir Arnold T. Wilson disagreed with this appreciation, and later defended himself in *Mesopotamia*, chs. 12. 13; see also Marlowe, *op. cit.*, ch. 11.
63 WO–GOC Mes, 13 July 1920, WO 32/5227
64 Wilson Diary, 15 July 1920.
65 Conference of Ministers, 21 July 1920, CAB 23/22.
66 Wilson Diary, 30 July 1920.
67 General Staff memorandum, 27 July 1920, WO 32/5745.
68 CIGS—Secretary of State, 30 July 1920, WO 32/5745.
69 24th and 25th meetings of Finance Committee, 3 August 1920, WO 32/5745.
70 Wilson Diary, 4 August 1920.
71 Churchill—Lloyd George, 5 August 1920, LGP F/9/2/37.
72 Wilson Diary, 6 August 1920.
73 Finance Committee, 12 August 1920, CAB 23/22; WO 32/5745.
74 WO—IO, 12 August 1920, WO 32/5745; Minute by Secretary of State, 13 August 1920, WO 32/5745; Minute by Secretary of State, 13 August 1920, WO 32/5745; Cab 49 (20), 17 August 1920, CAB 23/22.
75 Churchill—Lloyd George (not sent), 31 August 1920, Ch.P.
76 Idem.
77 For example, Parliamentary Debates, Commons, 23 June 1920; Churchill–Caird, 23 August 1920, Ch.P. 16/52.
78 For the dispute with the India Office, Churchill—DCIGS, 26 July 1920, WO 32/5232; Henry Wilson minute, 22 September 1920, WO 32/5232; 3 November 1920, WO 32/5232; Secretary of State for India—WO, 3 December 1920, WO 32/5232.
79 October 1920, WO 33/969; "The Bolsheviks and Persia 1920," 13 October 1920, WO 136/14.
80 Appendix 11, WO 33/969.
81 Appendix 12, WO 33/969.
82 See FO 371/5178.
83 Appendix 20, WO 33/969.
84 Ivar Spector, *op. cit.*, 24–32.
85 Military Intelligence Report, 13 October 1920, WO 136/14.
86 Winston S. Churchill on the Communist Conspiracy, *Daily Telegraph*, 5 November 1920.
87 Idem.
88 Extract from *Bairaq-i-Adalat*, 7 November 1920, WO 157/1262.
89 Churchill memorandum for Cabinet, 16 November 1920, Ch.P. 16/53.
90 Churchill memorandum for Cabinet, 23 November 1920, Ch.P. 16/53.
91 2 December 1920, CAB 23/23.
92 The other points were an autonomous Thrace under Turkish suzerainty, the addition of Turkish delegates to the Straits Commission, modification of controls, and the separation of the Khalifate from the sultanate. Mustafa Kemal—Turkish Government, 1 November 1920, WO 32/5773.
93 Churchill—Lloyd George, 4 December 1920, Ch.P. 2/111.
94 Churchill memorandum to Cabinet, 16 December 1920, Ch.P. 16/53; C.P. 2387, CAB 24/117; LGP, F/206/4/24.
95 Churchill—Prime Minister, 10 November 1920, Ch.P. 16/50; LGP F/9/2/45.
96 Conference of Ministers, 1 December 1920, CAB 23/23.

97   Cab 67 (20), 8 December 1920, CAB 23/23.
98   GOC Mes—WO, 29 November 1920, WO 32/5236.
99   DMO—CIGS—Secretary of State, 7/8 December 1920, WO 32/5235.
100 Cab 70 (20), 13 December 1920, CAB 23/23.
101 Cab 72 (20), 17 December 1920, CAB 23/23; also WO 32/5235. By this time Cox was in full control of Iraq and had established a Provisional Council of State with the Naqib of Baghdad as its president. He was not about to agree to any kind of withdrawal. Busch, *op. cit.*, 443–51; Ireland, *op. cit.*, 227–87; Graves, *op. cit.*, 266–71; Burgoyne, *op. cit.*, 174–92.
102 Cab 82 (20), 31 December 1920, CAB 23/23.
103 CAB 21/186.
104 1 May 1920, CAB 24/106; LGP, F/205/6/1; see also Busch, *op. cit.*, 435–43; Klieman, *op. cit.*, 86–91.
105 17 May 1920, FO 371/5255.
106 8 June 1920, FO 371/5255; CAB 21/186.
107 26 May 1920, CAB 21/186; Parliamentary Debates, Commons, 19 July 1920.
108 See Young memorandum, 3 July 1920, FO 371/5255; Curzon memorandum for Cabinet, 16 August 1920, FO 371/5255, CAB 21/186; Cab 49 (20), 17 August 1920, CAB 23/22.
109 Cab 82 (20), 31 December 1920, CAB 23/23. Klieman describes this meeting but makes no mention of Churchill's role. Klieman, *op. cit.*, 89.
110 Martin Gilbert claims that Lloyd George offered the post on New Year's Day and that Churchill officially accepted 4 January, three days after tentatively doing so. Gilbert, *op. cit.*, 507–8.
111 Quoted in Marlowe, *op. cit.*, 238.

Chapter 5

1   Churchill—Lloyd George, 4 January 1921, LGP, F/9/12; see also Busch, *op. cit.*, 456. On creating the Middle East Department, see Gilbert, *op. cit.*, ch. 29.
2   Curzon—Churchill, 2 January 1921; Churchill—Curzon, 3 January 1921, Ch.P. 16/72; 4 January 1921, Sir Henry Wilson's Diary, Wilson Papers, copies in Ch.P.
3   See note 1.
4   Churchill—Prime Minister, 8 January 1921, LGP E/9/2.
5   Hankey—Creedy, 8 January 1921, WO 32/5897; Churchill had actually drawn all this up 1 January; WO—Hankey, 1 January 1921, CAB 21/186.
6   S/SW—High Commissioner Mes. (hereafter HC Mes.), General Officer Commander-in-Chief, 8 January 1921, W.P. 2571, CAB 24/119. On Cox's administration until Iraq's transfer to Colonial Office control, Longrigg, *op. cit.*, 126–27; Ireland, *op. cit.*, chs. 16, 17; Graves, *op. cit.*, ch. 20; Marlow, *op. cit.*, ch. 12. For a historical summary by Sir Percy Cox of his career in the Middle East, see Bell, *op. cit.*, vol. 2, 504–41.
7   S/Sw—HC Mes., GOCinC, 8 January 1921, C.P. 2571, CAB 24/119.
8   Supra, Chapter II. Two scholars on the Middle East who analyze and try to prove that these many instruments are not in conflict one with the other are Kedourie, *op. cit.*, Chs. 2, 5, 7; and Friedman, *op. cit.*, chs. 6, 7, 17. The texts of these documents can be found in J. C. Hurewitz, *Diplomacy*, Vol. 2.

9 Friedman, *op. cit.*, 304.
10 See JC Hurewitz, *op.cit.*, Vol. 2.
11 Churchill—AG, 9 January 1921, WO 32/5234.
12 Churchill—Secretary, AG, CIGS, 8 January 1921, WO 32/5234.
13 Churchill—PM, 8 January 1921, LGP F/9/2.
14 An excellent analysis of Lawrence is in Kedourie, *The Chatham House Version*, Chs. 4, 5.
15 Ibid., 206. Friedman disproves the claim of gratitude because the general Arab uprising in the Fertile Crescent promised by the Sharif failed to materialize, and the British promise of recognition of Arab independence in the Fertile Crescent therefore lapsed. Friedman, *op.cit.*, chapter 6.
16 Curzon—Churchill, 9 January 1921, Ch.P. 17/2.
17 28 October 1920, WO 32/5769. Another important partisan of Faysal was Gertrude Bell, Cox's Oriental Secretary; her conversion to this point of view is traced in Kedourie, *England and the Middle East*, 199–204; Marlowe, *op. cit.*, 202–6. On the Sharifian solution in general, see Klieman, *op. cit.*, 96–101.
18 Churchill—Lloyd George, Curzon, D'Abernon, Hardinge, 12 January 1921, Ch.P. 16/71; Curzon papers, Box 65, F/4/13, India Office Library, London.
19 Churchill—Lloyd George, 12 January 1921, Ch.P. 17/2; LGP F/9/54; also letter of 14 January 1921, LGP F/9/2.
20 Churchill—Cox, 15 January 1921, Ch.P. 17/16; Curzon Papers, F/9/2/60.
21 For details see Busch, *op. cit.*, 453–56.
22 Lawrence—Marsh, 17 January 1921, Ch.P.
23 Churchill—Curzon, 8 January 1921, Curzon P. Box 65, F/3/3.
24 Churchill—Clementine Churchill, 16 February 1921, Spencer Churchill Papers, Martin Gilbert, Oxford.
25 Curzon—Churchill, 9 January 1921, Ch.P. 17/2.
26 Churchill—Curzon, 12 January 1921, Curzon P., Box 65, F/4/3.
27 Curzon—Churchill, 17 January 1921, Ch.P. 17/2.
28 See note 6.
29 High Commissioner, Baghdad—Churchill, 13 January 1921, C.P. 2571, CAB 24/119.
30 Haldane—S/SW, 13 January 1921, A.P. 2571, CAB 24/119.
31 S/SW—HC Mes., 10 January, 15 January 1921, C.P. 2571, CAB 24/119.
32 Minutes, 9 January–22 January 1921, WO 32/5234.
33 HC Mes—S/SW, 15 January 1291, C.P. 2571, CAB 24/119.
34 S/SW—HC Mes, 23 January 1921, C.P. 2571, CAB 24/119.
35 Idem.
36 HC Mes—S/SW, 26 January 1921, C.P. 2571, CAB 24/119.
37 HC Mes—S/SW, 24 January 1921, C.P. 2571, CAB 24/119.
38 S/SW—Haldane, 26 January 1921, C.P. 2571, CAB24/119.
39 S/SW—Haldane, 28 January 1921, C.P. 2571, CAB24/119.
40 19,360 British; 86, 117 natives, 46,400 native followers; 23,746 native laborers; 13,501 local laborers; 3,310 civilians, 33,351 refugees.
41 S/SW—HC Mes, 7 February 1921, C.P. 2571, CAB 119.
42 Milner—Samuel, 5 February 1921, Samuel Papers, St. Anthony's College, Oxford.
43 Samuel—Curzon, 30 January 1921, Curzon Papers, Box 65, F/3/3. On Samuel's administration until Palestine's transfer to Colonial Office control, see Klieman, *op cit.*, 64–67,

72–76; E. Kedourie, *The Chatham House Version and Other Middle Eastern Studies* (New York: 1970), 55–57; Bowle, *op. cit.*, 198–203; Esco, *op. cit.*, Vol. 1, 261–63; A. Cohen, *op. cit.*, 181.
44 Wilson—Cox, 21 January 1921, A. T. Wilson Papers, ADD 52455, British Museum, London.
45 7 February 1921, C.P. 2545, CAB 24/119; WO 32/5897; also Busch, *op. cit.*, 260–61.
46 DMO—DCIGS, 18 February 1921, WO 32/5897.
47 Creedy—S/SW, 16 March 1921, Wo 32/5897.
48 Idem.
49 10 February 1922, C.P. 2571, CAB 24/119; Busch, *op. cit.*, 463.
50 Cab 7(21), 14 February 1921, CAB 23/24. See Klieman, *op. cit.*, 91–93.
51 *The Times*, 20 January 1921.
52 25 February 1921, CO 732/3. Klieman, *op. cit.*, 93–94.
53 Churchill—Hirtzel, 23 January 1921, Ch.P. 17/14.
54 Churchill—Fiddes, 17 February 1921, Ch.P. 17/1.
55 Churchill—Curzon, 16 February 1921, Curzon Papers, Box 65, F/4/3.
56 End of January 1921, Colonial Office Papers (hereafter CO) 732/3, Public Record Office, London.
57 17 February 1921, CO 732/3.
58 Shuckburgh—Churchill, 17 February 1921, CO 730/13; CO 732/3.
59 Congreve—Churchill, 15 November 1920, WO 32/5770.
59a 17 February 1921, CO 732/3; contrast with those who claim that it was not until Churchill's trip to Palestine that this decision was made. Cf. Shwadran, *op. cit.*, 136–38.
60 Shuckburgh—S/S, 19 February 1921, CO 727/3.
61 Churchill note, 23 February 1921, CO 727/3; Shuckburgh—Secretary of State Colonies (hereafter S/SC) 23 February 1921, CO 727/1.
62 22 February 1921, CO 727/3. Few writers mention this crucial interview: Klieman, *op. cit.*, 96–102; Busch, *op. cit.*, 465. Antonius does mention it, but comes to his own interpretation as to its meaning. Antonius, *op. cit.*, 316.
63 Sir Reader Bullard, *The Camels Must Go* (London: 1961), 117.
64 Churchill—Curzon, 16 February 1921, Curzon Papers Box 65, F/4/3.
65 Idem.
66 S/SC—Sir George Ritchie, 25 February 1921, CO 732/3. Klieman, *op. cit.*, 95.
67 Churchill—Shuckburgh, 18 February 1921, CO 732/4. Klieman, *op. cit.*, 94–95; for details on the preliminaries to the conference, Gilbert, *op. cit.*, ch. 30.
68 S/SC—HC Mes, 7 February 1921, C.P. 2571, CAB 24/119.
69 Memorandum by Middle East Dept. prior to Cairo Conference, Appendix II, C.P. 3123, CAB 24/126.
70 Churchill—Shuckburgh, 18 February 1921, CO 732/4.
71 See note 69.
72 Weizmann—Churchill, 1 March 1921, Weizmann Archives. For details on the drawing up of Palestine's frontiers, see Frischwasser-Ra'anan, *op.cit.*, ch. 5.
73 Note by Hirtzel, 28 January 1921, CO 730/13.
74 Harris—S/SW, 8 February 1921, CO 730/13.
75 Churchill-Shuckburgh, 18 February 1921, CO 730/13.
76 "The Work of the R.A.F. in Mesopotamia," 25 November 1920, circulated to the Cabinet 19 February 1921, CAB 24/120.

77 Trenchard—Geoffrey Salmond, AOC, Middle East, mid-February 1921, in Boyle, *op.cit.*, 380.

Chapter 6

1. The British Mission included Churchill, Trenchard, Lt. Gen. Sir W. Congreve, Sir George Barstow (Treasury), Maj. Gen. Sir P. P. de B. Radcluffe (CMO, WO), J. B. Crosland (Director of Finances, WO), Col. T. E. Lawrence, Maj. H. W. Young.
2. For details see C.P. 3123, CAB 24/126; see also Klieman, *op. cit.*, ch. 6.
3. The historical term "Mesopotamia" included only the Basrah and Baghdad vilayets; the addition of the Mosul vilayet complicated the use of the term and gradually "Iraq" became the accepted term. Busch, *op. cit.*, 23n39.
4. First meeting of Political Committee, Mesopotamia, 12 March 1921, Appendix VI, C.P. 3123, CAB 24/126.
5. Churchill—CO and Prime Minister, 14 March 1921, C.P. 2742, CAB 24/121.
6. Idem.
6a. Klieman writes that Trenchard chose the Conference as an opportune time for presenting his scheme for RAF control of Iraq when this was a central part of Churchill's plans as early as 1919. Klieman, *op. cit.*, 111.
7. Churchill—CO, MP, 14 March 1921, C.P. 2742, CAB 24/121. Klieman agrees that Churchill set the tone for the committees on Iraq. Klieman, *op. cit.*, 107–10.
8. Hankey—Worthington Evans, 16 March 1921, WO 32/5233.
9. Prime Minister—Churchill, 16 March 1921, C.P. 2742, CAB 24/121; LGP F/25/1/16.
10. Churchill—Prime Minister, 16 March 1921, C.P. 2743, CAB 24/121.
11. S/SC—Prime Minister, 18 March 1921, LGP F/9/3/11; F/25/1/28.
12. Prime Minister—Churchill, 18 March 1921, C.P. 2744, CAB 24/121.
13. Churchill—Prime Minister, 19 March 1921, LGP F/9/3/11.
14. First meeting of Palestine Political and Military Committee, 17 March 1921, Appendix 17, C.P. 3123, CAB 24/126.
15. Idem. Klieman claims that Churchill was swayed by the arguments of Samuel, Congreve and Lawrence to appoint 'Abdallah; but what of the plans made before Churchill left for Cairo? Klieman *op. cit.*, 119–20.
16. Churchill—Prime Minister, 20 March 1921, C.P. 2753, CAB 24/121; for details on 'Asir, Yemen, Nejd, see Busch, *op. cit.*, chapter 5.
17. S/SC—Prime Minister 18 March 1921, C.P. 2751, CAB/121.
18. Churchill—CO, 19 March 1921, WO 106/208.
19. Lawrence—Montague Robert Lawrence, 20 March 1921, T. E. Lawrence Papers, MSS. ENG. LETT C.147, Bodleian Library, Oxford.
20. Churchill—Prime Minister and Cabinet, 21 March 1921, C.P. 2755, CAB 24/121.
21. E. Marsh—J. T. Davies, 19 March 1921, LGP F/9/3/16.
22. Cab 14(21), 22 March 1921, CAB 23/24; Martin Gilbert completely ignores this tension between Churchill and Lloyd George over Faysal in his treatment of the material; see Gilbert, *op. cit.*, chapter 31.
23. Prime Minister—S/SC, 22 March 1921, LGP F/9/3/20.
24. Churchill—Prime Minister, 23 March 1921, C.P. 2770, CAB 24/121.
25. Idem.

26 Lawrence—Montague Robert Lawrence, 12 April 1921, T. E. Lawrence Papers, MSS. EMG. LETT. C. 147, 254.
27 28 March 1921, Appendix 19, CP 3123, CAB 24/126; see also "Trans-Jordania," Memorandum by S/SC, 2 April 1921, C.P. 2815, CAB 24/122. See Klieman, *op. cit.*, 129–31, 209–10; Esco, *op. cit.*, Vol. 1, 264–65; Shwadran, *op. cit.*, 132–33; Gilbert, *op. cit.*, ch. 32.
28 King Abdullah, *Memoirs* (New York: 1950), 204. For the importance of Sharifian-Sa'udi relations, see Busch, *op. cit.*, 321–34, 354–55, 424–31.
29 See note 27.
29a Klieman's interpretation of the material is that Churchill was not to ask 'Abdallah to control Transjordan and that he therefore changed the Cairo decision in doing so. To this author's understanding of the material this offer was not precluded from the Colonial Secretary; it is just that most officials were sure that 'Abdallah would not settle for so small a territory. Klieman, *op. cit.*, 132.
30 28 March 1921, Appendix 23, C.P. 3123, CAB 24/126. Texts of Churchill's meetings with the Arabs and Zionists are in Klieman, *op. cit.*, Appendices B, C, D, E, 259–81.
31 28 March 1921, Appendix 23, C.P. 3123, CAB 24/126.
32 Idem.
33 See in chapters IX, XI.
34 See note 30.
35 "Zionism versus Bolshevism: A Struggle for the Soul of the Jewish People," *Illustrated Sunday Herald*, 8 February 1920, LGP H/45/4.
36 18 December 1920, FO 371/5257; C.P. 2324, CAB 24/117.
37 See note 30.
38 Idem.
39 29 March 1921, Appendix 21, C.P. 3123, CAB 24/126.
40 Norman Bentwich, *My 77 Years* (Philadelphia: 1961), 71; Gilbert, *op. cit.*, 536, 573, 584; see also Sara Reguer, "Rutenberg and the Jordan River: a Revolution in Hydroelectricity," *Middle Eastern Studies* vol. 31, no. 4, October 1995, 691–729.
41 "Trans-Jordania," Memorandum by S/SC, 2 April 1921, C.P. 2815, CAB 24/122.
42 Churchill—Gouraud, 31 March 1921, C.P. 2132, CAB 14/126.
43 Quoted in P. Knightley and C. Simpson, *The Secret Lives of Lawrence of Arabia* (London: 1969), 140; also in Kedourie, *The Chatham House Version*, 207.
44 R.W. Thompson, *Winston Churchill: The Yankee Marlborough* (New York: 1963), 213.
45 29 October 1918, CAB 27/24.
46 W. S. Churchill, *Great Contemporaries* (London: 1937), 160.
47 Ibid.
48 Ibid., 163.
49 Kedourie, *op. cit.*, 207.
50 Elizabeth Burgoyne, *Gertrude Bell* (London: 1961), 211. See also Busch, *op. cit.*, 467–74; Boyle, *op. cit.*, 378–81; Graves, *op. cit.*, ch. 21; Kedourie, *England and the Middle East*, 207; Ireland, *op. cit.*, 311–18.

Chapter 7

1 Hankey—Prime Minister, 14 June 1921, LGP F/25/1/39.

2   Churchill—Lloyd George, 2 June 1921, LGP F/9/3/48. Klieman skips from the Cairo Conference to the Parliamentary presentation with an aside or two that Churchill "wished first to gain Cabinet approval before, reporting publicly on his mission," and that because Churchill had "to convince his colleagues and to clarify minor differences with his successor at the War Office, "his speech to Commons was postponed from April to June. Klieman, *op. cit.*, 133–34.
3   High Commissioner—S/SC, 12 April 1921; S/SC—HC Mes, 14 April 1921, CO 730/1.
4   HC Mes—S/SC, 12 April 1921; S/SC—HC Mes, 14 April 1921, CO 730/1.
5   Bullard minute, 13 April 1921, CO 730/1.
6   HC Mes—S/SC, 17 April, 18 April 1921, CO 730/1.
7   S/SC—HC Mes, 20 April 1921, CO 730/1. Klieman, *op. cit.*, 139–48.
8   S/SC—Lawrence, 19 April 1921, CO 730/1.
9   Lawrence note, 18 May 1921; HC Mes—S/SC, 7 May 1921; S/SC—HC Mes, 12 May 1921; HC Mes—S/SC, 18 May 1921, CO 730/1; Lawrence note, 18 May 1921; Shuckburgh—S/SC, 19 May 1921; HC Mes—Colonial Office, 24 May 1921; HC Mes—Colonial Office, 25 May 1921; S/C—HC Mes, 27 May 1921; HC Mes—S/SC, 28 May 1921, CO 730/2.
10 Minutes, 18 April 1921; S/SC—Hc Mes, 21 April 1921, CO 730/1.
11 Minutes, 27 April–3 May 1921, CO 733/2.
12 HC Mes—S/SC, 9 May 1921; S/SC—HC Mes, 4 June 1921, CO 730/2.
13 HC Mes—S/SC, 19 April 1921, CO 730/1.
14 S/SC—Mes, 22 April 1921, CO 730/1.
15 HC Mes—S/SC, 29 April 1921, CO 730/1.
16 S/SC—HC Mes, 4 May 1921, CO 730/1.
17 Memorandum by S/SC, 10 May 1921, C.P. 2925, CAB 24/123.
18 General Officer Commander-in-Chief—C.O., 10 May 1921, C.P. 2941, CAB 24/123.
19 HC Mes—S/SC, 20 May 1921, S/SC—HC Mes, 25 May 1921, CO 730/2; Colonial Office—Director of Military Operations, 23 May 1921, WO 32/5227.
20 Despatch Churchill—Cox, 20 July 1921, CO 730/2.
21 Vernon memorandum, 27 April 1921, CO 732/3; WO 32/5898.
22 Churchill—Worthington Evans, 27 April 1921, WO 32/5898.
23 Worthington Evans—Churchill, 6 June 1921, WO 32/5898; CO 730/14.
24 Meinertzhagen—Vernon, Young, Shuckburgh, 21 June 1921, CO 730/14.
25 Shuckburgh—S/SC, 22 June 1921, CO 730/14.
26 23 June 1921, CO 730/14.
27 Churchill note, 4 June 1921, CO 730/2; note by S/SC, 2 April 1921, Appendix 16, C.P. 3123, CAB 24/126; CO—Treasury, 2 May 1921, CO 730/1; Minutes 17–22 April 1921, CO 730/1; HC Mes—S/SC, 5 June 1921; Minutes, 7–9 June 1921; S/SC—HC Mes, 9 June 1921, CO 730/2.
28 Conference of Ministers, 11 April 1921, CAB 23/25.
29 Minutes, 11–13 April 1921, WO 32/5237.
30 HC Palestine—S/SC, 12 April 1921, CO 733/2; WO 32/5237.
31 HC Mes—S/SC, 13 April 1921, CO 730/1; WO 32/5237.
32 Churchill—Hankey, 13 April 1921, CO 733/2; WO 32/5237.
33 Conference of Ministers, 19 April 1921, CAB 23/25.
34 1 April–14 April 1921, CO 732/1; CO 733/2.

35 HC Pal—S/SC, 21 April 1921, CO 733/2.
36 Churchill note, 22 April 1921, CO 733/2.
37 HC Pal—S/SC, 14 May 1921, CO 733/3.
38 Despatch HC Pal—S/SC, 28 May 1921, CO 733/3. Klieman, *op. cit.*, 211–12.
39 Conference of Ministers, 11 April 1921, CAB 23/25.
40 HC Pal—S/SC, 2 May 1921, CO 733/3. See Gilbert, *op. cit.*, 585–88, 617, 636–37; Esco, *op. cit.*, vol. 1, 269–70; Andrews, *op. cit.*, 75–79.
41 HC Pal-S/SC, 4 May 1921, CO 733/3; 2 ships were sent from Egypt, 3 from Malta.
42 Despatch Samuel—Churchill, 8 May, 15 May 1921, CO 733/3. See Esco, *op. cit.*, vol. 1, 271–72; Andrews, *op. cit.*, 80.
43 Despatch Samuel—Churchill, 8 May 1921, CO 733/3.
44 S/SC—HC Pal, 12 May 1921, CO 733/3.
45 HC Pal—S/SC, 12 May 1921, CO 733/3.
46 S/SC—HC Pal, 14 May 1921, CO 733/3.
47 HC Pal—S/SC, 13 May 1921, CO 733/3.
48 Minutes, second meeting, Middle East Committee, 12 May 1921, CO 537/826.
49 S/SC—HC Pal, 20 May 1921, CO 537/826.
50 HC Pal—S/SC, 22 May 1921, CO 733/3.
51 See note 46.
52 HC Pal—S/SC, 25 May 1921, CO 733/3.
53 S/SC—HC Pal, 27 May 1921, CO 733/3. For an analysis of the Palestine situation between March and June 1921 as a microcosm for studying the entire period of the British mandate, see Klieman, *op. cit.*, 173–85.
54 HC Pal—S/SC, 29 May 1921, CO 733/3.
55 Pressure had been mounted by the Zionists regarding the desperate plight of emigrants stranded in transit, and Churchill had passed instructions along to Samuel to announce this.
56 S/SC—HC Pal, 2 June 1921, CO 733/3. For Zionist and Palestine Arab actions as a result of Samuel's 3 June speech, see Klieman, *op. cit.*, 185–202; see also Esco, *op. cit.*, vol. 1, 274–75; Hanna, *op. cit.*, 80.
57 HC Pal—S/SC, 3 June 1921, CO 733/3.
58 S/SC—HC Pal, 4 June 1921, CO 733/3.
59 Despatch HC Pal—S/SC, 26 May 1921, CO 733/3.
60 S/SC—HC Pal, 14 June 1921, CO 733/3.
61 Memorandum by S/SC, 9 June 1921, C.P. 3030, CAB 24/125.
62 Churchill—Lloyd George, 2 June 1921, LGP, F/9/3/48; Appendix, Committee on Future of Constantinople, 2 June 1921, CAB 27/133. Esco traces seven stages in drafting the Palestine mandate, starting in Spring 1919 and reaching its final form August 1921. Esco, *op. cit.*, vol. 1, 164–77.
63 See J. C. Hurewitz, *Documents*, 77.
64 See M. Beloff, *op. cit.*, 293.
65 Conference, 1 June 1921, CO 732/5; S/SC—HCs Mes and Pal, 1 June 1921, C.P. 3040, CAB 24/125.
66 HC Mes—S/SC, 4 June 1921, C.P. 3040, CAB 24/125.
67 HC Pal—S/SC, 4 June 1921, C.P. 3040, CAB 24/125; CO 733/3.
68 Note on Palestine and Mesopotamian Mandates, 8 June 1921, C.P. 3040, CAB 24/125.
69 Note by S/SC, 14 June 1921, CO 732/5.

70   Idem; incorporates Young's suggestions of 10 June 1921, CO 732/5.
71   Churchill—Prime Minister, 9 June 1921, LGP, F/9/3/51.
72   Prime Minister—Churchill, 11 June, LGP, F/9/3/54.
73   CAB 49(21), 14 June 1921, CAB 23/26.
74   M. Gilbert, *op. cit.*, 894. On the Middle East settlement as a whole, ch. 33.
75   Churchill—Shuckburgh, 13 April 1921, CO 732/4.
76   Question in Parliament, 19 April 1921, CO 732/3; Cab 25(21), 20 April 1921, CAB 23/25.
77   Prime Minister—Churchill, 23 May 1921, LGP, F/9/3/42.
78   Churchill—Prime Minister, 25 May 1921, LGP, F/9/3/43.
79   Cab 44(21), 31 May 1921, CAB 23/25.
80   Cab 45(21), 31 May 10921, CAB 23/245.
81   Churchill—Secy (M), Vernon, 1 June 1921, CO 732/5.
82   Churchill—Worthington Evans, 1 June 1921, CO 732/5.
83   HC Mes—CO; 25 May 1921, CO 730/2; HC Mes—S/SC, 10 June 1921, CO 730/2.
84   S/SC—HC Mes, 10 June 1921, CO 730/2. For Britain's role in preparing for Faysal's entry into Iraq, see Klieman, *op. cit.*, 149–55.
85   Churchill-Shuckburgh, 14 June 1921, CO 732/5.
86   Parliamentary Debates, vol. 143, 14 June 1921, 265–334. Klieman, *op. cit.*, 135–37.
87   Parliamentary Debates, vol. 143, 14 June 1921, 265–334.
88   Idem.
89   Idem.
90   Idem.
91   Chamberlain—Prime Minister, 14 June 1921, LGP, F/7/4/10.
92   Churchill—Prime Minister, 17 June 1921, LGP, F/9/3/58.
93   *The Times*, 16 June 1921.
94   *Nation*, 18 June 1921, LGP, H/46/6.
95   *New Statesman*, 18 June 1921, LGP, H/46/6.

Chapter 8

1   See M. Gilbert, *op. cit.*, chs. 37–40; on Iraq, see ch. 44. How important this was is reflected in the space devoted to the Irish issue in history books on modern Britain as compared with Middle Eastern issues. Cf. Mowat, *op. cit.*, 57–108; Taylor, *op. cit.*, 204–12.
2   For a good biography, see Ralph G. Martin, *Jennie: The Life of Lady Randolph Churchill* (Englewood Cliffs, N. J.: 1971), 2 vols.
3   Churchill—Secy (M), 9 July 1921, CO 730/3; Imperial Conference, 22 June 1921, CAB 32/2.
4   M. Kinnear, *The Fall of Lloyd George* (Toronto: 1973), 24. See Mowat, *op. cit.*, 129–32.
5   HC Mes—S/SC, 29 June 1921, CO 730/2.
6   HC Mes—S/SC, 2 July 1921, CO 730/3. Kedourie writes a scathing analysis of how Faysal was pushed onto Iraq by Britain against the will of the people. Kedourie, *The Chatham House Version*, ch. 9; also Kedourie, *England and the Middle East*, 208–12.
7   Cab 57(21), 3 July 1921, CAB 23/26.
8   HC Mes—S/SC, 13 July 1921, CO 730/3. Klieman, *op. cit.*, 155–62.
9   HC Mes—S/SC, 1 August 1921, CO 730/3.
10 Cab 62(21), 2 August 1921, CAB 23/26; for details see Ireland, *op. cit.*, ch. 18.

11 S/SC—HC Mes, 9 August 1921, CO 730/3.
12 S/SC—HC Iraq, 15 August 1921, CO 730/4; LGP, F/9/3/78.
13 Churchill—Cox, 15 August 1921, LGP, F/9/3/78.
14 Churchill—Prime Minister, 15 August 1921, LGP, F/9/3/78.
15 Cabinet Committee, 19 August 1921, CAB 23/27. Klieman, *op. cit.*, 162–65.
16 Cabinet Committee, 19 August 1921, CAB 23/27; also CO 730/4. For a description of the situation internal to Iraq, see Longrigg, *op. cit.*, 134–39; Longrigg & Stoakes, *op. cit.*, 83–89; Ireland, *op. cit.*, ch. 18; Graves, *op. cit.*, ch. 22.
17 29 August 1921, C.P. 3273, CAB 24/127.
18 HC Iraq—S/SC, 26 August 1921, CO 730/4.
19 S/SC—HC Iraq, 3 September 1921, CO 730/4.
20 Balfour—Churchill, 8 September 1921, CO 730/16; C.P. 3440, CAB 24/129.
21 Churchill—Balfour, 20 September 1921, CO 730/16; C.P. 3440, CAB 24/129.
22 Churchill—Shuckburgh, 11 October 1921, CO 730/16.
23 Churchill—Balfour, 12 October 1921, CO 730/16.
24 Idem. Klieman, *op. cit.*, 167–68.
25 Shuckburgh—Masterton Smith—S/SC, 28 October–1 November 1921, CO 732/5; see Winston Churchill, *World Crisis* (New York: 1921), vol. 5, 493.
26 S/SC— Cox, 19 October 1921, CAB 24/129. To complete his story in 1921 and on an optimistic note, Klieman skims over the treaty negotiations and does not mention Faysal's stubbornness in seeking to attain real independence which caused these discussions to continue for over a year. Klieman, *op. cit.*, 166, 169–70.
27 Young—Shuckburgh, 23 October 1921; seen by Churchill 15 November 1921, CO 730/16.
28 Churchill—Cox, 21 July 1921, CO 732/1.
29 Young—Meinertzhagen, 28 October 1921, CO 730/7.
30 Meeting of Middle East Committee, 3 November 1921, CO 537/829; S/SC—HC Iraq, 11 November 1921, CO 730/7.
31 Churchill—Worthington Evans, 23 June 1921, CO 32/5898.
32 WO—CO, 4 July 1921, CO 730/13.
33 CO—WO, 13 July 1921, WO 32/5899.
34 Shuckburgh—S/SC, 19 July 1921, CO 730/13.
35 Churchill—Vernon, 22 July 1921, CO 730/15.
36 Vernon—S/SC, 23 July 1921, CO 730/15.
37 Churchill—Vernon, Meinertzhagen, 26 July 1921, CO 730/15.
38 Churchill—Secy (M), 26 July 1921, CO 730/15.
39 Shuckburgh—S/SC, 28 July 1921, CO 730/15.
40 Churchill—Prime Minister, 28 July 1921, LGP, F/9/3/71.
41 Cf. *The Times*, editorial, 18, July 1921.
42 S/SC—Cox, 2 August 1921, CO 730/15
43 Idem.
44 Memorandum by S/SC, "Policy and Finance in Mesopotamia, 1922–23," 4 August 1921, WO 32/5899.
45 Idem.: appeared as C.P. 3197, 17 August 1921, CAB 24/127.
46 Memorandum by S/SW, "Policy and Finance in Mesopotamia," 7 August 1921, C.P. 3240, CAB 24/127.
47 Churchill— Prime Minister, 7 August 1921, LGP, F/9/3/75.

48 Cab 70 (21), 18 August 1921, CAB 23/26
49 Young—S/SC, 29 August 1921, CO 730/13.
50 Worthington Evans—Churchill, 10 October 1921, WO 32/5899.
51 Conference, 31 October 1921, WO 32/5899.
52 Interdepartmental Conference, 3 November 1921, WO 32/5899.
53 11 November–21 November 1921, CO 730/13.
54 Minutes of conference at CO, 19 December 1921, CO 730/16; WO 32/5899.
55 CO—Treasury, 22 July 1921, CO 732/3. On the Geddes Committee, see Taylor, *op. cit.*, 240; Mowat, *op. cit.*, 130–31; Gilbert, *op. cit.*, 768–70.
56 Treasury—CO, 1 October 1921, CO 732/3.
57 Answers written 23 December 1921, sent to Treasury 10 January 1922, CO 732/3.
58 Cox—S/SC, 12 November 1921, CAB 24/129; 20 November 1921, CO 730/17; 22 November 1921, CO 730/16.
59 Memorandum by S/SC, "French Negotiations with Angora," 26 October 1921, C.P. 3447, CAB 24/129; the treaty was signed 20 October 1921, text in Hurewitz, *Diplomacy*, vol. 2, 97–100.
60 Cab 84 (21), 1 November 1921, CAB 23/27.
61 Cab 95 (21), 22 November 1921, CAB 23/27.
62 Churchill—Cox, 28 November 1921, CO 730/16.
63 Churchill—Secy, Secy (M), 24 November 1921, CO 730/16.
64 For example, HC Mes—S/SC, 5 August 1921, CO 730/4; LGP, F/9/3/77.
65 Memorandum by S/SC, "Greece and Turkey," C.P. 3328, 26 September 1921, CAB 24/128.
66 Cox—S/SC, 29 September 1921, CO 730/5; C.P. 3378, CAB 24/128.
67 Cox—S/SC, 7 October 1921, CO 730/16; C.P. 3390, C/128.
68 Cox—S/SC, 16 October 1921; C.P. 3420, CAB 24/129.
69 Memorandum by Curzon, "Intervention Between Greece and Turkey," 7 October 1921, Curzon Papers Box on Middle East, F/12/1.
70 HC Iraq—S/SC, 21 November 1921, C.P. 3511, CAB 24/131.
71 HC Iraq—S/SC, 13 December 1921, C.P. 3565, CAB 24/131.
72 Middle East Department memorandum, "Foreign Incitement of the Turks to Attack Iraq," 13 December 1921, C.P. 3566, CAB 24/131.
73 Conference of Ministers, 21 December 1921, CAB 23/27.
74 Cf. Beaverbrook, *The Decline and Fall of Lloyd George* (London: 1963), 40.
75 Churchill—Shuckburgh, 9 July 1921, CO 732/2.
76 Churchill—Curzon, 12 July 1921, CO 732/2.
77 Committee Imperial Defense—Churchill, 30 November 1921, CO 537/830.
78 13 December 1921, CO 537/830.
79 31 July 1921, CO 730/15.
80 16 December 1921, CO 730/7.
81 *The Times*, 27 December 1921, 28 December 1921, and 29 December 1921.
82 *The Times*, editorial, 30 December 1921.

Chapter 9

1 E.g., Imperial Conference, 22 June 1921, CAB 32/2.
2 Congreve—Young, 16 June 1921, CO 733/17A.

3   Salmond—Trenchard, 17 June 1921, CO 733/17A.
4   Report n. 5, 1 July 1921, CO 733/4.
5   S/SC—HC Pal, 11 July 1921, CO 733/3.
6   HC Pal—S/SC, 13 July 1921, CO 733/4.
7   HC Pal—S/SC, 25 July 1921, CO 733/4; see also for this period, Klieman, *op. cit.*, 212–27; Shwadran, *op. cit.*, ch. 8.
8   Churchill—Young, 25 August 1921, sent to FO, 30 August 1921, CO 732/2. Klieman, *op. cit.*, 213–15.
9   Shuckburgh—Masterton Smith, 29 September 1921, CO 733/11.
10 Young—Shuckburgh, 8 October 1921, CO 733/6. For a laudatory description of 'Abdallah, see Kirkbride, *op. cit*, ch. 4; Morris, *op. cit.*, 90–92.
11 Churchill—Secy, Secy M, 8 October 1921, CO 733/6. See also Shwadran, *op. cit.*, 139–40.
12 Churchill note, 26 October 1921, CO 733/6. For 'Abdallah's reasons for wanting to stay on, see Klieman, *op. cit.*, 226–27.
13 HC Pal—S/SC, 25 October 1921, CO 733/7.
14 Written 24 October, dispatched 4 November, arrived 15 November 1921, CO 733/7.
15 Memorandum by HC's Secretariat, 4 November, arrived 15 November 1921, CO 733/7.
16 Churchill note, 21 November 1921, CO 733/7. On this debate, see Klieman, *op. cit.*, 215–28.
17 Despatch HC Pal—S/SC, 24 November 1921, CO 733/7.
18 28 November 1921, Diary, Vol. 1, Box I, Philby papers, St. Anthony's College, Oxford.
19 R. Meinertzhagen, *Middle East Diary* (New York: 1960), 24 December 1921, 33–34.
20 Ibid., 21 June 1921, p. 99; 5 July 1921, 102. For an analysis of the factors going into the shaping of British policy, see Esco, *op. cit.*, vol. 1, 256–65.
21 Churchill—Sec (M), 15 June 1921, CO 732/5; for a brief discourse on Palestine in this period, see Klieman, *op. cit.*, 176–204.
22 Shuckburgh—S/SC, 17 June 1921, CO 732/5.
23 Despatch HC Pal—S/SC, sent 26 May 1921, CO 733/3.
24 Churchill—Secy (M), 18 June 1921, CO 732/5.
25 Idem. For a description of the contrasting communities in Palestine, see J. C. Hurewitz, *The Struggle for Palestine* (New York: 1950).
26 S/SC—HC Pal, 21 June 1921, CO 732/5.
27 Samuel—Churchill, 18 July 1921, LGP, F/9/3/72.
28 Weizman—Schmarya Levin (NY), 15 July 1921, Weizmann Archives.
29 Idem.
30 Notes of conversation at Balfour's house, 22 July 1921; Weizman—Deedes, 31 August 1921, Weizmann Archives.
31 Weizmann—Sam Untermeyer (Carlsbad), 28 July 1921, Weizmann Archives.
32 Shuckburgh—S/SC, 9 September 1921, CO 733/15.
33 HC Pal—S/SC, 9 September 1921, CO 733/6.
34 Young minute, 9 September 1921, CO 733/6.
35 S/SC—HC Pal, 12 September 1921, CO 733/6.
36 Shuckburgh—S/SC, 12 September 1921, CO 733/6.
37 HC Pal—S/SC, 17 September 1921, CO 733/6.
38 Shuckburgh—S/SC, 17 September 1921, CO 733/15.
39 Pinhas Rutenberg—Shuckburgh, 17 September 1921. CO 733/15; CO 733/6.
40 Shuckburgh—S/SC, 17 September 1921, CO 733/15.

41 Churchill—Shuckburgh, 20 September 1921, CO 733/6.
42 S/SC—HC Pal, 21 September 1921, CO 733/6. Gilbert, *op. cit.*, 620, 633–34.
43 Shuckburgh—S/SC, 25 July 1921, CO 733/13. See Esco, *op. cit.*, vol. 1, 227–29; Klieman, *op. cit.*, 190–97, 202; Andrews, *op. cit.*, vol. 2, p. 83; Hanna, *op. cit.*, 80.
44 Young minute, 11 August 1921, CO 733/14.
45 Conversation of S/SC and Palestine Arab Delegation, 12 August 1921, CO 733/17B; Gilbert, citing the Central Zionist Archives, says this discussion took place 15 August. Gilbert *op. cit.*, 625; on Palestine in 1921, see ch. 35; see also Esco, *op. cit.*, vol. 1, 279; Klieman, *op. cit.*, 192–94.
46 Conversation of S/SC and Palestine Arab Delegation, 22 August 1921, CO 733/14.
47 Idem.
48 Musa Kazim al-Hussayni—Churchill, 1 September 1921, CO 733/16.
49 Minutes, 2 October—10 October 1921, CO 733/6.
50 Supra, note 30.
51 HC Pal—S/SC, 4 June 1921, CO 733/3; HC Pal—S/SC, 23 June 1921, CO 733/4; Shuckburgh—S/SC, 7 July 1921, CO 733/4.
52 Young—Vernon, 25 August 1921, CO 733/13; Young—S/SC, 31 August 1921, CO 733/15.
53 Churchill—Secy (M), Young, 2 September 1921, CO 733/15.
54 Churchill—Secy (M), Young, 2 September 1921, CO 733/15.
55 Churchill—Lloyd George, 3 September 1921, LGP, F/9/3/86.
56 Congreve—Young, 16 June 1921, CO 733/17A. See also Klieman, *op. cit.*, 200–2.
57 Despatch HC Pal—S/SC, rcv 22 November 1921, CO 733/7.
58 Mond—Churchill, 15 December 1921, Weizmann Archives.
59 HC Pal—S/SC, 16 November 1921, CO 733/7.
60 Memorandum by S/SC, "Palestine," November 1921, C.P. 3515. CAB 24/131; WO 32/5840.
61 General Tudor, the commander of the "Black and Tans" Constabulary in Ireland, proposed transferring some companies to Palestine in the event of an Irish peace.
62 Wilson—S/SW, 10 December 1921, WO 32/5840.
63 Conference, 19 December 1921, WO 32/5840, WO 32/5899, CO 730/16.
64 Meinertzhagen, *op.cit.*, 19 December 1921, 114.
65 Conference of Ministers, 21 December 1921, CAB 23/27; WO 32/5840.
66 Churchill answer to Sir Eric Geddes Treasury Committee, 23 December 1921, CO 732/3.
67 Meinertzhagen, *op.cit.*, 16 November 1921, 110.
68 Memorandum by Weizmann, 21 July 1921, CO 733/16.
69 Young minute, 1 August 1921, CO 733/14.
70 Meinertzhagen memorandum, 31 July 1921, CO 733/14.
71 Shuckburgh minute, 3 August 1921, CO 733/14.
72 Young—S/SC, 4 August 1921, CO 733/14.
73 Memorandum by S/SC, "Palestine," 11 August 1921, C.P. 3213, CAB 24/127.
74 Idem.
75 Cab 70(21), 18 August 1921, CAB 23/26.
76 S/SC—Weizmann, 8 September 1921, CO 733/17B; *The Times*. 13 September 1921; see also Minutes, 17 August 1921, CO 733/16; Young—S. Landman, 29 August 1921, Weizmann Archives.

77 Despatch HC Pal—S/SC, 14 October 1921; HC Pal—S/SC, 16 November 1921, CO 733/7. Kedourie analyzes Samuel's methods and concludes that they were totally geared toward reconciling the Arabs to Zionism. Kedourie, *The Chatham House Version*, ch. 4.
78 Resume, 11 September 1921, CO 733/5.
79 Despatch HC Pal—S/SC, 19 October 1921, CO 733/6.
80 S/SC—HC Pal, 4 November 1921, CO 733/6.
81 HC Pal—S/SC, 11 November 1921, CO 733/7.
82 Churchill—Secy, Secy (M), 17 November 1921, CO 733/7.
83 S/SC—HC Pal, 13 December 1921, CO 733/8.
84 Meinertzhagen—Shuckburgh, 15 November 1921, CO 733/7. Klieman, *op. cit.*, 195–96.
85 Memorandum on Jewish immigration into Palestine, 12 October 1921, CO 733/6.
86 Minutes, 30 November–6 December, CO 537/855, CO 733/16, CO 537/854; minutes, 18th meeting of Zionist Executive, 30 November 1921, Weizmann Archives. For a description of the disillusionment of all parties concerned at the close of 1921, see Klieman, *op. cit.*, 199–204.

Chapter 10

1 For detailed information, see Gilbert, *op. cit.*, chs. 37–40; on Iraq, see ch. 44.
2 Interdepartmental Conference, 19 January 1922, CO 732/7; WO 32/5840.
3 Churchill—Prime Minister, 3 February 1922, LGP, F/10/2/41.
4 CO-WO, 3 February 1922, CO 730/14.
5 Conference of Ministers, 9 February 1922, CO 732/8.
6 9 March 1922, Parliamentary Debates, Commons.
7 Kedourie, *The Chatham House Version*, 242. See also Burgoyne, *op. cit.*, 270–71.
8 Kedourie, *The Chatham House Version*, 242–43; Ireland, *op. cit.*, 356–57; for details see chapter 19. For a personal view of events, see Bell, *op. cit.*, ch. 22; see also Gilbert, *op. cit.*, 797–819, 824, 855–56.
9 CO final draft of treaty, 10 January 1922, CO 730/33.
10 Minutes, 6–10 February 1922, CO 730/28.
11 Memorandum S/SC, 17 February 1922, C.P. 3748, CAB 24/133.
12 Curzon—Prime Minister, 5 April 1922, Cab 23(22), Appendix 4, CAB 23/30.
13 Cab 12(22), 21 February 1922, CAB 23/29.
14 S/SC—HC Iraq, 23 February 1922, CO 730/33.
15 HC Iraq—S/SC, 3 March 1922, CO 730/20.
16 S/SC—HC Iraq, 16 March 1922, CO 730/20; C.P. 3923, CAB 24/136.
17 Shuckburgh—Masterton Smith, S/SC, 30 March 1922, CO 730/33.
18 Churchill—Marsh, 1 April 1922, Ch.P. 17/27. See Gilbert, *op. cit.*, ch. 43; Mowat, *op. cit.*, 112; Taylor, *op. cit.*, 247.
19 Memorandum by S/SC, 31 March 1922, C.P. 3903, CAB 24/136.
20 HC Iraq—S/SC, 31 March 1922, C.P. 3924, CAB 24/136.
21 The Arabic word for "mandate," *'amr*, connotes subservience to a ruling power or person.
22 HC Iraq—S/SC, 2/3 April 1922, CO 730/21.
23 HC Iraq—S/SC, 1/2 April 1922, CO 730/21.
24 Cab 23(22), 5 April 1922, CAB 23/30.
25 Churchill—Cox, 6 April 1922, C.P. 3953, CAB 24/136
26 HC Iraq—S/SC, 7 April 1922, C.P. 3953, CAB 24/136.

27 Ireland, *op. cit.*, 351.
28 HC Iraq—S/SC, 5 April 1922, C.P. 3953, CAB 24/136.
29 Churchill—Cox, 19 April 1922, Ch.P. 17/26; S/SC—HC Iraq, 20 April 1922, C.P. 3953, CAB 24/136.
30 HC Iraq—S/SC, 22 April 1922, CO 730/21; C.P. 3953, CAB 24/136.
31 Churchill—Curzon, 24 April 1922, Curzon Papers Box 65, F/5.
32 S/SC—HC Iraq, 27 April 1922, CO 730/21; C.P. 3953, CAB 24/136.
33 Note Churchill—Young, 3 May 1922, CO 730/21; S/SC—HC Iraq, 5 May 1922, CO 730/21; C.P. 3953/136. Britain was still in the midst of the "anti-waste" campaign and as Iraq had been a prime target since 1920, Churchill did not wish to draw any more attention than necessary to it. Klieman, *op. cit.*, 84–85.
34 S/SC—HC Iraq, 15 June 1922, CO 730/22; C.P. 4178, CAB 24/138.
35 HC Iraq—S/SC, 27 June 1922, C.P. 4178, CAB 24/138.
36 HC Iraq—S/SC, 28 June 1922, C.P. 4178, CAB 24/138.
37 HC Iraq—S/SC, 9 July 1922, C.P. 4178, CAB 24/138.
38 S/SC—HC Iraq, 13 July 1922, C.P. 4178, CAB 24/138.
39 HC Iraq—S/SC, 12 July 1922, C.P. 4178, CAB 24/138.
40 Davidson (legal Secretary in Baghdad)—Young, quoting minutes, 2 August 1922, CO 730/23.
41 HC Iraq—S/SC, 16 July 1922, C.P. 4178, CAB 24/138.
42 S/SC—HC Iraq, 18 July 1922, C.P. 4178, CAB 24/138.
43 S/SC—HC Iraq, 18 July 1922, C.P. 4178, CAB 24/138.
44 HC Iraq—S/SC, 21 July 1922, C.P. 4178, CAB 24/138.
45 HC Iraq—S/SC, 29/30 July 1922, CO 730/23; C.P. 4178, CAB 24/138.
46 Minutes, 2 August 1922, CO 730/23. See Burgoyne, *op. cit.*, 288.
47 HC Iraq—S/SC, 10 August 1922, C.P. 4178, CAB 24/138.
48 Idem.
49 Memorandum by Young, 15 August 1922, CO 730/23.
50 Masterton Smith—HC Iraq, 16 August 1922, C.P. 4178, CAB 24/138.
51 HC Iraq—Masterton Smith, 17 August 1922, C.P. 4178, CAB 24/138.
52 S/SC—HC Iraq, 19 August 1922, CO 730/23.
53 S/SC—HC Iraq, 22 August 1922, C.P. 4178, CAB 24/138.
54 Kedourie, *op. cit.*, 244; Ireland, *op. cit.*, 357.
55 HC Iraq—S/SC, 23 August 1922, CO 4178, CAB 24/138. See also Kedourie, *The Chatham House Version*, 243–44; Longrigg, *op. cit.*, 141.
56 Churchill—Prime Minister, 23 August 1922, LGP, F/10/3/37.
57 HC Iraq—S/SC, 24 August 1922, C.P. 4178, CAB 24/138. See Graves, *op. cit.*, ch. 23.
58 Young—S/SC, 24 August 1922, CO 730/24.
59 HC Iraq—S/SC, 26 August 1922, C.P. 4178, CAB 24/138; CO 730/24. See Longrigg, *op.cit*, 141–42.
60 HC Iraq—S/SC, 27 August 1922, C.P. 4178, CAB 24/138.
61 Churchill—Cox, 28 August 1922, CO 730/24.
62 Conference of Ministers, Cab 56(22), 28 August 1922, CAB 23/31. On the slump and unemployment, see Mowat, *op. cit.*, 125–29.
63 S/SC—HC Iraq, 28 August 1922, C.P. 4178, CAB 24/138.
64 S/SC—HC Iraq, 29 August 1922, C.P. 4178, CAB 24/138.
65 Idem.

66 S/SC—HC Iraq, 30 August 1922, C.P. 4178, CAB 24/138.
67 Churchill—Lloyd George, 1 September 1922, LGP, F/10/3/41.
68 HC Iraq—S/SC, 31 August 1922, C.P. 4178, CAB 24/138.
69 S/SC—HC Iraq, 2 September 1922, C.P. 4178, CAB 24/138.
70 Lloyd George—Churchill, 5 September 1922, LGP, F/10/3/44.
71 Idem.
72 Churchill—Lloyd George, 6 September 1922, LGP, F/10/3/45.
73 Idem.
74 HC Iraq—S/SC, 7 September 1922, C.P. 4178, CAB 24/138; LGP, F/10/3/47.
75 S/SC—HC Iraq, 7 September 1922, C.P. 4233, CAB 24/139.
76 HC Iraq—S/SC, 10 September 1922, C.P. 4233, CAB 24/139.
77 S/SC—HC Iraq, 14 September 1922, C.P. 4233, CAB 24/139; CO 730/24.
78 Idem.
79 HC Iraq—S/SC, 17 September 1922, C.P. 4233, CAB 24/139.
80 HC Iraq—S/SC, 18 September 1922, C.P. 4233, CAB 24/139.
81 S/SC—HC Iraq, 19 September 1922, C.P. 4233, CAB 24/139.
82 HC Iraq—S/SC, 25 September 1922, C.P. 4233, CAB 24/139; CO 730/24.
83 Cab 56(22), 5 October 1922, CAB 23/31.
84 S/SC— HC Iraq, 7 October 1922, CO 730/34.
85 HC Iraq—S/SC, 10 October 1922, CO 4274, CAB 24/139; CO 730/25; in J. C. Hurewitz, *Diplomacy*, vol. 2, 111–14.
86 S/SC—HC Iraq, 16 October 1922, CO 730/25. For a negative assessment of what Britain created in Iraq, see Kedourie, *The Chatham House Version*, 258–65.

Chapter 11

1 Meinertzhagen—Shuckburgh, Masterton Smith, S/SC, 16 January 1922, CO 733/33. On Palestine, 1922, see Gilbert, *op. cit.*, ch. 36.
2 Churchill—Secy, Secy (M), 11 January 1922, CO 537/831; Minutes, 16–20 January 1922, CO 733/33.
3 Group Council, 11 January 1922, CO 733/33; Churchill—Shuckburgh, 14 January 1922, CO 733/33.
4 Communique to the Press, 14 January 1922, CO 733/33.
5 S/SC—HC Pal, 25 February 1922, CO 733/18; C.P. 3826, CAB 24/134. On the Palestine administration, see Esco, *op. cit.*, vol. 2, 296–328; Andrews, *op. cit.*, 107; for actions taken by this administration to widen the Arab-Jewish gulf, see Cohen, *op. cit.*, 75–91.
6 HC Pal—S/SC, 27 February 1922, C.P. 3826, CAB 24/134.
7 S/SC—HC Pal, 2 March 1922, CO 732/8; C.P. 3826, CAB 24/134.
8 Churchill note, 5 March 1922, CO 732/3.
9 HC Pal—SC, 6 March 1922, CO 733/19; C.P. 3826; CAB 24/134.
10 Vernon, Shuckburgh—S/SC, 10 March 1922, CO 733/19.
11 S/SC—HC Pal, 11 March 1922, CO 733/19.
12 Churchill—Secy, Secy (M), 22 February 1922.
13 IO—Under S/SC, 7 February 1922, CO 733/32; Montagu—Churchill, 6 March 1922, CO 733/19.
14 Worthington Evans—Churchill, 21 February 1922, CO 733/33.
15 Churchill—Shuckburgh, 24 February 1922, CO 733/33.

16 Interdepartmental Conference, 1 March 1922, WO 32/5840; 11 May 1922, WO 32/5841.
17 Shuckburgh—Masterton Smith, S/SC, 31 January 1922, CO 733/8.
18 Churchill—Shuckburgh, 2 February 1922, CO 733/8; Despatch S/SC—HC Pal, 7 February 1922, CO 733/8. For a summary of factors contributing to the emergence of the Amirate of Transjordan, see Klieman, *op. cit.*, 235.
19 Lawrence—Shuckburgh, 5 January 1922, CO 733/33; HC Iraq—S/SC, 10 January 1922, CO 730/19.
20 Minutes, Shuckburgh—Masterton Smith, S/SC, 16 January 1922, CO 730/19; Churchill—Secy, Secy (M), 26 January 1922, CO 730/19.
21 9 March 1922, Parliamentary Debates, Commons. Klieman describes him as the "architect of Britain's New Arab policy," and claims that he "relied heavily on the advice" of Lawrence. Klieman, *op. cit.*, 237–38, 247–48. Compare, supra, 158–59.
22 Churchill—Clementine Churchill, 4 February 1922, C.S., Ch.P. See Andrews, *op.cit.*, 80; Hanna, *op. cit.*, 80; Abu-Lughod, ed., *The Transformation of Palestine* (Evanston: 1971), 222–23.
23 Shuckburgh—Masterton Smith, S/SC, 7 February 1922, CO 733/33.
24 Minutes, 21–24 February 1922, CO 733/36.
25 Letter no. 1, Palestine Arab Delegation—S/SC, 21 February 1921, C.P. 1700. On the formulation of the anti-Zionist position, see Esco, *op. cit.*, vol. 1, 473–83. On how both the British and Zionists erred in thinking they could reconcile the Arabs to the Balfour Declaration, see Halpern *op. cit.*, 340; Hanna, *op. cit.*, 86.
26 Shuckburgh—Masterton Smith, S/SC, 28 February 1922, CO 733/36.
27 Idem.
28 Idem.
29 Shuckburgh—Musa Kazim, 1 March 1922, Zionist Central Archives; Letter no. 2, CO—Pal Arab Delegation, 1 March 1922, C.P. 1700. For comments; see, Andrews, *op. cit.*, 86–92.
30 Letter no. 3, Pal Arab Delegation—S/SC, 16 March 1922, C.P. 1700. See Andrews, *op. cit.*, 92–96.
31 Shuckburgh—Masterton Smith, 5 April 1922, CO 733/36.
32 Letter no. 4; CO—Pal Arab Delegation, 11 April 1922, C.P. 1700. See Andrews, *op. cit.*, 96–98.
33 Letter no. 4, CO—Pal Arab Delegation, 11 April 1922, C.P. 1700.
34 The Secretariat was the center around which revolved the whole of administrative machinery in Palestine. Its primary duty was initiation of all executive action required to bring legislation into operation. At this time Sir Wyndham Deedes was about to retire as Chief Secretary and negotiations were afoot to replace him with Sir Gilbert Clayton. Minutes, 17 May–25 August 1922, CO 733/24, 34.
35 Meeting of S/SC and HC Pal, 1 June 1922, CO 732/7; for an analysis of Sir Herbert Samuel, see Kedourie, *The Chatham House Version*, ch. 4.
36 Shuckburgh—Masterton Smith, Wood, S/SC, 24 May 1922, CO 733/34.
37 Minutes, 18 May–24 May 1922, CO 733/34.
38 Esco guessed that Samuel had a great part in formulating the White Paper, but that it was probably influenced by Churchill in the first place. Esco, *op. cit.*, vol. 1, 259; others write that it was written in "close collaboration with Samuel" Bowle, *op.cit.*, 220–21 or that it was issued 'over Churchill's signature," Hanna, *op. cit.*, 81.

39　Minutes, 18 May–24 May 1922, CO 733/34. On Samuel's London visit, see Esco, *op. cit.*, vol. 1, 280–81; Bowle, *op. cit.*, 220–21; Hanna *op. cit.*, 81.
40　Shuckburgh—S.SC, 24 May 1922, CO 733/34.
41　Shuckburgh—Weizmann, 27 May 1922, CO 733/34.
42　Shuckburgh—Samuel, 3 June 1922, CO 733/34.
43　Letter no. 5, CO—Zionist Organization, 3 June 1922, C.P. 1700. Esco, *op. cit.*, vol. 1, 282–84; Andrews, *op. cit.*, 98–101; on the Churchill White Paper in general, see Esco, *op. cit.*, vol. 1, 281–88; Klieman, *op. cit.*, 204; Halpern, *op. cit.*, 310–14; Hurewitz, *The Struggle for Palestine*, 21–22.
44　Letter no. 5, CO—Zionist Organization, 3 June 1922, C.P. 1700. For opposing views on whether the White Paper denied a Jewish state, see Esco, *op. cit.*, vol. 1, 284; Feiwel, *op. cit.*, 125; Halpern, *op. cit.*, 323. Hanna writes that the purpose of the policy paper was the creation of a binational but unitary state. Hanna, *op. cit.*, 69, 82.
45　Letter no. 5, CO—Zionist Organization, 3 June 1922, C.P. 1700; the lack of fear of a Jewish majority was based on two memoranda written by Mills summarizing Palestine's population statistics and his scientific forecasts and conclusions. 21 February 1922, CO 733/33; 12 June 1922, CO 733/21.
46　Shuckburgh—Vansittart, FO, 7 June 1922, CO 733/34.
47　Vansittart—Shuckburgh, 15 June 1922, CO 733/36.
48　Letter no. 7, Zionist Organization—CO, 18 June 1922, C.P. 1700. Esco, *op. cit.*, vol. 1, 286; Andrews, *op. cit.*, 104; some claim that the Zionists accepted because they were too weak to oppose Britain, cf. Cohen, *op. cit.*, 166, 173; Hanna *op. cit.*, 81–82. Weizmann wrote that he favored the "economic absorptive capacity" principle at that time and that "it was made clear to us that confirmation of the Mandate would be conditional on our acceptance of the policy as interpreted in the White Paper ... ." Weizmann, *op. cit.*, 290.
49　Letter no. 7, Zionist Organization—CO, 18 June 1922, C.P. 1700.
50　Shuckburgh—Masterton Smith, 22 June 1922, CO 733/36.
51　Letter no. 6, Pal Arab Delegation—S/SC, 17 June 1922, C.P. 1700. Esco, *op. cit.*, vol. 1, 286, 478–80; Andrews, *op. cit.*, 102.
52　Shuckburgh—Masterton Smith, 22 June 1922, CO 733/36.
53　Minutes, 23–28 June 1922, CO 733/36.
54　Letter no. 8, CO—Pal Arab Delegation, 23 June 1922, C.P. 1700. Andrews, *op.cit.*, 105.
55　Letter no. 9, S/SC—Officer Administrating Government of Palestine, 29 June 1922, C.P. 1700. Some writers claim that the White Paper is evidence of the change in spirit and modifications of emphasis which reduced the primacy of Jewish and increased the consideration of Arab interest; it is the first "whittling down" of the mandate quantitatively and qualitatively. Esco, *op. cit.*, vol. 1, 268, 285; Weizmann, *op. cit.*, 290. Others see it as the first major impediment to Jewish development which led to a growth in the contradiction between Zionist and British interests. Cohen, *op. cit.*, 172–74. Halpern sees it as an attempt to gain time to settle issues. Halpern, *op. cit.*, 339. For a scathing Zionist viewpoint, see W. Ziff, *The Rape of Palestine* (New York: 1938), 110–13; for an Arab viewpoint, S. Hadawi, *Bitter Harvest* (1967), 61–62.
56　21 June 1922, Parliamentary Debates, Lords. See Hanna, *op. cit.*, 82; P. Graves, *Palestine* (London: 1923), 72.
57　4 July 1922, Parliamentary Debates, Commons.
58　Meinertzhagen, *op. cit.*, 119.
59　4 July 1922, Parliamentary Debates, Commons.

60 Shuckburgh—Masterton Smith, 17 January 1922, CO 733/29. For more on Rutenberg, see Gilbert, *op. cit.*, 651–59; Bowle, *op. cit.*, 221–22; R. L. Taylor, *Winston Churchill* (Garden City: 1952), 304–5.
61 4 July 1922, Parliamentary Debates, Commons.
62 Kerensky telegram enclosed in Nathan—Vernon, 4 July 1922, CO 733/39.
63 4 July 1922, Parliamentary Debates, Commons. See Hanna, *op. cit.*, 83.
64 *The Times*, 6 July 1922. See Klieman, *op. cit.*, 239–40.
65 Churchill—Sec M, 10 July 1922, CO 733/36.
66 Memorial given to Churchill, 18 July 1922, CO 733/38.
67 Churchill—Islington 20 July 1922, CO 733/38; *The Times*, 18 August 1922.
68 Churchill—Balfour, 21 July 1922, CO 733/38.
69 Islington—Churchill, 16 August 1922, CO 733/38; *The Times*, 18 August 1922.
70 Sydenham—editor of The Times, 24 August 1922.
71 Churchill—Sydenham, 29 August 1922, *The Times*.
72 Sydenham—Churchill, 29 August 1922, *The Times*.
73 Churchill—Sydenham, 31 August 1922, *The Times*.
74 Charles E. Hughes—Balfour, 27 January 1922, CO 733/37.
75 Cecil Harmsworth, Acting British Representative on Council of League—Churchill, 18 January 1922, CO 733/33.
76 Churchill—Shuckburgh, 18 July 1922, CO 733/35.
77 Minutes, 17 March–18 March 1922, CO 733/37; CO—FO, 27 April 1922, CO 733/34.
78 Churchill—Balfour, 15 May 1922, CO 733/34.
79 Minutes, 19–22 June 1922, CO 733/34.
80 Report by Samuel on interview with Pope, 6 July 1922, CP 730–29.
81 Minutes, 30 June–4 July 1922, CO 733/34.
82 Conversation between Britain and Italy, 3 July 1922, CO 732/8.
83 Shuckburgh—Masterton Smith, Wood, S/SC, 19 July 1922, CO 733/35.
84 Shuckburgh—S/SC, 22 July 1922, CO 733/35. See Andrews, *op. cit.*, 106; Cohen, *op. cit.*, 173; Weizmann, *op. cit.*, 292. For details on Article 25 separating Transjordan from Palestine, see Bowle, *op. cit.*, 22; Klieman, *op. cit.*, 228–34; Kirkbridge, *op. cit.*, 27; Andrews, *op. cit.*, 107; Cohen, *op. cit.*, 173; Feiwel, *op. cit.*, 102–3; Hanna, *op. cit.*, 76–77.
85 Weizmann—Churchill, 26 July 1922, Weizmann Archives.
86 HC Pal—S/SC, 2 September 1922, CO 733/25.
87 HC Pal—S/SC, 14 September 1922, CO 733/25.
88 S/SC—Young, 15 September 1922, CO 733/25.
89 Minutes, 11 January 1922, CO 733/18; Minutes, 31 July 1922, CO 733/23; Young—S/SC, 8 September 1922, CO 733/25; Young—S/SC 14 September 1922, CO 733/28.
90 Churchill—Young, 15 September 1922, CO 733/25.
91 Idem.
92 Minutes, young—S/SC, 15 September 1922, CO 733/25.
93 Idem.
94 S/SC—HC Pal, 16 September 1922, CO 733/25.
95 HC Pal—S/SC, 17 September 1922, CO 733/25.
96 Young—S/SC, 20 September 1922, CO 733/25.
97 S/SC—HC Pal, 28 September 1922, CO 733/25; HC Pal—S/SC, 30 September 1922, CO 733/25; Young—Masterton Smith, 3 October 1922, CO 733/35; Young—S/SC, 10 October 1922, CO 733/35.

98 M. Kinnear, *The Fall of Lloyd George* (Toronto: 1973). For the party crisis and the fall of Lloyd George, see Gilbert, *op. cit.*, ch. 46; Mowat, *op. cit.*, 132–42; Taylor, *op. cit.*, 251.
99 Kinnear, *op. cit.*, 21–24. See Taylor, *op. cit.*, 244–45, 252.
100 On Chanak, see D. Walder, *The Chanak Affair* (London: 1964); Mowat, *op. cit.*, 116–19; Taylor, *op. cit.*, 248–50; R. R. James, *Churchill, A Study in Failure*, 1900–1939 (Cleveland: 1970), 155–62; Gilbert, *op. cit.*, ch. 45.

Bibliography

I. Unpublished Primary Sources
A. Great Britain, Official Correspondence

Public Record Office:
Air Ministry files, in Foreign Office Series 371:
Turkey: Political, 1906–
Cabinet Office Papers, Series 1: Committee of Imperial Defence, Misc. Records
Series 2: Committee of Imperial Defence, Meetings
Series 4: Committee of Imperial Defence, Misc. Records
Series 5: Committee of Imperial Defence, Colonial Defence
Series 6: Committee of Imperial Defence, Indian Defence
Series 8: Committee of Imperial Defence, OverseasSubcommittee
Series 9: Committee of Imperial Defence, Overseas Defence
Series 10: Committee of Imperial Defence, Minutes
Series 15: Committee of Imperial Defence,Coordination
Series 16: Committee of Imperial Defence, Papers, 1907–10
Series 17: Committee of Imperial Defence, Correspondence and Misc. Papers
Series 21: Cabinet, registered files, 1917–19
Series 22: Cabinet minutes: War Council, 1914–16
Series 23: Cabinet minutes: War Council, 1916–19
Series 24: Cabinet papers: 'G' series
Series 27: Cabinet Committees, minutes and memoranda
Series 37: Cabinet papers: confidential prints, 1912–16
Series 41: letters to His Majesty
Colonial Office Papers, Series 323: Correspondence of Secretary of State for the Colonies
Series 537: Misc.
Series 725: Aden
Series 727: Arabia
Series 730: Iraq
Series 732: Middle East
Series 733: Palestine

Foreign Office Papers, Series 371: Turkey: Political, 1906–
Munitions Papers, Series 1: Munitions Council Daily Reports
Series 5: Ministry of Munitions Records, Meetings and correspondence
War Office Papers, Series: 32 Registered papers and correspondence
Series 33: Misc. reports
Series 106: Correspondence and Papers: Defence and Operational Plans
Series 157: Intelligence reports and summaries
Series 158: Correspondence and Papers of Military Headquarters
Series: 159: Private Office Papers
Series 163: Army Council
Foreign and Commonwealth Office: India Office Records: Political Department, Political and Secret Subject files (L/P & S/10)

B. Private Papers

(A. J.) Balfour Papers, British Museum, London
Churchill Papers, Chartwell Papers, Cambridge
Curzon Papers, India Office Library, London
(T. E.) Lawrence Papers, Bodleian Library, Oxford
Lloyd George Papers, Beaverbrook Library, London
Lothian Papers, Scottish Record Office, Edinburgh
Philby Papers, St. Anthony's College, Oxford
Samuel Papers, St. Anthony's College, Oxford
(A. T.) Wilson Papers, British Museum, London

II. Published Primary Sources

A. Official Publications

Great Britain, Parliamentary Debates, House of Commons. Fifth Series, 1919–1922.
Great Britain, Parliamentary Papers, 1919–1922.
Great Britain, Report on 'Iraq Administration October 1920–March 1922. London: H. M.'s Stationery Office, 1923.
Woodward, E. S. & R. Butler, eds., *Documents on British Foreign Policy 1919–1939*. London: H. M.'s Stationery Office 1952.

B. Private Publications (Memoirs, Correspondence, Contemporary Studies)

Abdullah, King. Memoirs. New York: Philosophical Library, 1950.
Bell, Lady, ed. *The Letters of Gertrude Bell*. London: Ernest Benn Ltd., 1927. 2 vols.

Bentwich, Norman. *My 77 Years*. Philadelphia: The Jewish Publication Society of America, 1961.

Bullard, Sir Reader. *The Camels Must Go: An Autobiography*. London: Faber & Faber, 1961.

Burgoyne, Elizabeth. *Gertrude Bell: From Her Personal Papers, 1914-1926*. London: Ernest Been Ltd., 1961. 2 vols.

Callwell, C. E. *Field Marshal Sir Henry Wilson: His Life & Diaries*. London: Cassel & Co., Ltd., 1927. 2 vols.

Churchill, Sarah. *A Thread in the Tapestry*. New York: Dodd, Mead & Co., 1967.

Churchill, Winston S. *Amid These Storms: Thoughts and Adventures*. New York: Charles Scribner's Sons, 1932.

_____. *A Roving Commission: My Early Life*. New York: Charles Scribner's Sons, 1930.

_____. *Great Contemporaries*. London: Thornton, Butterworth Ltd., 1937.

_____. "Reflections on the Strategy of the Allies," *Century* 94, (May 1917), 117-21.

_____. *The World Crisis*. New York: Charles Scribner's Sons, 1923. 6 vols.

Eade, Charles, ed. *Churchill by his Contemporaries*. London: Hutchinson & Co., 1953.

Hurewitz, J. C. *Diplomacy in the Near and Middle East: A Documentary Record 1535-1956*. New York: Van Nostrand Co., 1956. 2 vols.

Ingrams, Doreen. *Palestine Papers 1917-1922: Seeds of Conflict*. New York: George Braziller, 1973.

Lloyd George, David. *War Memoirs*. Boston: Little, Brown & Co., 1933. 6 vols.

McGowan, Norman. *My Years with Churchill*. New York: British Book Centre, 1958.

Meinertzhagen, Richard. *Middle East Diary, 1917-1956*. New York: Thomas Yoseloff, 1960.

Samuel, Edwin. *A Lifetime in Jerusalem*. London: Vallentine, Mitchell, 1970.

Storrs, Sir Ronald. *The Memoirs of...* New York: G. P. Putnam's Sons, 1937.

Thompson, W. H. *Assignment: Churchill*. New York: Farrar, Straus & Young, 1955.

Weizman, Chaim. *Trial and Error*. Philadelphia: The Jewish Publication Society of America, 1949. 2 vols.

Wilson, Sir A. T. *Mesopotamia 1917-1920: A Clash of Loyalties*. London: Oxford University Press, 1931.

C. Books, Articles and Periodicals

Abu-Lughod, Ibrahim, ed. *The Transformation of Palestine: Essays on the Origin and Development of the Arab-Israeli Conflict*. Evanston: Northwestern University Press, 1971.

Adelson, Roger. *London and the Invention of the Middle East: Money, Power, and War, 1902-1922*. New Haven: Yale University Press, 1995.

Alon, Yoav. *The Making of Jordan: Tribes, Colonialism and the Modern State*. New York: J.B. Tauris, 2007.

Andrews, Fannie Fern. *The Holy Land under Mandate*. Boston: Houghton Mifflin Company, 1931. 2 vols.

Antonius, George. *The Arab Awakening*. New York: J. B. Lippincott Co., 1939.

Atia, Nadia. *World War I in Mesopotamia: the British and the Ottomans in Iraq*. London: I.B. Taurus, 2016.

Avery, Peter. *Modern Iran*. New York: Frederick A. Praeger, 1965.

Barbour, Nevill. *Nisi Dominus, a Survey of the Palestine Controversy*. London: George G. Harrap & Co., 1946.

Bardens, Dennis. *Churchill in Parliament*. London: Robert Hale, 1967.

Barker, A. J. *The Bastard War: The Mesopotamian Campaign of 1914–1918*. New York: Dial Press, 1967.

Barr, James. *A Line in the Sand: Britain, France and the Struggle for the Mastery of the Middle East*. New York: Simon & Schuster, 2011.

Beaverbrook, Lord. *The Decline and Fall of Lloyd George*. London: Beaverbrook, Foundations, 1963.

Bell, H.T. Montague, "Great Britain and the Persian Gulf", *United Empire*, VI (April 1915), 274–80.

_____. "Churchill, the Life Triumphant," *American Heritage Magazine*, 1965.

Beloff, Max. *Imperial Sunset: Britain's Liberal Empire, 1897–1921*. New York: Alfred A. Knopf, 1970.

Bentwich, Norman. *England in Palestine*. London: Kegan Paul, Trench, Trubnert Co., Ltd., 1932.

Bickerton, Ian, & Carla Klausner. *A Concise History of the Arab Israeli Conflict*. New Jersey: Prentice Hall, 1998.

Birkenhead, Earl of. *Contemporary Personalities*. Freeport, New York: Books for Libraries Press, 1961.

Bishop, Donald. *The Administration of British Foreign Relations*. New York: Syracuse University Press, 1961.

Bloom, Cecil. "Sir Mark Sykes: British Diplomat and a Convert to Zionism," *Jewish Historical Society of England* vol. 43, 2011, 141–57.

Bocca, Geoffrey. *The Adventurous Life of Winston Churchill*. New York: Julian Messner, Inc., 1958.

Bonham Carter, Violet. *Winston Churchill: An Intimate Portrait*. New York: Harcourt, Brace & World, Inc., 1965.

Bowle, John. *Viscount Samuel, a Biography*. London: Victor Gollancz Ltd., 1957.

Boyle, Andrew. *Trenchard*. London: Collins, 1962.

British Information Services. *Britain and Palestine*. New York: 1947.

Broad, Lewis. *Winston Churchill 1874–1951*. New York: Philosophical Library, 1952.

Bullard, Sir Reader. *Britain and the Middle East*. London: Hutchinson's University Library, 1952.

Busch, Briton. *Britain, India, and the Arabs, 1914–1921*. Los Angeles: University of California Press, 1971.

Caplan, Neil. *Palestine Jewry and the Arab Question, 1917–1925*. New York: Frank Cass, 1978.
Carrington, C. E. *The British Overseas*. Cambridge: The University Press, 1950.
Chester, D. N., ed. *The Organization of British Central Government, 1914–1956*. London: George Allen & Unwin Ltd., 1957.
Churchill, Randolph S. *Winston S. Churchill: Young Statesman, 1901–1914*. Boston: Houghton Mifflin Company, 1967. Vol. 2.
Cohen, Aharon. *Israel and the Arab World*. New York: Funk & Wagnalls, 1970.
Cohen, Michael J. *Britain's Moment in Palestine, 1917–1948*. London: Routledge, 2014.
_____. *Churchill and the Jews, 1900–1948*. London: Routledge, 1985.
Commager, Henry S., "Winston Churchill: An Appreciation," *The American Mercury* 61 (August 1945), 135–46.
Constantine, Stephen. *The Making of British Colonial Development Policy 1914–1940*. London: Routledge, 1985.
Cooper, Duff. *Old Men Forget*. New York: E. P. Cutton & Co., 1954.
Cowles, Virginia. *Winston Churchill, the Era and the Man*. New York: Harper & Brothers, 1953.
Cox, Jafna L. "A Splendid Training Ground: The Importance to the Royal Air Force of Its Role in Iraq, 1919–32," *The Journal of Imperial and Commonwealth History"* vol. 13, 1985, no. 2.
Cummings, Henry H. *Franco-British Rivalry in the Post-War Near East*. London: Oxford University Press, 1938.
Dann, Uriel. *Studies in the History of Transjordan, 1920–1949: The Making of a State*. New York: Routledge, 2019.
Davenport, E. H. and Sidney R. Cooke. *The Oil Trusts and Anglo-American Relations*. New York: the Macmillan Company, 1924.
Davies, Joseph. *The Prime Minister's Secretariat, 1916–1920*. Newport, Great Britain: R.H. John, Ltd., 1951.
Dawisha, Adeed. *Iraq: A Political History from Independence to Occupation*. Princeton: Princeton University Press: 2009.
De Mendelssohn, Peter. *The Age of Churchill: Heritage and Adventure, 1874–1911*. London: Thames-Hudson, 1961. Vol. 1.
Dodge, Toby. *Inventing Iraq: the Failure of Nation Building and a History Denied*. New York: Columbia University Press, 2003.
Dunner, Joseph. *The Republic of Israel; Its History and Its Promise*. New York: McGraw-Hill Book Co. Inc., 1950.
Esco Foundation for Palestine. *Palestine: A Study of Jewish, Arab, and British Policies*. New Haven: Yale University Press, 1947. 2 vols.
Farmer, Bernard J. *Bibliography of the Works of Sir Winston S. Churchill*. London: 1962.
Feiwel, T. R. *No Ease in Zion*. London: Secker & Warburg, 1938.
Fiddes, George V. *The Dominions and Colonial Office*. London: G. P. Putnam's Sons Ltd., 1926.
Fisher, John. *Curzon and British Imperialism in the Middle East, 1916–1919*. London: Routledge, 1999.

Fishman, Jack. *My Darling Clementine, The Story of Lady Churchill.* New York: David McKay Co., Inc., 1963.

Fitzsimons, M. A. Empire by Treaty: *Britain and the Middle East in the Twentieth Century.* Indiana: University of Notre Dame Press, 1964.

Foster, Henry A. *The Making of Modern Iraq.* Norman Oklahoma: University of Oklahoma Press, 1935.

Friedman, Isaiah. *The Question of Palestine, 1914–1918: British-Jewish-Arab Relations.* London: Routledge & Kegan Paul, 1973.

Frischwasser-Ra'anan, H. F. *The Frontiers of a Nation.* London: The Batchworth Press, 1955.

Frye, Richard. *The Near East and the Great Powers.* New York: Kennikat Press, Inc., 1951.

Gardiner, a. G. *Prophets, Priests, and Kings.* London: J. M. Dent & Sons Ltd., 1914.

Gilbert, Martin. *Churchill—A Life.* New York: Henry Holt & Co., 1991.

_____. *Churchill and the Jews: A Lifelong Friendship.* New York: Henry Holt & Co., 2007.

_____. *In Search of Churchill: A Historian's Journey.* London: Harper Collins, 1994.

_____. *Winston S. Churchill: Volume 3, The Challenge of War 1914–1916.* Boston: Houghton Mifflin Co., 1971.

_____. *Winston S. Churchill: Volume 4, The Stricken World 1916–1922.* Boston: Houghton Mifflin Co., 1975.

_____, ed. *Churchill.* Englewood Cliffs, N. J.: Prentice Hall, Inc., 1967.

_____. *Winston Churchill.* London: Oxford University Press, 1966.

Glubb, Sir John Bagot. *Britain and the Arabs: A Study of Fifty Years, 1908–1958.* London: Hodder & Stoughton, 1959.

_____. *Syria, Lebanon, Jordan.* New York: Walker & Co., 1967.

Goldstein, Erik. *The First World War Peace Settlements, 1919–1925.* London: Routledge, 2013.

Gordon, Hampton. *The War Office.* London: Putnam, 1935.

Graves, Philip. *The Life of Sir Percy Cox.* London: Hutchinson & Co., Ltd., (1938)

_____. *Palestine, the Land of Three Faiths.* London: Jonathan Cape, 1923.

Groseclose, Elgin. *Introduction to Iran.* New York: Oxford University Press, 1947.

Guedalla, Philip. *Mr. Churchill.* New York: Reynal & Hitchcock, 1942.

Guinn, Paul. *British Strategy and Politics 1914 to 1918.* Oxford: Clarendon Press, 1965.

Hadawi, Sami. *Bitter Harvest: Palestine between 1914 and 1967.* The New World Press, 1967.

Hall, Henry. *The Colonial Office.* London: Longman's Green & Co., 1937.

Halpern, Ben. *The Idea of the Jewish State.* Cambridge, M.A.: Harvard University Press, 1961.

Hanky, Lord. *Diplomacy by Conference.* London: Ernest Benn Ltd., 1946.

Hanna, Paul L. *British Policy in Palestine.* Washington, D.C.: American Council on Public Affairs, 1942.

Hassall, Christopher. *Edward March.* London: Longmans, Green & Co. Ltd., 1959.

Hoskins, Halford L. *The Middle East: Problem Area in World Politics.* New York: The Macmillan Co., 1955.

Bibliography | 217

Howard, Harry N. *The Partition of Turkey: A Diplomatic History, 1913–1923*. New York: Howard Fertig, 1966.

Howse, A.L., "Churchill Considered Historically," *Encounter* 26 (January 1960), 45–50.

Hughes, Emrys. *Winston Churchill, British Bulldog*. New York: Exposition Press, 1955.

Hughes, Matthew. *Allenby and British Strategy in the Middle East, 1917–1919*. London: Routledge, 1999.

Hurewitz, J. C. *Middle East Dilemmas, The Background of United States Policy*. New York: Harper & Brothers, 1953.

_____. *The Struggle for Palestine*. New York: W.W. Norton & Co., Inc., 1950.

Hyamson, Albert M. *Palestine under the Mandate, 1920–1948*. London: Methuen & Co., Ltd., 1950.

Ireland, Philip W. *'Iraq: A Study in Political Development*. London: Jonathan Cape, 1937.

James, Robert Rhodes. *Churchill, Study in Failure 1900–1939*. Cleveland: The World Publishing Co., 1970.

Johnson, Franklyn Arthur. *Defence by Committee: the British Committee of Imperial Defence, 1885–1959*. London: Oxford University Press, 1960.

Joseph, Barnard. *Ha-Shilton Ha-Briti Be-Eretz Yisrael*. Jerusalem: Mosad Bialik, 1948.

Katzburg, N. *Mishtar ha-Mandat be-Eretz Yisrael*. Tel Aviv: University of Tel Aviv, 1967–68.

Kedourie, Elie. *The Chatham House Version and other Middle Eastern Studies*. New York: Praeger Publishers, 1970.

_____. *England and the Middle East: the destruction of the Ottoman Empire 1914–1921*. London: Bowes & Bowes, 1956.

Kinnear, Michael. *The Fall of Lloyd George: The Political Crisis of 1922*. Toronto: University of Toronto Press, 1973.

Kirkbride, Alec Seath. *A Crackle of Thorns*. London: John Murray, 1956.

Klieman, Aaron S. *Foundations of British Policy in the Arab World: The Cairo Conference of 1921*. Baltimore: Johns Hopkins Press, 1970.

Koestler, Arthur. *Promise and Fulfillment—Palestine, 1917–1949*. New York: The Macmillan Co., 1949.

Kraus, Rene. *Winston Churchill*. New York: J. B. Lippincott Co., 1940.

Lenczowski, George. *Russia and the West in Iran, 1918–48: A Study in Big-Power Rivalry*. Ithaca: Cornell University Press, 1949.

Loder, J. de V. *The Truth about Mesopotamia, Palestine and Syria*. London: George Allen & Unwin Ltd., 1923.

Longrigg, Stephen H. *'Iraq, 1900 to 1950: A Political, Social, and Economic History*. London: Oxford University Press, 1953.

_____, and Frank Stoakes. *Iraq*. London: Ernest Benn Ltd., 1958.

McCormick, Donald. *The Mask of Merlin: A Critical Study of David Lloyd George*. London: MacDonald, 1963.

Mackintosh, John P. *The British Cabinet*. Toronto: University of Toronto Press, 1962.

McMeekin, Sean. *The Ottoman Endgame: War, Revolution, and the Making of the Modern Middle East, 1908-1923*. New York: Penguin, 2015.

Main, Ernest. *Palestine at the Crossroads*. New York: W.W. Norton & Co. Inc., 1937.

Manning, Paul & Milton Bronner. *Mr. England: The Life Story of Winston Churchill*. Chicago: The John C. Winston Co., 1941.

Marchant, James, ed. *Winston Spencer Churchill: Servant of Crown and Commonwealth*. London: Cassell & Co. Ltd., 1954.

Marlowe, John. *Late Victorian: The Life of Sir Arnold Talbot Wilson*. London: The Cresset Press, 1967.

_____. *The Persian Gulf in the Twentieth Century*. New York: Frederick A. Praeger, 1962.

Marsh, Edward. *A Number of People*. New York: Harper & Brothers, 1939.

Martin, Hugh. *Battle: The Life Story of Winston S. Churchill*. London: Victor Gollancz Ltd., 1940.

Martin, Ralph G. *Jennie: The Life of Lady Randolph Churchill*. Englewood Cliffs, N. J.: Prentice Hall, INC., 1971. Vol. 2.

Masterson, Lucy, *C. F. G. Masterman: A Biography*. London: Frank Cass & Co., Ltd., 1968.

Mathew, William M. "The Balfour Declaration and the Palestine Mandate, 1917-1923: British Imperialist Imperatives," *British Journal of Middle Eastern Studies* vol. 40, 2013, no. 3, 231-50.

Medlicott, W. N. *British Foreign Policy since Varsailles 1919-1963*. London Methuen & Co., Ltd., 1968.

Millard, Candice. *Hero of the Empire: the Boer War, a Daring Escape, and the Making of Winston Churchill*. New York: Doubleday, 2016.

Miller, Rory, ed., *Britain, Palestine and Empire: The Mandate Years*. Farnham: Ashgate Publishing, 2010.

Monroe, Elizabeth. *Britain's Moment in the Middle East 1914-1956*. Baltimore: The John Hopkins Press, 1963.

Moorehead, Alan. *Winston Churchill in Trial and Triumph*. Boston: Houghton Mifflin Co., 1955.

Morin, Relman. *Churchill: Portrait of Greatness*. Englewood Cliffs, N. J.: Prentice Hall, Inc., 1965.

Morris, James. *The Hashemite Kings*. New York: Pantheon Books Inc., 1959.

Mowat, Charles L. *Britain between the Wars, 1918-1940*. Chicago: University of Chicago Press, 1955.

Neilson, Francis. *The Churchill Legend*. Appleton, Wisconsin: C.C. Nelson Publishing, Co., 1954.

Nevakivi, Jukka. *Britain, France and the Arab Middle East 1914-1920*. London: Athlone Press, 1969.

Owen, Frank. *Tempestuous Journey: Lloyd George, His Life and Times*. London: Hutchinson & Co., Ltd., 1954.

Pappe, Ilan. *A History of Modern Palestine: One Land, Two People.* Cambridge: Cambridge University Press, 2004.

Paris, Timothy J. *Britain, the Hashemites and Arab Rule, 1920–1925: The Sherifian Solution.* London: Frank Cass, 2003.

_____. "British Middle East Policy-Making after the First World War: The Lawrentian and Wilsonian Schools", *The Historical Journal* vol. 41, no. 3, September 1998, 773–93.

Parkinson, Sir Cosmo. *The Colonial Office from Within, 1909–1945.* London: Faber & Faber Ltd., 1947.

Patai, Raphael. *The Kingdom of Jordan.* Princeton, N. J.: Princeton University Press, 1958.

Peretz, Don. *The Middle East Today.* New York: Holt, Rinehart & Winston, Inc., 1965.

Philby, H. St. John. *Sa'udi Arabia.* New York: Frederick A. Praeger, 1955.

Rabinowicz, Oskar K. *Winston Churchill on Jewish Problems.* New York: Thomas Yoseloff, 1960.

Reguer, Sara, "Churchill's Role in the Dardanelles Campaign," *The British Army Review*, no. 8 (December 1994), 70–80.

_____, "The Ottoman Empire's Declaration of War, 1914: A Chapter in British Naval History," *The Middle East and North Africa: Essays in Honor of J.C. Hurewitz*, ed. By Reeva S. Simon. New York: Columbia University Press, 1990, 409–31.

_____, "Persian Oil and the First Lord: A Chapter in the Career of Winston Churchill," *Military Affairs* vol. 46, no. 3 (October 1982), 134–38.

Robins, Philip. *A History of Jordan.* Cambridge University Press, 2019.

Rogan, Eugene. *The Fall of the Ottomans: The Great War in the Middle East.* New York: Basic Books, 2015.

Roskill, Stephen. *Hankey: Man of Secrets.* London: Collins, 1970–73. 2 vols.

Royal Institute of International Affairs. *The Middle East: A Political and Economic Survey.* London: 1954.

Rutledge, Ian. *Enemy on the Euphrates: the British Occupation of Iraq and the Great Arab Revolt, 1914–1921.* London: Saqi Books, 2014.

Safran, Nadav. *Israel: The Embattled Ally.* Cambridge, M. A.: Harvard University Press, 1978.

Sharabi, H. B. *Governments and Politics of the Middle East in the Twentieth Century.* New York: Van Nostrand Co., Inc., 1962.

Shwadran, Benjamin. *Jordan, a State of Tension.* New York: Council for Middle Eastern Affairs Press, 1959.

Sieff, Martin. *The Politically Incorrect Guide to the Middle East.* Washington, D. C.: Regnery Publishing, 2008.

Simon, Reeva S. & Eleanor Tejirian, eds. *The Creation of Iraq, 1914–1921.* New York: Columbia University Press, 2004.

Soustelle, Jacques. *The Long March of Israel.* New York: American Heritage Press, 1969.

Spector, Ivar. *The Soviet Union and the Muslim World, 1917–1956.* Washington: University of Washington Press, 1956.

Taylor, A. J. P. *Churchill Revised: A Critical Assessment.* New York: The Dial Press, Inc., 1969.

_____. *English History 1914–1945.* Oxford: Oxford University Press, 1965.

Taylor, Robert Lewis. *Winston Churchill: An Informal Study of Greatness.* Garden City, N. Y.; Doubleday & Co. Inc., 1952.

The Times, London, 1919–1922.

Thompson, R. W. *Winston Churchill: The Yankee Marlbourough.* Garden City, N. Y.: Doubleday & Co. Inc., 1963.

Thomson, Malcolm. *Churchill, His Life and Times.* London: Oldhams Books Ltd., 1965.

Touken, B. U. *A Short History of Trans-Jordan.* London: Luzac & Co., 1945.

Townsend, John. *Proconsul to the Middle East: Sir Percy Cox and the End of Empire.* New York: I.B. Taurus, 2010.

Tuchman, Barbara. *The Proud Tower.* New York: Bantam Books. 1972.

Walder, David. *The Chanak Affair.* London: Hutchinson, 1964.

Watt, D. C. *Personalities and Policies.* London: Longmans, Green & Co. Ltd., 1965.

Westrate, Bruce. *The Arab Bureau: British Policy in the Middle East, 1916–1920.* Pennsylvania: Pennsylvania State University Press, 1992.

Wibberley, Leonard. *The Life of Winston Churchill.* New York: Farmar, Straus & Siroux, 1965.

Williams, Ann. *Britain and France in the Middle East and North Africa, 1914– 1967.* New York: St. Martin's Press. 1968.

Wilson, Mary C. *King Abdullah, Britain, and the Making of Jordan.* Cambridge: Cambridge University Press, 1987.

Woodward, David R. *Hell in the Holy Land: World War I in the Middle East.* Lexington: University of Kentucky Press, 2006.

Young, Kenneth. *Churchill and Beaverbrook.* London: Eyre & Spottiswoode, 1966.

Ziff, William B. *The Rape of Palestine.* New York: Longmans, Green & Co., 1938.

Index

A
'Abdallah, 5, 13, 58, 60, 68–70, 73–74, 77, 79–84, 88–89, 96–97, 106–107, 127–129, 162, 175, 177, 180, 195n15, 196n29a
'Ali, 60, 88
1936 Arab Revolt, 182
Abramson, Julius, 127, 129
Aden, 61, 65–66, 78, 81
Afghanistan, 17–19, 29, 50
Air Ministry, 25, 65, 96, 103, 114–115, 119–120, 144, 153, 159–160
Aitken, Max (Lord Beaverbrook), 177, 185n2
Aleppo, 12, 44, 61
Alexandria, 88
Allenby, Edmund, 9–10, 27, 30, 38, 43–44, 88, 129
Anatolia, 7, 14, 26, 34, 46, 51
Anglo-Persian Agreement, 48
Ankara, 14, 46, 94, 156
anti-Zionism, 77, 138, 140, 163, 170, 172–173, 181
Aqaba Gulf, 72
Arabian Peninsula, 2, 7, 10, 65, 68–69, 78, 81
Armenia, 12, 30, 50
Arslan, Mazhar, 129
Asia Minor, 33, 35, 174, 178, 181
'Asir, 78
Asquith, Herbert H., 177
as-Salt, 44, 81
Auja concession, 134

B
Baghdad, 22, 24–25, 40, 47–48, 50, 62–63, 74, 88, 92–93, 110, 113–114, 119, 122, 124, 147, 153, 156–157, 162, 187n49, 192n101, 195n3

Baku, 51
Balfour Declaration, 5, 10, 74, 84, 99, 106, 132–133, 135–137, 141–142, 160, 163–167, 169–170, 172–173, 181–182, 184n13, 207n25
Balfour, Arthur J., 8, 26–27, 101, 112–113, 132–133, 140–141, 146–147, 168–169, 172–173
Basrah, 8, 22, 47, 49, 54, 55, 61, 63–64, 74, 92–93, 110, 145, 195n3
Batum, 45
Beersheba, 72
Beirut, 99Bell, Gertrude, 74–76, 88, 90, 193n17
Bir Yaakov, 88
Birkenhead, 18
Bolsheviks, 4, 8, 17–18, 29, 32–35, 39, 44, 50–51, 56, 79, 86, 106, 126, 144, 172
Bonar Law, Andrew, 33, 40, 177
Bonham-Carter, Edgar, 110
Bouillon, Franklin, 122
Bullard, Reader, 66
Bunsen, Maurice, de, 7
Bursa, 27

C
Cabinet, 4–5, 9, 13, 16–17, 20, 22, 24, 26, 29–30, 33–43, 45–56, 58, 60–61, 63, 65–66, 73, 79–82, 91, 94–96, 100–104, 110–111, 115–116, 118, 122–124, 127, 129–130, 133, 138–141, 145–148, 152–155, 157–159, 178, 180–181, 184n31, 185n7, 197n2
Cairo Conference, 70, 73–90, 105, 180, 197n2
Cairo, 4, 10, 26, 67, 72–73, 75–76, 81, 88–89, 91, 93–94, 97, 103, 116, 180, 184n21, 187n49, 196n29a, 197n2Caix, M., le, 88

Carslbad, 113
Caucasus, 17, 123
Ceylon, 92, 154
Chamberlain, Austen, 97, 108, 177
Chanak Crisis, 178
Christianity, 86, 99, 132, 135, 137, 167, 183n9
    Catholic, 174
Churchill White Paper, 5, 160, 167, 208n43
Churchill, Clementine, 109
Churchill, Marigold, 109
Cilicia, 12–13, 30, 60, 100, 187
Clark, Travers E., 23
Clauson, Gerard, 127
Clemenceau, George, 11, 13, 32
Cockran, Bourke, 4
Colonial Office, 4, 35, 41, 43, 54–59, 65–66, 69, 71, 79, 81, 94–95, 104, 114–115, 117–121, 124, 130, 139, 143, 145–146, 148, 152, 161, 163, 166–167, 169–174, 180, 182, 192n6, 193n43
    Middle East Department, 4, 35, 57, 71, 79–80, 89, 93, 95, 101, 105, 109, 113, 123, 125, 127, 129, 133, 137, 142, 160, 162, 163, 166, 168, 171–175, 180, 182, 201n72
Congreve, Walter Norris, 68, 74, 127, 129, 138, 195n15
Conservative party, 52, 177
Constantine (King), 52–53, 178
Constantinople, 6, 16, 29–31, 33, 35–36, 38, 45–46, 49, 52, 100, 178, 181, 198n62
Constantinople Agreement, 7Cornwallis, Kinahan, 78, 88, 93, 156–158
Cox, Percy, 40, 50, 59, 61, 92, 105, 144, 154, 192n6
Crane, Charles R., 12
Creedy, Herbert, 65
Curzon, George, 10–11, 22–24, 43–44, 48, 50, 53, 55–56, 58, 60, 62, 67–68, 101, 108, 123–124, 146, 149, 159, 192n108

D

Daily Express, 177
Daily Mail, 177
Daily Mirror, 177
Daily Telegraph, 51
Damascus, 12–13, 38, 40, 44, 61, 68, 71, 88, 111, 187n49
Dardanelles, 5, 159
Declaration to the Seven, 10

Deedes, Wyndham, 81, 129, 170, 207n34
demobilization, 4, 10, 15–16, 18–21, 29, 33, 56, 179, 185n7, 187n51
Dickson, John (Lord Islington), 172
Dominions, 14, 25, 64, 132, 141

E

Eastern Committee, 10–11, 88
economizing, 4, 16, 19, 20, 26, 29–30, 32, 38, 41, 44, 46, 62, 70, 78, 93, 100, 109, 114, 117, 120, 139, 160, 162, 179–180, 182
Egypt, 2, 7–10, 19, 27–31, 36–38, 41, 43, 52, 55, 58, 64, 66, 68, 71, 73, 77, 91, 96, 114, 124, 126–127, 137, 140
Enver, Ismail, 33

F

Faysal, 10, 12–13, 29–30, 38, 41, 58, 60–62, 64, 67–70, 74, 76–77, 79–82, 88–89, 92–93, 104, 106, 108–112, 114, 116, 121–123, 128, 144–159, 176, 180–181, 188n66, 193n17, 195n22, 199n6, 200n26
Fertile Crescent, 2–3, 6, 8, 12, 33–34, 57, 125, 179–182, 193n15
Fisher, Herbert, 101, 147–148
Flanders, 19
Forbes Adam, Eric, 66
Foreign Office, 7, 9, 12, 23, 30, 38, 40, 42–44, 50, 54–56, 58, 60–62, 65–67, 94, 103, 114, 128, 146, 148–149, 151, 173–174
France, 4, 6–14, 19, 27, 30, 32, 43, 46, 50, 53, 59–62, 67–69, 79–80, 83, 93, 100–102, 107, 121–122, 151–152, 186n20

G

Geddes Committee, 119–121, 139, 144
Genoa Conference, 144, 147, 177
Georges-Picot, Charles François, 7
Germany, 10, 16, 19, 60, 178
Gilbert, Martin, 2, 192n110, 195n22, 207n34
Gouraud, Henri, 81, 88, 93, 111, 127, 153
Greece, 30–31, 45–46, 53, 101, 123
Guest, Frederick, 129, 139

H

Hague Convention, 9

Haifa Congress, 84
Haifa, 12
Haldane, Aylmer, 39-40, 46-47, 49-50, 53-54, 58-59, 62, 64, 74-75, 115-116, 118
Hama, 12, 44, 61
Hankey, 30, 132
Harmsworth, Alfred (Lord Northcliffe), 177
Harmsworth, Harold (Lord Rothermere), 141
Harrington, C.H., 22
Haycroft, Thomas, 98
Hebrew University of Jerusalem, 87
Hedera, 98
Hewitt, John, 24
Hijaz, 10, 65, 68-69, 78, 87-89, 92-93, 104, 154
Hillah, 22
Hirtzel, Arthur, 66, 72
Hogarth, D.G., 10
Holy Places Commission, 87, 141, 173-174
Homs, 12, 44, 61
House of Commons, 42, 52-53, 91, 105, 145, 149, 170-171
House of Lords, 58, 170
Husayn, 7-8, 10, 58, 60, 67, 74, 76, 78, 81, 84, 88, 106, 137, 65, 168
Husayn-McMahon letters, 165

I
Ibn Sa'ud, 12, 69, 74, 76, 78, 81-82, 93, 148, 154, 175-176
Idrisi, al, 78
Illustrated Sunday Herald, 86
Imam of Yemen, 76, 78
India Office, 9, 28, 33, 50, 56, 58, 66, 71, 186n32, 188n12
India, 7, 9, 12, 14, 17, 19, 21, 28-29, 33, 35-39, 47-50, 52, 56-60, 62-63, 66-67, 70-72, 119, 124, 145, 162, 180, 184n18
Interdepartmental Committee on Middle Eastern Affairs, 10, 22, 55, 59-60
Interdepartmental Committee on Palestine, 44
Iraq Treaty, 144, 147, 181
Iraq, 5, 9, 12-14, 65, 74-82, 88-89, 91-94, 96-97, 101-102, 104-106, 108-117, 120-126, 128, 130, 133, 137-138, 140-141, 144-153, 155-160, 162, 174, 176, 180-182, 186n32, 187n41, 188n66, 192n101, 192n6, 195n3, 195n6a, 199n6
Iraqi Revolt, 38-40, 101
Ireland, 5, 14, 19, 56, 109, 126, 141, 144, 181
Irish Treaty, 109, 144, 177
Ironside, Edmund, 64, 116
Islam, 29, 50-51, 123, 183n9
  Shiah, 67, 104
  Sunni, 67, 104
Ismid, 45, 101
Italy, 7-8, 31, 46, 53, 100, 173-174

J
Jabotinsky, Vladimir, 43
Jackson, Sadlier, 94
Jaffa riots, 100, 140, 142
Jaffa, 97, 134, 142, 171
Jauf oasis, 175-176
Jerusalem, 61, 73, 81, 88, 128-129, 142, 171, 180
Jewish National Home, 12, 71, 84, 86, 89, 106, 108, 132, 136, 142, 168, 171, 175
Jiddah, 93
Jordan concession, 134

K
Kantara, 139
Karachi, 26, 124, 187n49
Karbala, 148
Kazim, Musa, 84, 131, 137
Kemal, Mustafa, 5, 12, 14, 26, 29-30, 32-34, 46, 50, 52-53, 56, 61, 94, 100, 106, 121-124, 178, 181, 191n92
Kerak, 44
Kermanshah, 23
King, Henry C., 12
Kirkuk, 94
Kitchener, Herbert, 1, 8
Kunaytra, 127
Kurds, 23, 29, 71, 75-76, 78, 80, 89, 106, 114, 123
Kut, 119

L
Lawrence, T.E., 60-61, 66-69, 74-76, 78-79, 81, 88-89, 92, 95-96, 127-130, 147, 151, 193n14, 195n1, 195n15
League of Nations, 14, 31, 59, 97, 101-102, 109, 113, 130, 147, 150, 160, 73-174, 182

Lebanon, 7, 9, 11–13Lenin, Vladimir, 17–18, 32, 50
Levant, 6
Liberal party, 106, 144, 177
Lloyd George, David, 1, 5, 11–13, 15–17, 19, 21, 27–28, 32, 36, 39, 43–46, 49, 52–53, 55–59, 61, 74–77, 79–81, 89, 102–103, 108–109, 111, 116, 118–119, 132–133, 138, 144, 146, 156–157, 177–178, 181, 186n20, 187n54, 192n110, 195n22, 197n2
London Agreement, 7
London Conference, 67
London, 7, 38, 47, 60, 67, 69, 73, 79, 81, 84, 87–88, 91, 93, 96, 98–99, 110, 119, 124, 127–129, 132, 135, 137–138, 140, 143, 146, 148–149, 151–152, 156, 165–166, 174–177, 180, 186n32, 190n58
Ludd, 96

M
Macdonogh, George, 40
MacMunn, G., 21–22, 24, 28–30
Marsh, Edward, 80
Masterton-Smith, James, 58–59, 66, 72
Maude, Stanley, 9McMahon, Henry, 8, 165, 168
Mecca, 7–8, 58, 60, 80–81, 106
Medina, 7, 58
Meinertzhagen, Richard, 43, 95, 116, 127, 129–130, 139–140, 142, 151
Mesopotamia, 9, 12, 18, 20, 22–26, 28–31, 36–42, 44–54, 58–64, 66–69, 71–72, 79–80, 88, 94, 96, 104–106, 108, 116–117, 121, 124, 186n22, 186n32, 188n11, 195n3
Millerand, Alexander, 60–61
Milne, G.F., 30
Milner, Alfred, 44, 48, 50, 55, 64
Mond, Alfred, 138
Montagu, Edwin, 44, 50, 54–56, 139
Morning Post, 163
Mosul, 8, 11–14, 22–23, 37, 39, 45, 47, 49, 59, 63, 74–76, 88, 94, 120–121, 123, 145, 190n58, 195n3
Mudros, 9
Muhammarah, 92

N
Naqib of Baghdad, 92, 192n101
Nasrieh, 22
Nation, 108

New Statesman, 108
New York, 4
Noel, E.W.C., 75
Nugent, W.F., 24

O
oil, 11, 14, 37, 54, 70, 101, 124, 157, 188n11
Ottoman Empire, 6–9, 16, 40

P
Palestine, 5, 8–9, 11–14, 18–20, 26–31, 36–38, 41–45, 49, 53, 61, 64–68, 71–73, 77–79, 82, 84–87, 89, 91, 96–97, 99–108, 114, 121, 126–127, 129–143, 160–175, 177, 180–182, 187n52, 189n35, 198n53, 198n62, 202n21, 207n34
pan-Arabism, 29
pan-Islamism, 29
Paris Conference, 145, 185n7
Paris, 10–11, 26–27, 60, 145, 184n31
Peake, Frederick, 97
Persia, 2, 7, 17–19, 24, 29, 36–37, 40, 42, 44–53, 55, 58–59, 65, 67, 124
Persian Gulf, 24
Petach Tikva, 98
Philby, John B., 128–129, 162, 175–176
Pope, 174
Prinkipo, 17

R
Radcliffe, Percy, 25, 37, 40, 42
Rafa, 139
railroads, 6, 12–13, 22–25, 29, 33, 40, 47, 49, 64, 75–76, 79, 89, 119–122, 128, 134, 139, 171
Ramla, 98
Rapallo Treaty, 178
Rehovot, 98
Reuters, 104
Rhine, 19, 36, 49
Richmond, Ernest, 129
Rishon le-Zion, 88
Ritchie, George, 70
Rothschild, Lionel, 8
Rumaitha, 47
Russia, 6–8, 17, 21, 27–28, 32, 35–36, 39, 44, 50–52, 86, 172, 178
Russian Civil War, 17
Rutenberg concession, 87, 133, 135, 140, 170–172

S

Saint-Jean de Maurienne Agreement, 8
Sakarya, 123
Salis, John Francis, de, 174
Salmond, Geoffrey, 127
Samawa, 47
Samuel, Herbert, 43-44, 64, 77, 81–82, 84–85, 88, 92, 97–100, 106, 127–129, 132, 134–135, 137–139, 142–143, 160–161, 166–169, 173–176, 195n15, 198n55, 207n38
San Remo Conference, 14, 40, 50, 59, 101–102, 141, 189n28
Scotland, 134
Sèvres Treaty, 46, 52–53, 67
Sharifian policy, 58, 60, 62, 68–69, 74, 76–77, 81, 83, 88–89, 92, 106–107, 122, 129, 156, 182, 188n66
Shuckburgh, John, 66–69, 71–72, 95, 115–116, 122, 124, 129, 134, 137, 140, 143, 151, 161, 163–169, 174–175
Smyrna, 26, 30–31, 40, 45-46, 52, 75, 178
Somaliland, 71, 81
South Persian Rifles, 124
Soviet Union, 17–18, 32, 50–51, 144, 177
Stalin, Joseph, 17
Stevenson, James, 58
Storrs, Ronald, 129
Straits, 6–7, 14, 31, 35–36, 38, 45, 100, 181, 191n92
Sudan, 1
Suez Canal, 70
Sunday Pictorial, 177
Sunderland, 35
Sydenham, George, 173
Sykes, Mark, 7, 184n19
Sykes-Picot Agreement, 7–13
Syria, 7–9, 11–13, 19, 26, 29–31, 38–39, 42–44, 51, 55, 59–60, 68, 81, 88, 100, 107, 121, 127–128, 151, 174, 187n54
Syrian Congress, 12–13, 38–39

T

Talib, Sayid, 92
Tashkent, 18
Tehran, 40, 49
Tel Afar, 47
Tel-Aviv, 88
Third International (Comintern), 51
Thrace, 26, 30, 40, 45–46, 75, 191n92
Thwaites, William, 42

Times, the, 67, 70, 125, 172, 177
Transjordan, 5, 8, 44, 68–69, 71–74, 77–79, 81–84, 87–89, 92, 96–97, 107, 127–129, 133, 160, 162, 175–176, 180, 182, 196n29a, 207n18, 209n84
Trenchard, Hugh, 45, 72, 97, 144, 176, 195n6a
Trotsky, Leon, 17, 33, 86
Trouville, 12
Tudor, Henry, 161–162, 175–176
Turkey, 2, 5, 7–8, 12–13, 16, 18, 23, 26–27, 29–39, 41–42, 44, 46, 50–52, 56, 62, 75–76, 83, 97, 100–101, 103–104, 107–108, 122–123, 126, 159
Turkish Petroleum Company, 11, 13

U

Ulster, 144
United States, 12, 14, 32, 91, 102, 132, 173
Vatican, 173–174
Venizelos, 45, 51, 53
Vernon, Roland, 67, 95, 104, 113–116, 118, 134–135, 140, 151, 161
Versailles Treaty, 12

W

Wadi Sirhan, 162
Wahhabis, 12
Wales, 108, 118
War Office, 9, 16, 19–23, 25–27, 38, 42–45, 47, 50–58, 65, 72, 76, 94–96, 103–104, 110, 114–121, 138–139, 153, 159–160, 180, 185n3, 188n11, 197n2
Weizmann, Chaim, 132–133, 135–137, 140–141, 143, 164, 167, 169, 174, 208n48
Wilson, Arnold, 9, 12, 24, 28, 37, 40, 56, 64, 117, 188n66, 190n58, 191n62
Wilson, Henry, 41, 44–46, 48, 50, 96, 139, 170
Wilson, Woodrow, 11
Wingate, Reginald, 10
World War I, 1–2, 58, 90, 181, 184n18
Worthington Evans, Laming, 95, 103–104, 114–115, 117–120, 139, 145

Y

Yemen, 76, 78
Young, Hubert, 55, 60, 66–68, 74–75, 81, 88, 95, 97, 113–114, 118, 127–128, 134–135, 137, 140, 151–152, 154, 174–176

Z
Zinoviev, Grigory, 51
Zionism, 6, 8, 43, 61, 68, 73, 77, 82, 84–87,
    98–100, 106, 126–128, 130, 132–133,
    136, 138–143, 160–174, 181, , 196n30,
    198n55, 204n77